SHERMAN LEAD

Flying the F-4D Phantom II in Vietnam

GAILLARD R. PECK, JR

OSPREY PUBLISHING
Bloomsbury Publishing Plc
PO Box 883, Oxford, OX1 9PL, UK
1385 Broadway, 5th Floor, New York, NY 10018, USA
E-mail: info@ospreypublishing.com
www.ospreypublishing.com

OSPREY is a trademark of Osprey Publishing Ltd

First published in Great Britain in 2019

ISBN: HB 978 1 4728 2937 5; eBook 978 1 4728 2938 2;
ePDF 978 1 4728 2939 9; XML 978 1 4728 2940 5

19 20 21 22 23   10 9 8 7 6 5 4 3 2 1

Edited by Tony Holmes
Map and diagrams by Bounford.com
Index by Zoe Ross

Typeset by Deanta Global Publishing Services, Chennai, India
Printed and bound in Great Britain by CPI (Group) UK Ltd, Croydon CR0 4YY

Front cover: Gail Peck dressed for combat in front of his assigned aircraft, F-4D tail-number
750; it was named *Kayte Baby* for his eldest daughter. (*Gail Peck collection*)
Back cover: F-4Ds from the 435th, 25th and 433rd TFSs (left to right). The central aircraft,
66-8795, became a wartime loss on September 22, 1973, although both 25th TFS crew
members were rescued. (*Peter E. Davies collection*)
Title page: (top) 433rd TFS F-4D 65-0705 leads 435th TFS F-4D 66-0234, both loaded with
LGBs, target-bound in 1969. (*Peter E. Davies collection*); (bottom) The 433rd TFS patch.
(*Gail Peck collection*)

Osprey Publishing supports the Woodland Trust, the UK's leading
woodland conservation charity.

To find out more about our authors and books visit **www.ospreypublishing.com**.
Here you will find extracts, author interviews, details of forthcoming events
and the option to sign up for our newsletter.

Contents

CONTENTS

Forewords

This book is a must-read for anyone interested in knowing the demands placed on a young fighter pilot during his first test in combat. It explains how skilled crews extracted the maximum performance from their F-4D Phantom IIs so that they could become a truly effective fighting force.

Capt Peck was a fast learner whose flying skills and abilities enabled him to make the best of the opportunities on offer in combat and quickly become a seasoned veteran.

I know Gail Peck, and it has been a pleasure for me to see what started out as a pinpoint of light grow into a glaring beacon that not only brightened his USAF career, but enhanced our fighter force many fold.

Lt Gen Walter D. (Dan) Druen, Jr (USAF) Ret.

No history of America's long and painful war in Vietnam would be complete without the story of how our military prepared and equipped its airmen to carry the fight to North Vietnam and to Laos through which they infiltrated forces to the south. In *Sherman Lead*, Gail Peck tells that story in a captivating way and with a level of detail that is unmatched. Gail and I both flew the F-4D and later the F-15C. We served together three times, though he would likely recall only our time together in the 18th Tactical Fighter Wing in the mid 1980s. But two decades earlier, Gail flew his first combat sortie out of Ubon Royal Thai Air Base. On nearly the same day in September of 1968 I flew my first combat sortie in the O2-A out of Pleiku Air Base in Vietnam, about two hundred miles to the southeast of Ubon. And a few years earlier Gail was one of my upper classmen at the Air Force Academy.

If you share an interest in airplanes, military aviation, air combat or the air war in Vietnam you will find this book captivating. You will gain insights into how the Air Force trains its pilots and prepares them for combat. The complexity of the F-4D and the tactics used to make it effective in combat are revealed in amazing detail. The anecdotes describing some of Gail's most memorable missions are vivid and capture the emotions that every pilot who has experienced combat has felt. The tributes to those who helped us along the way, and to those who made the ultimate sacrifice while answering their country's call to arms, are heartfelt and moving.

The US Air Force flew more than 5 million sorties during the war in Vietnam and lost 1,737 aircraft to hostile action. More than 20 percent of those were F-4s. Our military commitment to the war was near its peak when Gail and I deployed in the fall of 1968. By the time we returned home a year later the drawdown that culminated in the truce of January 27, 1973 was unfolding at a rapid pace. The lessons from that experience shaped the military that serves this nation so well today. Gail Peck was one of those who helped capture those lessons and put them to work in the training programs that served us so well in *Desert Storm* and every subsequent combat operation.

Gail earned his spurs as a fighter pilot flying combat missions over North Vietnam and Laos. He went on to be one of the select few chosen to attend the Air Force's graduate school for fighter pilots at Nellis Air Force Base in Nevada, and later to instruct in that same prestigious program, the Fighter Weapons Instructor Course. He helped give birth to a then-classified program using Soviet-built fighter aircraft to train post-Vietnam generations of fighter pilots in air-to-air combat, the subject of his earlier book, *America's Secret MiG Squadron*. I served alongside Gail in the 18th Tactical Fighter Wing at Kadena Air Base, Okinawa, Japan. It was the best assignment of my 35-year Air Force career.

Gen Richard E. Hawley (USAF) Ret.
Former commander of US Forces in Japan,
US Air Forces in Europe, Allied Air Forces
Central Europe, and Air Combat Command.

Introduction

WHAT THIS BOOK IS AND
WHAT IT ISN'T

My goal in writing this book is simply to share some of my personal experiences and describe my impressions of the experiences of some of my colleagues while, as American fighter pilots, we lived through a year or so of war in Vietnam flying the F-4D Phantom II jet fighter. We flew in combat with the 433rd TFS "Satan's Angels," a part of the famous 8th Tactical Fighter Wing (TFW) "Wolf Pack." Everyone should know I love my mother and can guess how badly I wanted to date the head cheerleader in high school. So, there is none of that in this book.

My children have asked the question, "Why were Americans involved in the Vietnam War?" It is not my intent to go into details as to how the war was fought. Nor will I delve into policy, the role of the White House, the Pentagon or other Washington agencies, except to share my observation that the Washington leadership appeared to be unable to keep their noses out of the daily operations and leave the prosecution of the war to the generals and their warriors.

It is important to note the outstanding quality of the leadership in the 433rd TFS, starting with Lt Col Ralph

"Hoot" Gibson, the commander when I arrived, and then extending to Lt Col Dick O'Leary, who replaced "Hoot," and then on to Lt Col Jack Bennett, the CO at the end of my tour. It is hard to imagine better leaders, officers or fighter pilots. Without exception, these men, who are now all deceased, were outstanding. The leadership quality extended to the other senior officers who worked for the commanders. Notable was Lt Col Bill "The Padre" Strand, with whom I had an especially close bond. There were so many more men of the same stature in that squadron.

I would be remiss if I did not shine a special bright light on Cols Dan Druen and Skip Stanfield. At 8th TFW level, these two officers were beyond exceptional. Druen, who retired as a (three-star) Lieutenant General, was the 8th TFW Deputy Commander for Operations, while Stanfield, who should have "made general," was the 8th TFW CO. I owe so much to both of these men. We recently celebrated Gen Druen's 91st birthday in Las Vegas.

So, with that said, let us begin.

The time period of this book runs from August 1968 through to September 1969. The location from which we launched combat operations was Ubon RTAFB. The mission was to do what were told to do, on a daily basis, while flying combat operations over North Vietnam and Laos in support of operations *Rolling Thunder* (North Vietnam), *Steel Tiger* (Laos) and *Barrel Roll* (also Laos).

Prologue

Okay, the mid-air refueling of my F-4D Phantom II was complete. I pushed the button on the stick and we disconnected from the air-refueling boom of the KC-135 tanker immediately above and ahead of us. I moved the stick ever so slightly to the right, applying a little right aileron. The spoiler on the right wing opened slightly and the mighty F-4 slid to the right from the air-to-air refueling receiver position. I pressed the throttles gently forward, and responding to that slight increase in power, my Phantom II moved up on the right wing of the KC-135. We were on the "Cherry Anchor" air-to-air refueling track about 100 nautical miles northeast of Ubon, parallel to and just west of the Mekong River. It was September 19, 1968.

My move made room for my flight lead, Maj Bud Marconi, to maneuver into the pre-contact position for his pre-strike air refueling. My mind wandered as I took up my spot while Bud refueled. I was tucked in tight on the right wing of the tanker.

Nearly five years had passed since my mother and my wife had pinned the silver wings of a USAF pilot onto my chest at Laughlin AFB, Texas. Finishing pilot training was phase two of my grand plan. Graduating from the Air Force Academy in Colorado Springs a little more than a year before had been the completion of phase one. I had wanted to be a USAF fighter pilot more than anything else in life. It was not to be at the end of phase two, however. I had graduated first in my class at pilot training but there was not a single F-100 Super Sabre fighter assignment for the graduates of Class 64B at Laughlin. Was I disappointed? Incredibly so! However, I made a clear and conscious decision, passing up an F-102 Delta Dagger interceptor assignment, to stay in Air Training Command (ATC) and "bet the farm" that I could eventually get into fighters.

While a cadet at the Air Force Academy I had a summer assignment with Air Defense Command (ADC) at Hamilton AFB, just north of San Francisco, California. At the time it seemed like a glamorous job flying supersonic interceptors whose mission it was to defend North America. But, while there, I realized that I didn't want to do that. I wanted to fly "hot jets," dogfight, shoot the gun, drop bombs and fire rockets and missiles – all part of my fighter pilot fantasy. Thus, phase three started with me teaching people how to fly. The term FAIP (first assignment instructor pilot) hadn't yet been invented, but that is what I was. At the end of phase three I was a pretty good instructor pilot (IP), being skilled at flying the supersonic T-38 Talon jet trainer. So, when the chance to fly fighters finally came, I was ready.

My reverie was broken as the wisp of fuel from the refueling boom of the KC-135 indicated that the F-4 had disconnected from the tanker. Bud, having finished refueling his jet, moved under me and then positioned himself off my right wing. He then banked away and I followed, moving into close formation. His rudder, moving back and forth, told me to adopt a more widely spread tactical formation. This was followed by a crisp command over the radio, instructing me to switch frequency for the ABCCC (Airborne Battlefield Command & Control Center) EC-130E.

"'Olds,' let's go Button 8."

"'Olds,' check!"

"Two," I immediately responded.

Next, Bud called the ABCCC, stating, "'Cricket.' 'Olds' with a flight of two for mission No. 19868 [or some such similar number]." The EC-130E ABCCC aircraft answered, "Roger 'Olds,' you are cleared into Route Package I as fragged [briefed]." Our preflight planning told us to expect clearance into North Vietnam's route packages for armed reconnaissance against targets starting at a specific Delta Point or geographic position on the ground, the coordinates of which had been plotted on our maps. The mission was unfolding as expected. In this case, the initial target area was a truck park nestled next to the mountainous karst on the coastal plain in southern North Vietnam.

Phase four of my dream was unfolding. I had completed fighter training and I was now on my first combat mission to North Vietnam. Earlier in 1968, our forces had been restricted from going "Downtown" to Hanoi in Route Package VI, but in September the war in the southern route packages of North Vietnam was still raging.

Bud made a slight heading change and I moved into position about 4,000ft line abreast of the leader and about 1,500ft above him, and we began crossing Laos en route to our target area in North Vietnam. We were carrying CBU-24 cluster bomb munitions. These weapons, designated BLU-26, were like little hand grenades that were carried in a canister about 16in. in diameter and 7ft 9in. long. Each canister carried 665 of the bomblets. The canister was dropped from the fighter in a high-angle 30- to 45-degree dive-bombing attack. Each canister had a fuse in the nose that was connected to a small propeller, which was held in place by an arming wire hooked directly to the aircraft while the weapon was attached to a stores pylon beneath the wing of the fighter. When the weapon was released, the wire extracted from the propeller, allowing it to spin. This in turn armed the fuse for the CBU-24 canister.

When the fuse went off, it split the CBU-24 canister, spilling the BLU-26 bomblets into the slipstream. Ripples on the surface of the bomblets caused them to spin, and the spinning motion armed the bomblets – like pulling the pin on a hand grenade. The fuses could be set for various times, and the pilots had figures on their kneeboards giving them various dive angle and release altitude parameters. Ideally, the canister would split at an altitude above the ground that would give the bomblets time to spin-arm and then impact the ground, exploding on contact. If the canister was dropped with perfect release parameters of dive angle, airspeed and altitude, it would create an explosive pattern some 800ft in diameter on the ground. If the pilot dropped low, there was a chance the bomblets would not have time to spin-arm and they would dud. On the other hand, if the pilot dropped higher than planned, a hole opened up in the middle of the pattern, creating a doughnut-like ring of explosions. The higher the drop above the ideal release altitude, the larger the hole in the doughnut.

Suddenly, the dense green of the Laotian jungle gave way to the karst typical of the foothills of the North Vietnamese mountain ranges, and further east were the rice paddies and vegetable fields between the mountains and the beach. The Gulf of Tonkin was dead calm and there wasn't a cloud in the sky.

Bud switched us to mission frequency and we immediately heard the radio calls of "Scuba" flight. As we overflew our target, we saw two F-105 Thunderchiefs dropping their ordnance. There were several fires burning on the ground, and Bud maintained an easterly heading until we were several miles "Feet Wet," or over the Gulf of Tonkin. He set up a holding pattern while we waited for the F-105s to finish their work on the same target that we had been assigned. Listening to the radio calls and grabbing quick looks at the target area got my adrenalin flowing. This was phase four, for real. I WAS a fighter pilot and this was WAR! "Scuba" Lead and No. 2 made radio calls indicating they were in sequence, commencing strafing attacks – the F-105 had an awesome M61A1 20mm cannon capable of firing 100 rounds a second. "Scuba 1" called "Bingo," indicating that he had reached a fuel state mandating that they depart the target area and head for the post-strike tanker.

"Scuba 2" called in "Hot strafe, last pass." I sneaked a peek just in time to see the F-105 on a northerly heading right next to, and flying parallel with, the mountains. There were several miles of rice paddies and open fields to the east and then the beach. As he completed his pass, the pilot called "'Scuba 2' is off, HIT." A lucky North Vietnamese gunner had managed to predict the F-105's flightpath and fire a lethal burst of antiaircraft artillery. There were no more radio calls.

The jet pulled up in what otherwise would have been a normal recovery from a strafing pass, and then instead of banking and leveling off, it continued up in a lazy arc across the sky. With my attention fixed on the jet, I took only enough time to crosscheck my formation position with Bud. The jet continued up and then started to level off, and as it did so I saw two bright flashes from the cockpit area, indicating the pilot had jettisoned the canopy and ejected. Almost instantly, the eerie sound of the emergency beeper blasted into our headset from our auxiliary radio. The emergency beeper, when activated, was set up to turn on and start transmitting a blaring signal like a pulsating police siren on 243.0 MHz – the emergency UHF radio frequency (known as "Guard"). The beeper activated at the moment of the pilot's ejection from the aircraft. Then, his white parachute blossomed. The jet continued its arc across the sky, nose down now, until it crashed on the beach in a mighty explosion of fire and smoke.

The F-105 flight leader called "Mayday" and Bud answered that we were in position to take up the on-scene command, as the lone Thunderchief flight leader was out of fuel.

The parachute floated down into a rice paddy or cabbage patch very near an intersection of what appeared from the air to be dikes. The intersection created an "X" on the ground, with green semi-flooded fields in all four of the adjacent quadrants. Moments later, the near hysterical pilot started transmitting on the Guard 243.0 MHz emergency radio frequency, reporting to all that his leg was broken and the "gomers are all around me!"

By this time Bud had maneuvered our flight directly overhead the downed pilot's parachute, while simultaneously commanding the launch of the search and rescue force of A-1E Skyraider aircraft and H-3 Jolly Green Giant helicopters. A C-130 with the call-sign "King" was the rescue commander. Meanwhile, Bud and I circled momentarily before he barked out orders for our attack – it wasn't really an attack, but rather an effort to keep the enemy at bay while the rescue forces responded. Bud directed me to select my CBU munitions and "bombs single," to plan 45-degree dive attacks and to put the gunsight pipper on the parachute, then "Pickle" off the CBU 1,000ft high and create a "doughnut of lethality," with the pilot in the center of the hole.

This was my first combat mission to North Vietnam. Only a year to go.

The Operational Report for that day, as documented by a National Museum of the Air Force Fact Sheet, reads as follows:

Tail Number: 60-0428*
Date Lost: 9/19/1968
Country: North Vietnam
Model: F-105D
Base/Squadron: 469th TFS, Korat AB, Thailand
Mission: Strike
Target: Storage site six miles northwest of Thon Cam Son
Cause: Guns
Where Lost: Flew three miles short of coast
Pilot: Maj Elwyn Rex Capling
Pilot Status: KIA [Killed In Action]

In August and again in September, tragedy struck two members of the 469th (TFS). On August 17, 1968, [Capt

---

*Editor's Note: this aircraft was the first F-105D to reach 3,000 flying hours, and it had flown more than 500 missions prior to being shot down.

Noble Ray Koontz] was killed in a freak landing accident at Da Nang Air Force Base in South Vietnam. On September 19, 1968, [Maj Elwyn Rex Capling] was shot down just north of the DMZ [demilitarized zone] in North Vietnam. He ejected successfully from his disabled F-105 but was taken captive shortly after.* Our sympathies go out to these men and to their families.†

---

*Editor's Note: the pilot was actually killed in action shortly after surviving the ejection, for his name did not appear in any of the listings for the known PoW camps. Maj Capling's remains were returned to the USA on March 18, 1977.
†http://www.nationalmuseum.af.mil/factsheets/factsheet.asp?id=1363.

I

Earning my Wings

JUMP WINGS

Air Force Academy cadets in the early classes had no glider or fixed wing aircraft programs that enabled them to earn wings, in the form of badges worn on the cadet uniform. Indeed, the only badges that we could earn, as cadets, were parachute wings! To earn those Jump Wings, the cadet was required to attend the US Army paratrooper school at Fort Benning, Georgia, during a forfeited summer vacation. I coveted those parachute wings and therefore applied for, and was accepted into, the program. I was scheduled to attend during the summer of my 1st Class year (rising senior) in 1961.

That spring I got sick and spent a week or so in the hospital. I also had a major break up with a girlfriend that further distracted me. A consequence was that I failed the Air Force Academy's "Strength of Materials" course (administered by the Mechanics Department) during that 2nd Class spring semester. To avoid washing out of the Academy altogether I had to forego jump school and forfeit summer leave while taking the course over again. I passed the repeat with an A.

"Oh well," I reflected, "I'm still here at the Academy, and I'll get those parachute wings some other time, maybe."

Following graduation from the Air Force Academy on June 6, 1962, I reported to the 3646th Pilot Training Wing at Laughlin AFB in Del Rio, Texas, for pilot training or UPT (undergraduate pilot training) in class 64B. Here, I flew the T-37, which was a fun little airplane to fly. My instructor, 1Lt Jim Martin, prepared me well to progress from primary training to basic training flying, which was undertaken in the T-33 Shooting Star, which we knew as the "T-Bird." Pilot training was great, and I sailed through the program, even though I took time about halfway through to marry Jean Hilger, the daughter of Brig Gen John A. "Jack" Hilger. "General Jack," as I called him, had been, as a major, Jimmy Doolittle's vice commander on the famous Doolittle Raid against the Japanese homeland on April 18, 1942. That was less than five months after the Japanese attack on Pearl Harbor. Jeannie and I settled into married life, and UPT continued with a change of squadrons and a transition onto the T-33.

Career fighter pilot Capt Robin Nierste was my instructor in the "T-Bird," and we really "grooved!" At graduation in September 1963, my mother and Jeannie pinned the wings of a USAF pilot onto my uniform. Normally, graduating first in the class permits the graduate to select just about any aircraft in the USAF inventory to fly. This was not the case with my class, however, as 89 percent of the assignments were to Strategic Air Command (SAC) flying tankers (KC-97s or KC-135s) or bombers (B-47s or B-52s). I wanted no part of SAC. The only options left open to me were T-33 instructing back at Laughlin with the 3646th, two slots flying F-102 interceptors (with a follow-on assignment to ADC) and a single helicopter slot. I also wanted no part of ADC or helicopters, which left me facing the unwelcome prospect of selecting the T-33 and an assignment back to Laughlin as an instructor.

Nos. 2 and 3 in the class, Jerry Jones and Air Force Academy classmate Mike Williams, took the F-102s and rejoiced. Joe Guilmartin, also an Air Force Academy classmate, took the helicopter. Over the years I lost track of Jerry Jones, but Mike Williams only served briefly with the USAF before spending many years with the airlines. Joe Guilmartin was a multiple Silver Star recipient for combat rescues in Vietnam. As Dr. Joseph Guilmartin (now sadly deceased), he had a follow-on career as a history professor at Ohio State University.

One might ask why I didn't want the F-102. The answer rests with one summer TDY (temporary duty) I had while still a cadet. I attended a program called 3rd Lieutenant, the goal of which was to expose cadets to two weeks in the "real Air Force." My assignment was to Hamilton AFB, which, in those days, was an active duty air force base just north of San Francisco. Hamilton is now closed. The unit I was assigned to was the 83rd Fighter Interceptor Squadron (FIS). The 83rd, and its sister squadron the 84th, had just completed transitioning from the F-104 Starfighter to the F-101 Voodoo. That sounded like a dream assignment to an aspiring fighter pilot. I even flew in the back seat of an F-101 and also got a couple of rides in the T-33 that was used as a target for the Voodoo interceptor pilots.

The mission itself was what turned me off about flying jets for ADC. Firstly, I didn't like the idea of a career sitting air defense alert. Secondly, the idea of overwater low-altitude intercepts at night in all weather conditions didn't sound like as much fun as going to a gunnery range and dropping bombs, shooting rockets and strafing on one day, followed by air-to-air dogfighting the next. The final straw that "broke the camel's back" and soured me on ADC was the orange flightsuits the pilots wore. I could not imagine me wearing one of those, even though I did have one during my first assignment. There is photographic evidence of me in orange with my son Jack getting his first haircut. Nevertheless, I still didn't like the orange flightsuit.

So, for my first assignment as an Air Force pilot I became a "T-Bird" instructor and returned to Laughlin to fly with the same squadron and flight that I had graduated from. I had only taught one class of students in the T-33 when I was selected to check out in the brand new supersonic T-38 Talon. I spent almost a year making frequent trips to Palmdale, California, where I picked up T-38s fresh off the production line and flew them back to Laughlin as the 3646th transitioned from the "T-Bird" to the Talon for basic training. It was pretty nifty flying jets that still had paint on the rudder pedals.

Living on a lieutenant's pay, we were pretty poor in those days and no one could afford two cars. I found a great deal on a motor scooter, however, and it became my transportation on base, leaving Jeannie with our Chevrolet convertible. The scooter became the mechanical love of my life. It required regular maintenance, and I figured out fixes for all of the mechanical needs of my "beloved" scooter. More about the scooter later.

Once we were fully equipped with T-38s, I started instructing in the aircraft, beginning with Class 66A. I had only completed the instruction of that one class of T-38 students when I was directed to attend Squadron Officer's School (SOS) at Maxwell AFB, Alabama. While I was at SOS, ATC transferred me to Randolph AFB, Texas, to serve as a T-38 instructor with the 3510th Flying Training Wing (FTW). I was specifically tasked with tutoring new instructors as part of the Pilot Instructor Training (PIT) school. The students at PIT were either recent pilot training graduates or, for the most part, aviators returning from Southeast Asia fresh from completing a combat tour. Randolph would ultimately prove to be a great assignment, even if I didn't appreciate that fact at the time. I would have been a lot happier in those days if I had known how my good fortune was going to lead me on to a great career as a fighter pilot. I consoled myself at the time with the fact that at least I was riding in the front seat of T-38s while the student instructors worked their way through the PIT curriculum from the rear cockpit.

I worked for a Canadian officer at Randolph who was on an exchange tour with the USAF. Flt Lt Al Brown had been a fighter pilot flying CF-5 Freedom Fighters with the Royal Canadian Air Force before the consolidation of the Canadian military into a single force. Al and I got along very well, with give and take on both sides. One day he told me that my student's check ride scheduled for the following day had been pushed back to the following week. I protested with all the rationale I could muster, while stressing that the weather was finally giving us a break and that Maj Merlyn Dethlefsen was ready for the check ride. Al calmly told me it wasn't his "call." He said, "Gail, you see, your President will be awarding Maj Dethlefsen the Medal of Honor at the White House." End of discussion. I was stunned. I knew that Merlyn had had a distinguished tour in F-105s as a *Wild Weasel*, hunting and killing North Vietnamese surface-to-air missile (SAM) sites, but I had no idea about the extent of his accomplishments.

One of my extra duties was that of the squadron information officer. In that capacity I worked with an author named

Herbert Malloy Mason, Jr, who was writing a book that he titled *The New Tigers – The Making of a Modern Fighter Pilot.*[*] Mason (a former Marine, whose father had flown with the *Lafayette Escadrille* in World War I prior to becoming one of the first pilots to join the US Army Air Corps) flew several times in the back seat of the T-38 with me and took all of the aerial photographs of the jet that were published in that book. He also featured me with my helmet on and oxygen mask attached on the dust cover of his book. Little did I know then that Mason would subsequently go on to Nellis AFB and feature my lifelong friend Jeff Cliver in the same book. Then-1Lt Cliver was undergoing F-105 training there at the time, and photographs of him were also included in Mason's book, along with a narrative about a typical Thunderchief training mission. Later, Jeff and I became acquainted when we served together at the FWS as instructors, and we have maintained a close relationship since then. Now retired, Maj Gen Cliver reviewed this manuscript for me in early 2018.

DECISION TIME

There were a lot of officers who came through the PIT pipeline that I was able to admire, look up to and learn from. After almost two years instructing at Randolph, I learned that the PIT mission was being moved to Tyndall AFB, near Panama City in the Florida panhandle. The Vietnam War was raging and most guys were either getting sent into combat or were getting out of the Air Force. I was stuck in ATC, facing another move for a third tour as an IP.

[*]Published by David McKay Company, Inc., New York, 1967, Library of Congress Catalog Card Number: 67-20972, Van Rees Press, New York, NY.

As best I recall, I had a very narrow window of time between the completion of my obligations to the military and my receipt of assignment notification. It seems like I had a four-year obligation after finishing pilot training, and therefore I could have left the Air Force in September 1967. By that time the 3510th FTW at Randolph was in the advanced stages of moving the T-38 PIT school to Tyndall. I did not want another back-to-back assignment in ATC and, therefore, when it appeared I would be forced to go to Tyndall or get out, I decided to leave the Air Force. Many of my other colleagues, including Air Force Academy classmate Roger Meyers, had decided to do that too.

Jeannie and the kids were in the new Plymouth station wagon waiting outside the "Taj Mahal" – the nickname for the Wing Headquarters and administrative building at Randolph AFB. I went inside to put my papers in to resign from the Air Force. When I entered the personnel office an NCO (non-commissioned officer) called me by name and exclaimed, "Capt Peck, where have you been? We've been looking for you all over the base!" I didn't know what was going on, or what to say. He filled the silence by further exclaiming, "We got that F-4 assignment for you. It came in today!" I was dumbfounded. But I quickly composed myself and asked if it was front seat or back seat. The NCO grinned and said, "Front seat, sir!" I signed the papers accepting the assignment to MacDill AFB, Florida, to train as an F-4 aircraft commander with the 45th TFS/15th TFW. Wow! Talk about a turn-around.

My reporting date was January 1968, and prior to heading to Florida I first had to go to survival school at Fairchild AFB, near Spokane, Washington, in December. That part of the deal wasn't too red hot as I soon remembered how cold it was there at that time of year. I had spent two full winters at Eielson AFB, southeast of the city of Fairbanks, Alaska, where, as a kid, I had gone to high school. And Spokane was a whole lot closer to Alaska than it was to Texas – or so it seemed climate-wise in December. Then, I had to go to water survival training at Homestead AFB, south of Miami. That was better, but it still meant getting wet in the Atlantic Ocean in winter! No rejoicing there either.

The family, however, was thrilled, and suddenly instead of an Air Force career falling apart, there was new energy and vigor in all that we did. I knew I was entering a pipeline to go to war. Where would my family stay while I was gone? What would we do for the holidays in Fairchild AFB in Washington before Christmas and Homestead and MacDill AFBs in Florida right after New Year's? What would I do with my beloved motor scooter? Where would we live in Florida? The questions raged and the answers were slowly fleshed out. To get started we packed up the family and headed for Las Vegas and Jeannie's parents' home, which became the designated family holding point while I attended survival school at Fairchild. The timing worked out well in that we arrived in Las Vegas, I went to survival school and then returned home to the family in time for Christmas.

There was good news and bad news about survival school. The bad news was that December is a "rugged" time of year to go to northeast Washington in respect to the weather. In a word it was COLD. The good news was that since my class was in the pipeline to Southeast Asia, and as potential survivors in the Vietnam jungle, we were not required to make the "arctic winter" survival trek at Fairchild. Those who made the trek described it as several days of unmitigated hell. No food to speak of, frozen water, and miles and miles of nothing but miles and miles in the mountains of the Pacific Northwest.

We didn't get off scot-free, however, as we had to complete the escape and evasion obstacle course. It was run at night, and it was cold. The uniform was a flightsuit, and the water bottle I had in my leg pocket froze. At times we were running and at times we were crawling. All the time, the "bad guys" were trying to capture us, hence the evasion aspect. There was barbed wire and other obstacles in our path. Occasionally, bright search lights would attempt to pin us down as we slithered on our bellies. At other times tracer bullets were fired over our heads. It was a dark, cold, eerie overall experience. I didn't get captured, and therefore had to run the whole obstacle course. As I recall, the guys that got scarfed up were taken straight to the PoW camp, sparing them some of the agony of the course. Skinned knees and bruised elbows were the reward for finishing uncaptured. Those of us that went the whole distance were thrown into the PoW camp anyway – finishers of the obstacle course simply entered captivity both later and more banged up than those who had been caught early.

The PoW camp was something that I will never forget. They put us in isolation cells with ceilings that were too low to fully stand erect. Nevertheless, we were ordered to stand. And they came by frequently to check. The cell was dark and cold, with a dirt floor. It had a latch on the outside of the door that looked and sounded like the handle latch opener on a freezer at the butcher's shop or at the entrance to the beer cooler in any convenience store. I quickly learned that I could sit down and get away with it because you could hear them coming, opening each cell door as they proceeded down the row, checking us out one at a time. Several times during that ordeal they jerked us out of our cell and took us to an interrogation room. It was a classic set up – small table and chair in the middle of the room, with a single very bright light right over the chair that made it impossible to see the walls of the room or the interrogator clearly. The interrogations were harsh. Our training included instructions to reveal only our name, rank, serial number and date of birth. We had the Code of Conduct hammered into us and we were expected to demonstrate that we could follow the code.

The interrogators were unrelenting in their attempts to get people to talk. Derogatory remarks about parents, especially mothers, was one popular line intended to create conversation or anger. Another was the suggestion that our wives were messing around while we were being held as prisoners. They didn't like much of my act and I was taken to a little cage and forced into it like an animal. I could see out but they were able to squeeze the top and sides so that there was no room to shift or maneuver and get comfortable. Soon, every muscle ached and my hands, feet and legs went to sleep.

The training stressed the mental discipline essential for surviving. In the academic preparation we were taught to occupy our minds totally and ignore the bodily discomfort. That worked for me. I had been an avid model airplane builder as a youth, and my mental diversion was to visualize cutting balsa wood and gluing together each part in an imaginary model airplane. It was elaborate, with all the parts of an aircraft. Formers were cut and notched and stringers were glued in place. Each rib of the wing and tail surface was similarly prepared and assembled, and on and on I went. I was afraid that I would "finish" the model before I was let out and then have to get on to building the next one while I suffered through the training ordeal.

Eventually, they let me out of the cage and returned me to a group holding pen. I was really stiff and cramped up, and it took a while before my legs worked properly. The holding pen was actually a shelter, and again this was dark and cold with a dirt floor and a low ceiling. It seemed to be partially dug into the ground, with a thatch-type roof on it. There were a lot of guys in there mingling around trying to find friends. It was possible to go outside of the shelter, which was surrounded by high wire fences and guard towers. Occasionally, a guarded gate in the fence line was left open for some unexplained reason. All of the activity during the two-day survival school took place at night.

At some point I was given an escape chit by someone long since forgotten. It meant that I had permission to attempt to escape, which I did. Upon arrival at the designated escape route end point I was greeted as a repatriated prisoner and given hot chocolate while sitting in the warmth of the cab of a pickup truck. Eventually, they told me I had to go back to the camp and finish that part of the survival school syllabus, but that I had done a good job in getting away. The big shock came when I was chosen to stay for a few extra days and attend a classified course. I had been selected because of my pipeline status to Southeast Asia. The course was aimed at better preparing me to be a prisoner in North Vietnam in the event that I got shot down. Fortunately, I would never need to put in practice what I was taught at survival school. I subsequently learned that my "survival training ordeal" didn't even come close to the horror experienced in the North Vietnamese PoW camps by those Americans that were shot down and captured during the conflict.

Later, in the mid-1980s, when I was the Wing Commander of the 26th Tactical Reconnaissance Wing at Zweibrücken

Air Base (AB) in West Germany, I had the opportunity to come back to Fairchild for an advanced survival school course designed to enhance resistance in the event that I was shot down while flying Phantom IIs in Europe as part of the Peacetime Aerial Reconnaissance Program. On these missions we flew routes in the RF-4C Phantom II that either paralleled the inner German border between East and West Germany or flightpaths over the Baltic that ran parallel with the eastern Baltic coastline, but were far enough offshore to be in international airspace. We flew at high altitude with a side-looking radar pod that peered into East Germany or over Estonia and the other eastern Baltic nations into the Soviet Union. The intelligence community devoured our radar recordings as they provided insight into military activity in East Germany and the Soviet Union.

There was always the risk that we could be shot down, captured and then held as spies like Francis Gary Powers in the earlier U-2 downing over the Soviet Union on May 1, 1960. Hence, I received the advanced training at Fairchild. My Deputy Commander for Operations at Zweibrücken, Col Jim Young, cleverly prevented me from ever actually flying one of these reconnaissance missions, even though I had completed the requisite training. Thanks Jim.

Finally, mid-December 1967 arrived and basic survival school was over. It was nearly time for Christmas before heading to MacDill and FIGHTERS!

What, one might ask, happened to the beloved motor scooter? Well, before leaving Randolph for Las Vegas and ultimately MacDill, I went down to the auto hobby shop and a couple of mechanical geniuses helped me make a rack for the scooter. It bolted onto the frame of our Plymouth station wagon and carried the scooter piggy-back in a similar fashion to the way motorized wheelchairs are carried today for the disabled. The scooter made it all the way to Las Vegas and then on to MacDill, where it served me well as base transportation while I was attending F-4 training. I then sold it for about what I paid for it, and the scooter may still be in a Tampa area junkyard.

Fighter time? No, not yet. I next had to go to Homestead AFB for water survival training. The two things that stand out in my memory of that course were para-sailing and surviving in a life raft. The water survival para-sailing was similar to the operational test I had participated in at Randolph AFB, when para-sailing was being considered as a part of pilot training. The exception was that at Homestead, we lifted off from a boat in a para-sail and were then actually cut loose from the tow cable, parachuting into the water. The latter was very different from achieving flight while being towed behind a truck, and remaining attached to the vehicle until brought back down to land on terra firma. The water landing gave us the opportunity to escape from under a collapsed parachute canopy and avoid drowning, as well as providing us with the opportunity to pull a life raft to us, instead of swimming after it – the life raft will always drift faster than one can swim. Since the raft was attached to the pilot by a tether, common sense demanded that you pull it to you. However, experience showed that, historically, some guys didn't get that point and exhausted themselves swimming after their rafts. The learning of this lesson was an important part of the water training.

The other memorable event was survival in the raft. I fished a little with the kit provided to us in our survival equipment. Then, it occurred to me that I had no idea what I would do with a fish if I caught one! A one-man raft didn't include facilities for filleting a fish (even if I had known how to), and it certainly didn't provide a grill for cooking the hapless creature. So, I abandoned the fishing and spent the rest of the time floating in Biscayne Bay cursing at the instructors, who were driving around us in circles in big boats trying to make waves to simulate the choppy open ocean. Having survived water survival, it was finally time to fly fighters.

F-4 SCHOOL

Jeannie and I and the little ones – now nearly five and three years old – felt fortunate to be assigned on-base housing at MacDill AFB. Our quarters were similar to the wherry houses we lived in at Randolph, being fairly small and certainly nothing to brag about. The house was located along Bayshore Drive, between the Officers' Club and the base hospital.

My training routine started with intense academics all aimed at learning about the F-4. We went to a maintenance training facility called FTD (Field Training Detachment) and learned about the jet's hydraulics, electrical and fuel systems. We studied the physics and operating principles for the aircraft radar and the air-to-air guided missiles. To operate the radar and select the right missile at the right time required mastery of a course called "Switchology," which referred to the switch positions that had to be selected in the cockpit prior to a given weapons delivery. It was the first time I had ever heard that word. Now, correct switchology is the magic that allows us to operate VCRs, HD TVs, microwaves, kitchen oven timers and myriad other home appliances, as well as our cell phones and the GPS in our automobiles.

Soon the emergency procedures for the F-4 had been mastered and demonstrated in the simulator and it was time to start flying. Upon reporting to the flightline for the first time, I was introduced to my instructor in the 45th TFS, Capt Tom Saylor, nicknamed "Sinbad" for obvious reasons. "Sinbad" had already completed a combat tour in Vietnam and we hit it off very well from the start – we remained lifelong friends up until his death. Over the next six months "Sinbad" taught me everything he could about the F-4, flying combat and generally about being a fighter pilot. Our first venture into the sky together in an F-4C didn't get off to a good start, however.

The preflight inspection of the aircraft was routine. Tom and I both looked at the aircraft Form 781 to be sure all preflight inspections had been complied with and that the jet was not still on a "Red X," indicating that it was not airworthy. There were several places to sign-off the 781, and when the crew chief completed his last inspection he signed off the "Red X." On the next line down he usually marked the form with a red diagonal, indicating that there were some minor discrepancies that needed to be taken care of in the future, but at the time the jet was safe to fly.

Tom and I had walked around an F-4 previously, so I knew what to look for. All was good, including the lengthy inspection of the ejection seat. There were a lot of parts to that Martin-Baker Mk H-7 ejection seat, and many moved, so it was vitally important that the pilot checked the seat closely. For example, in the ejection sequence there was a little guillotine that, at a certain point in the ejection sequence, severed some of the pilot's restraint lines, ultimately permitting the pilot to separate from the seat. The guillotine was concealed behind a yellow access "door" that was spring-hinged at the bottom. When the top of the spring-loaded "door" was flipped down the pilot could see that the guillotine had not fired and that the restraint lines were intact.

Getting strapped into an F-4 was quite an experience, especially for the first time. The ejection seat was rocket powered, and could be triggered either by pulling up on a lanyard between the pilot's legs on the front of the seat or by pulling dual lanyards slightly above and offset to either side of the pilot's head. These overhead lanyards were a part of a face screen, and if the pilot continued to pull forward and down, not only did the seat fire, but a fabric screen pulled out and down to protect the pilot's head and face from the rush of the slipstream air encountered upon ejection. The crew chief helping us to strap in usually pulled the safety pin from the face curtain and handed it to us just after we were seated in the jet. We left the safety guard up on the lanyard between our legs until the canopy was closed and we were taxiing onto the runway.

The pilot's parachute was mounted in the top of the seat and the pilot only wore a harness to the aircraft. Once seated and otherwise completely strapped in, the crew chief assisted the pilot with the connection of the parachute to his harness through devices called Koch fittings.

Each of the pilot's legs was constrained by a contraption aimed at pulling it back from the rudder pedals and snug against the seat as the latter went up the ejection seat rails. Each leg restraint included two straps, one of which went around the ankle and the other around the thigh just above the knee. On the back of each of these heavy duty straps was a ring about an inch in diameter. A heavy cord passed through these two rings, with one end hooked to the seat in a release fitting and the other attached to a retraction mechanism that pulled the cord tight as the seat went up the rails during ejection. So, when the pilot and seat traveled up the ejection rail the pilot's legs were pulled back and held firmly against the seat to prevent them flailing, especially at high airspeed. At the proper time before man-seat separation, the leg cord released and a "butt kicker" strap activated. The "butt kicker" was hooked to the front of the seat on one end, went aft under the seat cushion and then up, being attached to the top of the back of the seat. Thus, at seat separation, the pilot's legs were freed and the "butt kicker" ratcheted tight, kicking the pilot and his parachute out of the seat. The pilot thus took his parachute with him, since his harness was connected to it via the Koch fittings.

Usually, the ejection seat had been raised with its electric motor to its highest position prior to the pilot climbing into the cockpit. This allowed the crew chief to properly inspect both it and the surrounding cockpit area. So, the leg straps were usually hanging down nearly out of reach to a seated pilot. They were one of the big, or better said, many, differences between the Northrop-developed ejection seat in the T-38 that I had been used to flying and the Martin-Baker seat in the F-4.

So, in mounting the jet the pilot, facing aft, usually stepped off the aircraft ladder and into the seat, taking a last look at the top of the seat and the parachute prior to turning around and sitting down. Next came the reach for the leg straps. Once they were attached, the anti-g suit hose was usually connected next, followed by the lap belt – secured with a Koch-type fitting. Then, the aircraft's oxygen connector was attached to the CRU-60 fitting on the harness and the intercom/radio jacks were plugged in. If not already connected, the anti-g suit's inflation hose was attached to the hose emanating from the jet itself. The penultimate step in the ejection seat procedure was performed by the crew chief when he held out each parachute strap with its Koch fitting and the pilot snapped them securely to his harness. Finally, the upper ejection pin was pulled from the seat and handed to the pilot, after which it was time to get the engine pre-start checklist underway.

By this time external electrical power had usually been applied and the ejection seat could be electrically lowered (or raised) to the pilot's preferred seating height.

Meanwhile, the back seat instructor – or, in future days, the Weapon Systems Operator (WSO) – had also gone through the same boarding process, assisted by a second groundcrew member. The first step the backseater took after electrical power was connected was to start the alignment of the inertial navigation system (INS). This took nearly seven minutes to perform in the F-4C – later in life the Phantom II was modified with an INS that aligned more quickly.

To start the engines, the jet needed either an explosive cartridge that would spool them up or an external power unit we called a "Dash 60," which produced a high-pressure stream of air through a hose connected to the engine to initially spin up the aircraft's twin General Electric J79 turbojets. Except for exercises and other special events, we always used a "Dash 60" to crank up because it had electrical power that could be attached in advance of engine start, thus allowing the INS alignment to also commence, and to reduce the fire risk potential associated with cartridge starts. Over the long service life of the F-4, the USAF burned up a few when cartridge starts caused catastrophic fires rather than ignition of the J79s.

With the hose between the "Dash 60" and the jet hooked up, all the pilot needed to do was give the crew chief a standardized hand signal and the air from the external power unit was turned on. Immediately, the percent of RPM indicator in the cockpit showed motion, and at 12 percent RPM the throttle was moved from the stop-cock or off position to idle. With a slight rumble the engine "lit off," the exhaust gas temperature (EGT) gauge indicating an increasing tailpipe temperature as the J79 smoothly accelerated to the idle RPM of 65 percent. All of this happened with the fuel flow, EGT and RPM acceleration to idle automatically managed by the engine fuel control system. Sweet! I gave the signal to start the other engine and it too was soon purring at 65 percent.

Soon thereafter, Tom told me I was "cleared primary sync," indicating that he had completed the alignment of the INS. The controls to align the INS were in the back seat while the controls to select it were on a panel in my cockpit up front. "Primary" selected the INS as the reference system versus a less reliable and accurate gyro system. Moving the spring-loaded switch to "sync" after selecting "primary" completed the process of bringing the INS on line, hence the terminology, "cleared primary sync." The jet could not be moved until this final step was completed as the INS alignment would be lost if it was not stationary.

The F-4 was big, particularly when compared with a T-38. This was noticeable when it was first taxied. After the second crew chief pulled the chocks, the primary crew chief standing directly ahead of the jet gave the pilot a run-up signal with a twirl of the index finger, and the pilot in turn pushed the throttles forward, generating just enough thrust to get the F-4 rolling. Next, the brakes were tapped to check them, and then as the nose wheel steering button on the bottom front of the stick grip was pressed, the jet responded positively to the rudder input. As the turnout from parking was initiated, the power was pulled back to idle.

We were on our way to a great adventure!

The first stop was the quick check area, adjacent to the end of the takeoff runway – it was also known as the (weapons) arming and last chance inspection area. Here, a team of aircraft and armament technicians looked over the jet for leaks and cut tires and, if applicable, armed the weapons. Today was an unarmed training sortie, so the quick check went pretty fast and soon we changed radio frequencies and were cleared for takeoff by the MacDill AFB control tower.

Canopies were closed and the seats were armed by lowering the guards between our legs on the front of the seat. Last-minute adjustments were made to the air-conditioning system by adjusting a temperature knob to hot or above freezing and then putting a lever into the maximum flow position. Not turning the temperature up resulted in a fogged-up canopy or a combination of rain and snow blowing in one's face!

On the runway Tom read the pre-takeoff checklist to me and I checked each item. Each engine was first individually checked at 100 percent power and then chopped to idle to make sure the fuel flow didn't drop below 425lb per hour. Running both engines up to 100 percent with the brakes held could actually spin the tires on the wheels. With the checklist complete, it was time to go. Brakes firmly applied, power to 85 percent. Gauges were checked – all normal. Brakes were released and throttles smoothly pushed up to 100 percent, or military power. Gauges were checked again and throttles pushed over the resistance and advanced to the full afterburner position.

The jet leapt forward, startling me with the acceleration. Stick full back, and I waited for the nose to come up. There it was in a perfect takeoff attitude, and as I released a little back pressure on the stick in order to hold it there, I heard a loud

"BAM" just as we lifted off, followed by a mild but distinct vibration. Tom yelled, "OUT OF BURNER, leave the gear down. I think we blew a tire!" I complied as instructed and Tom told me to start a gentle right turn out over the bay before we got to the northern boundary of the air base. He then explained why he wanted me to head in that direction. "In case something is falling off the jet we don't want to trash 'Joe Six-pack's' Doughboy swimming pool down there." He was still trusting me to fly the jet, and I settled into the turn at about 230 knots, giving me a safe margin below the maximum landing gear extension airspeed of 250 knots.

The runway supervisory unit (RSU), also known as mobile control or just "mobile," was located at the approach end of the runway, and in those days was manned by an IP and a student. The former keyed his radio and said, "'Sinbad,' you might have blown a tire on takeoff. Hold her down below 250 and keep the gear down. Set up for a pass over the RSU so I can take a look." Tom replied, "Roger that. I think you are right. At least that's what it felt like right at the moment of lift off. Otherwise all is okay."

By this time, I was out over Hillsborough Bay between the MacDill AFB peninsula and Davis Island. At that point Tom said, "I've got it!" and shook the stick. I let go, feeling him on the controls. He made a big wide turn from what was essentially a downwind position and lined up with the RSU, while slowing to about 200 knots and descending to about 150ft. He then flew a pattern over the RSU and we waited for the report from the ground. The IP quickly came back on the radio after regaining his hearing from our low pass and stated, "It doesn't look awful but I think it is definitely blown. We have a crew headed out to check for tire debris on the runway. 'Sinbad,' are you in the front or back seat?" Tom replied, "Back chair with a 'Dollar Ride' student in front." A "Dollar Ride" denoted that this was a pilot's first trip in a new type of aircraft, for which the instructor was typically rewarded with one US dollar. This exchange also clarified that Tom was in back with a student in the front on his first flight in an F-4.

The IP responded with, "Well, that adds to the drama. Why don't you guys go off to the east, dump fuel and burn down some of the rest while I confer with the 'powers that be' on a recommended course of action. You might want to review your approach end barrier engagement procedures. Remain on this frequency. I'll call you." With a crisp, "Roger!" in reply, Tom turned the jet east and started a climb. After a while he instructed me on fuel-dumping procedures and switchology and gave me back control of the jet. After what seemed like a long time the IP called and said, "We think you should make an approach end barrier engagement. Can you do that from the back seat?" Tom replied, "I think that with this 500ft-wide runway that's two miles long, we should just land it and roll out straight ahead." The IP simply replied, "Your call!"

Tom coached me through my first F-4 landing from a modified straight-in. Gear was already down, so the flaps were lowered, and I slowed to 19.2 units angle-of-attack, which gave me an "on-speed" light on the indicator, and I stabilized there, trimming the jet hands off in pitch. With power, I could control my descent and maintain my attitude via the visual approach slope indicator. We weren't taught to flare out the F-4C. You just held that attitude till you hit the runway just like a navy carrier landing, and that's what I did. In later days we did learn to flare the aircraft and soften the touchdown. However, as a student on my first flight, I did exactly what Tom told me to do. Once on the ground I pulled the drag chute handle and the jet slowed rapidly. There was a tendency to turn toward the blown tire, but it was initially controllable with rudder. As we slowed down the nose wheel steering completed the job.

We stopped on the runway and the groundcrew, with a tug, came out and hauled us onto the taxiway. We went through a normal shut down procedure, safed-up our ejection seats, and I deplaned using the spring-mounted hand and foot ports built into the side of the jet. The last step would have been a big one if not for a mini-ladder that could be extended by stepping on a button in the bottom foot port. By the time I reached the ground, Tom had jumped out of the back seat, slid off onto a wing and jumped down. He was grinning like the Cheshire Cat in *Alice in Wonderland*, and as he shook my hand he asked me, "Where's my dollar?"

FLASHPOINTS

On January 23, 1968, shortly after my flight training had started on the F-4 at MacDill, the *Pueblo* incident occurred off the coast of North Korea. The intelligence-gathering ship USS *Pueblo* (AGER-2) and its entire crew – one of whom was killed when the vessel came under attack – were captured by North Korean armed forces despite being in international waters. The world held its breath and our training came to a screeching halt as negotiations started for the release of the crew, along with arrangements to release the ship. The crew eventually came home 11 months later, but the ship remains in North Korean hands to this day.

A year earlier, on January 2, 1967, high-scoring World War II ace Col Robin Olds, commander of the 8th TFW at Ubon, led the famous Operation *Bolo* raid into North

Vietnam. Through tactical deception wherein the air-to-air configured F-4s used the call-signs normally used by the bomb-hauling F-105s, the MiG-21s of the Vietnam People's Air Force (VPAF) were lured into the air and ambushed, resulting in Col Olds and his pilots shooting down no fewer than seven MiGs.

By this time North Vietnam had acquired SA-2 "Guideline" SAMs to aid in the defense of their homeland. Their growing arsenal of Soviet-supplied heavy-caliber anti-aircraft artillery (AAA), along with the MiGs and SAMs, were controlled by a sophisticated communications network as part of an integrated air defense system.

The *Pueblo* incident and Col Old's *Bolo* raid gave us would-be fighter pilots a sobering introduction to the reality of the times.

As we progressed in our F-4 training and the time was growing shorter before our first taste of combat, the academic instructors worked very hard to be sure we were as prepared as they could possibly make us. This turned out to be an oxymoron in that we weren't used in the way we had been trained once we arrived at our combat squadrons. Instead, those units in Thailand and South Vietnam viewed us simply as "warm bodies" trained to fly the F-4. The personnel "weenies" assigned us wherever we were needed from a manpower standpoint, without regard to the specialized training we had previously received. We later proved during the concluding years of the war, and in the period between the Vietnam War and Operation *Desert Storm* in 1991, that the entire approach to training for the Vietnam War was flawed. More on that later.

Meanwhile, the seemingly ceaseless hours of academic training at MacDill had a few real highlights, including the many lectures given to us by two captains who had recently completed combat tours. One was John Borchert and the other was Lawrence Glynn, Jr (who had shot down a MiG-21 flying with the 8th TFW during *Bolo*). These guys went overboard to make the information in their lectures interesting. Jokes and war stories filled in the attention-loss gaps while we were trying to learn the complex weapons delivery aspects of the F-4. One such course was named "Switchology," as I have already mentioned. Radar theory was equally "captivating." These subjects were new to us all, and mastery of them would be the key to our eventual effectiveness and potential survival in a combat environment.

My favorite war story from those dreadful academic hours has been repeated by me many times to other fighter pilots from the lecture platform, as well as to family and friends, and during Father's Day 1994 at Mom and Dad's home in Las Vegas. My second wife Peggy, oldest daughter Kayte and the little (not so little anymore) girls Jennifer and Elizabeth were all there. We had been talking about Saudi Arabia, and Kayte was reminiscing about surfing the sand dunes and water skiing and snorkeling in the Arabian (Persian) Gulf among the sea snakes when I commented about actually being able to paint the latter on radar off the coast of North Vietnam.

One night, we went out over the Gulf of Tonkin for some long-forgotten reason. We were getting ready to ingress inland over enemy territory when the backseaters started calling out "islands" in the gulf where we knew there were no islands. I took a look at the ground-mapping radar and it sure as hell looked like little islands several miles east of the North Vietnamese coast. It was totally dark so it was impossible to visually determine what the radar was seeing. Later, someone of exquisite knowledge and dubious character explained to us that sea snakes would "raft up" as part of their mating ritual, and the rafts could be painted by the F-4 radar, looking like islands in places in the Gulf of Tonkin where there were no islands. I still don't know whether that is true or not, but one thing is certain – the radar saw something and we couldn't explain what it was.

The family was amazed, as were we at the time, that these deadly poisonous reptiles would congregate by the millions, making an island-like surface on an otherwise flat ocean. I don't remember whether the rafts were an acre or two in size, but I do recall seeing small islands on the radar that weren't actually there.

This discussion led to my recollection of a war story, of unknown source and questionable truth, but nonetheless entertaining. It was first told by Capt Lawrence Glynn, Jr in academic training at MacDill in 1968.

It seems that an F-4 had become separated from the rest of its flight of four during a particularly hairy attack against a target near downtown Hanoi, in North Vietnam. The crew was glad to be alive, but terrified at being in that neighborhood alone. Although the WSO in an F-4 had most of the same flight controls that were in the front seat, his job was almost exclusively to operate the weapons system. The WSO was initially a pilot, but later pilots were replaced as backseaters by rated navigators. In the early days the USAF crewed the F-4 with an experienced pilot in the front seat and a young, comparatively inexperienced aviator in the back seat. The backseaters were affectionately referred to as "GIBs" by the frontseaters.

Well, these two aviators in the lonely F-4 were moving at the "Speed of Heat," or as fast as the Phantom II would go in Military power (no afterburner) in their effort to reach relative safety. The latter was known as going "Feet Wet," which was the term for leaving enemy territory behind as the aircraft crossed the east coast of North Vietnam and flew out over the Gulf of Tonkin.

The F-4 had a wonderful safety device in its ejection seat. Constructed by the Martin-Baker company, it was probably the most complicated device ever built which worked every time. One of the quirks of the early seats, including the Mk H-7 fitted in the Phantom II, was the interlock block. This was a connector containing the pilot's communications cables and oxygen source. It was designed to pull out from the aircraft in a single smooth motion of extraction in the event the pilot ejected from the aircraft. Unfortunately, the pilot or "GIB," through their movement while strapped into the seat in the cockpit, could inadvertently disconnect the block. This wasn't usually a problem in Vietnam, as we typically flew combat missions below altitudes at which we would have required oxygen. However, communication was vital between the crewmembers in the aircraft via the intercom and in order to maintain situational awareness through radio comms with other fighters in the strike mission, as well as the supporting airborne early-warning platforms and air-refueling tankers.

On this particular day the "GIB" had been really busy in the back seat, twisting from side to side looking as far behind him as the F-4's fuselage and tail would allow in a visual search for attacking enemy aircraft and any SAMs launched either at them or at members of their flight. The aircrew actually learned to coordinate the look-out pattern so as to clear their "dead six," "deep six" or just "six o'clock" in general. This is the area immediately behind and below a fighter. It may surprise some people, but you couldn't clear this area in an F-4 without weaving. Therefore, the pilot banked the aircraft and turned

20 or 30 degrees while the "GIB" cleared "six." Then, the pilot reversed his turn and the "GIB" cleared the other side. This went on continuously during both the ingress (into the target area) and the egress (exit from the target area). If one were to visualize four sailboats from above, each maintaining a parallel courses to the others while tacking back and forth into the wind, that would be the same pattern often flown by a four-ship formation of fighters ingressing and egressing a target area. The purpose of the sailboats' weaving pattern is to permit them to sail into the wind. The purpose of the fighters' weave was to clear their own, and each other's, six o'clock. This was called providing mutual support.

Well, on this day, there had been several SAMs launched at the formation, which had also been targeted by enemy aircraft. Several hard defensive maneuvers were made to avoid the threats, and as a result the formation was somewhat in disarray by the time they got to the target. Following their dive-bombing pass, one fighter lost sight of the other three and, hence, the F-4 was on its own when egressing. It was at about this time that the "GIB" realized that all of his twisting and turning to clear "six" had caused the interlock block on his ejection seat to become disconnected, leaving him without communications with the pilot, or anyone else for that matter.

He wanted to let the pilot know he was okay, so he started tapping the side of the control stick. This action was quickly felt by the pilot, who misinterpreted it to be a command from the "GIB" to turn defensively because they were again under attack by an unseen enemy, either fighter or SAM. The pilot reacted by immediately selecting full afterburner, which consumes four times as much fuel as full military power. He slammed the Phantom II into a hard defensive turn in the direction of the stick tap. While the pilot searched the sky for the nonexistent threat, the swell of fear, and panic, began to consume the "GIB." He had no idea what was happening, but was sure they were about to die.

Finally, the pilot reduced the power and rolled out of the defensive turn, satisfied that there was no immediate threat. He set up a course for the Gulf of Tonkin and the safety of "Feet Wet." By now he knew he did not have the fuel to make it back to the KC-135 tanker for the aerial refueling that was the key to them returning to base. He attempted to have the tanker come north from the normal track and meet him, but to no avail. Finally, the J79 engines sucked the last drops of fuel from the Phantom II's fuel tanks and everything went quiet as the engines flamed out.

The ejection sequence in a two-seat tandem fighter is critical, and is therefore highly automated to ensure each occupant has the chance to escape. A mechanical charge like an artillery shell starts the seat up the rails. This motion pulls a lanyard and, like a match, lights the ejection seat rocket. The rocket catapults each ejection seat clear of the aircraft, and high enough for the parachute to open if the ejection occurs on the ground. Without the complicated sequencing of the seats, the backseater would get fried by the front seat rocket in the event the frontseater initiated the ejection. The sequence of events following the frontseater's decision to eject (from an F-4), and his act of pulling the ejection handle between his legs or the face curtain above his head, is as follows. Firstly, the rear canopy is jettisoned and then the rear seat ejects, firing its own rocket. Following the rear seat by a split second, the front canopy is jettisoned and then the front seat ejects, firing its rocket. Both aircrew are then automatically separated from their seats and their parachutes open. There is a delay on the seat separation if the ejection has been performed at high altitude. The seat is smart and does everything automatically.

This was exactly what happened that day, except the "GIB" had no idea what was about to happen since he had no way of verbally communicating with the pilot! He was finally calming down from the "near death event" of the previous few minutes when suddenly the engines quit. There was no fuel gauge in the back seat of the F-4, so he was unaware of the jet's imminent demise. Then, suddenly, the canopy over his head disappeared and he was involuntarily ejected from the aircraft by the action of the pilot over the water off the coast of North Vietnam.

The "GIB's" parachute opened fine, he deployed his life raft and, after he was sure that it had fully inflated, he actually started to enjoy the parachute descent. The raft swings on a 20–30ft lanyard below the person in the parachute and, as a result, acts like a pendulum. In this case, the pendulum began to swing back and forth, and pretty soon the parachute and its occupant were in a fully blown oscillation, with the "GIB" swinging 45 degrees or more either side of the vertical like the weight on a grandfather clock. Then he became motion sick and started to throw up. I guess he must have thought, "What could come next and make things worse?" He didn't have to wait long to find out.

After what seemed like an eternity, he finally splashed into the salty sea water. He kept his composure, and his training paid off for he remembered to pop open his CO_2-inflated personal life vest, which were called "water wings" by the pilots. Then he found the lanyard attaching his parachute kit to the life raft and pulled it to him. Many before him had drowned attempting to swim to the life raft. The wind will blow a one-man life raft away from the swimmer as he generates slack in the lanyard. However, if the pilot remembers to stop swimming and find the lanyard, this difficult scenario can be reversed by simply pulling the life raft to you. Without training, as given at water survival school, a potentially dangerous situation exists, especially in a high sea state with waves breaking over your head.

It was dead calm that day, and the life raft was easily retrieved. The one-man life raft or dinghy is a rubberized craft with a big fat end and a small narrow end. It's about six feet long, and wide enough to lie in it on your back. The fat end acts as a pillow, the sides as armrests and the small end facilitates climbing into the life raft. Naturally, you take water on board the life raft when you crawl over the small end, but the buoyancy is adequate in spite of the water all around you. It comes with a thin layer of rubberized material that can be pulled up over the occupant to serve as either a sea spray or sun shield. These emergency devices were designed for survival, and were bright orange in color so as to help rescuers find them floating in the open ocean. Later, we got blue ones, which made it hard for the bad guys to find you. The good guys could still home in on your radio and find you, but by then the war was over. I'm sure some of our buddies were "scarfed up" by the bad guys because of those orange rafts.

Well, our friend made it into the life raft safely and was considering the situation when he looked out to his left and, barely 50ft away, saw a skinny head sticking up out of the water – I've seen turtles do this in the rivers and ponds in Texas. It was clear to the "GIB" that this was no turtle, however. It was a dreaded sea snake, the most deadly creature known to man, and it was swimming from left to right, barely 50ft away, when it suddenly stopped and looked at the raft.

The snake must have thought how silly it was for a "GIB" to be trying to hide in a bright orange life raft in the middle of the Gulf of Tonkin. So, it started swimming toward the life raft, obviously planning to check it out. Three things happened next, almost simultaneously. The snake crawled into the small end of the life raft just as the "GIB" was exiting over the fat end. At the same time, a US Navy helicopter arrived overhead to effect a rescue, amazed to see the snake in the life raft and the "GIB" in the water. They completed the rescue of the delirious aviator and, fortunately for him, were able to validate his hysterical story. The pilot, who was also rescued, didn't have much to add to the tale.

Sea snakes are much like coral snakes in that they have little mouths and are not known to be aggressive, except perhaps in mating season. Can you imagine coming down in a parachute and landing in the middle of one of their mating rafts? Brrr! Better to be lucky than good!

TRAINING PROGRESSION

On the flightline, things were a lot more fun, if not quite so entertaining! We learned to fly the jet and we learned to fly instruments and formation in the jet. No real challenges there for me or my classmates.

Amongst the latter was Lt Col Dick Horne, who was returning to the cockpit after completing a staff position somewhere deep in the Pentagon. And there were two majors, Pete Peeler and Bob Hicks, both of whom were former fighter pilots who had been with me at Randolph flying as instructors in the T-38. The remainder of the aircraft commanders were captains, some from the F-4 back seat and others, like me, from other backgrounds. One was my lifelong friend Bill

Ricks, who had just finished a combat tour in the F-105 and was being reassigned into the F-4. All of our backseaters were pilots fresh out of pilot training. It was a good group, and most of us ended up going to Ubon RTAFB as our follow-on assignment. Grant "Jeb" Stewart, Steve Mosier, Bill Schnittger, Tom Lennon and Bill Looke were five back seat pilots that went with Pete Peeler, Bob Hicks, Ed Durocher and me to Ubon. Steve and I were crewed together as nightfighters, while Bill was also a nightfighter, but assigned to the 497th TFS "Night Owls." Peeler, Hicks, Lennon and Looke were in the 435th as I recall. Sadly, "Jeb," who was in the same squadron as Steve and I, was lost near the end of his tour of combat duty.

Following the easy flying came intercepts, basic fighter maneuvers (BFM) and air combat maneuvering (ACM), where we learned the basics of employing the F-4 in the air-to-air arena. Such engagements usually started with a ground-controlled intercept (GCI) to a visual identification, followed by a radar missile shot and a stern conversion for an infrared (IR) or heat-seeking missile shot.

We started with 90-degree beam intercepts, during which the F-4 was vectored by a ground radar controller. The backseaters learned to operate the radar, slewing the antenna as needed and moving the tilt and radar gain to first acquire the target and determine the intercept geometry, and then provide maneuvering guidance to the aircraft commander, who was flying the F-4. The goal was to approach the target aircraft (which was another F-4) at an angle perpendicular to it, while accounting for the fact that the target was moving at 400+ knots. When you point out in front with a 90-degree track crossing angle, it is called lead pursuit. When the backseater locked up the target with the F-4 radar, the radar then self-tracked it and the aircraft commander made the subjective decision on when to fire the radar-guided missile based on "rules of thumb."

The radar display in both cockpits included a little circle in the center when locked onto a target. The circle expanded in diameter after lock-on until the missile-firing jet approached the heart of the envelope for the radar missile. Then, the circle shrunk as the aircraft approached each other, and at the minimum missile range the circle changed to a large X (called a break X), indicating that the attacking aircraft was at less than the minimum range capability of the missile. The F-4's missiles had minimum ranges usually based on the time it took after launch for the weapon's warhead to arm, and maximum ranges based on the kinematics of the missile – the latter was based on the amount of rocket fuel the weapon carried, as well as its lethal coast range after the fuel was exhausted.

On the F-4C/D, there was a little switch on the aircraft commander's instrument panel marked "radar" in one position and "IR," for the heat-seeking missiles, in the other. That switch, which had a plastic or hard rubber tube several inches long as an extender, was one of four that was key to a successful missile shot. The initial switch set up was always down, up, down, up, as viewed from left to right. The extender on the radar/IR switch permitted the pilot to easily find it by feel as the attack progressed, initially from a longer range radar missile shot to the shorter range IR missile shot. During this period, it was vital that the pilot not take his eyes off the target. And our F-4C/Ds had no internal gun, so the missile was the real deal.

After simulating firing a radar missile, the aircraft commander would move the radar/IR switch to IR and the entire attack display on the radar would change to parameters for an IR missile, usually an AIM-4 Falcon or AIM-9 Sidewinder. The early IR missiles needed to look right up the tail pipe of the target. This meant that from the 90-degree approach angle for the radar missile shot, the aircraft commander had to turn hard in the opposite direction of the target's heading and then almost immediately reverse back toward the tail of the target aircraft to put the IR missile into proper parameters looking up the tail pipe of the jet.

The 90-degree beam intercept was not a difficult attack geometry for the aircraft commanders to learn, and it was a useful starting point for the backseaters as they learned how to operate the radar and interpret the radar scope because the 90-degree beam intercept developed more slowly than the 135-degree (near head-on) and the 180-degree (head-on) intercepts, thus giving the inexperienced backseater more time to operate the radar and interpret the situation.

The radar antenna swept from 60 degrees either side of the nose of the jet. It could be set up by the backseater in different scan modes to widen or narrow the piece of sky that the radar could see. For example, if the radar made one scan (called a bar width) and then automatically lowered its look angle one bar width, it was looking at two bar widths of sky before it repeated itself. If it lowered four times before repeating, it would be a four-bar scan. These scans were called raster scans, and hence this example would be a four-bar raster scan. The switch for controlling the scan was on the radar control panel in the back seat of the jet. The entire scan could be adjusted up or down with a little wheel on the side of the radar antenna control stick, which was also in the back seat. When the entire scan was adjusted up or down, it was called adjusting the tilt of the antenna.

The aircraft commander and his backseater had to work as a true crew to be effective with the F-4C/D radar. Developing good crew coordination was the key to getting the full measure of combat capability out of the Phantom II.

The radar control stick located in the rear cockpit was used by the backseater to position two little vertical bars on the radar scope. Technically, these bars were the target acquisition symbol, but they were usually referred to as the "captain's bars" because they resembled the captain's military insignia. During the intercept, the backseater moved the captain's bars with the radar control stick, placing them over a target – the target was centered between the bars.

Finding a target was tricky. There was a knob on the radar control panel called "gain." With the gain fully up, the radar scope would be totally flooded with illumination. As the gain was turned down, the illumination subsided and eventually went away, except for the return from the target. The return was simply a reflection of the F-4's radar energy bouncing off of the target aircraft.

So, successful operation of the radar involved selecting the correct scan for the situation and then adjusting the antenna tilt and the gain until the target was broken out from the background. Only then could the backseater squeeze the trigger on the radar control stick to the first detent. At that point the radar antenna snapped to the target's azimuth angle off the nose, and the extra energy on the target from the radar made it "bloom." Squeezing the trigger fully commanded the radar to lock onto the target and track it wherever the target went. The tracking constraints were 60 degrees either side of the nose of the attacking aircraft and the upper and lower gimbal limits of the antenna.

After 90-degree beam intercepts, we advanced to 135- and 180-degree head-on attacks with our AIM-7 radar missiles, all followed by the stern conversion for the IR missile shot.

We hadn't learned to maneuver yet when engaging another aircraft in what would be euphemistically called a dogfight. That came next with BFM. The introduction to BFM was to assume the trail position like the slot man in the Thunderbirds' diamond formation and then take spacing back to 500 or 1,000ft while the leader flew climbing and descending turns. It took additional power to follow the leader up and a power reduction to keep from overrunning when the leader was going down. As the leader turned left or right, or simply reversed a direction of turn, quick reactions and, in some cases, anticipation were required to be able to maintain that position. If changes were not made quickly enough, the young pilot would, in an extended trail formation, quickly get out of synchronization with the leader's turns. Perfecting this kind of maneuvering was an early "building block" of training for air-to-air combat.

In the early 1960s we weren't very sophisticated in our understanding of more advanced dogfight maneuvers, or in our execution of them. Years of concentrating on the tactical nuclear mission and air defense against Soviet bombers had blunted the skills F-86 Sabre pilots had used to dominate the skies over Korea in the early 1950s. The instructors during the early days of the Vietnam War just weren't very good at teaching the science and art of aerial combat. Korean War ace "Boots" Blesse's volume *No Guts, No Glory* on how to fight and win in a dogfight was clearly not required reading in the US fighter community.

After achieving some skill level in the basics, we started with perch attacks, taking turns between attacking and defending.

The initial positioning for the attacker was 2,000 to 3,000ft back and about 1,000ft higher than the defender, offset 15 or 20 degrees to one side. Typically, a student was in the front seat of each aircraft, with his instructor in the seat behind him. As briefed, the attacking student would call "Ready" and the defender would call "Fight's On."

As previously noted, the F-4C/D of this time frame did not have an internal gun. One of two external gun pods – known as the SUU-16 or SUU-23 – could be carried on the centerline station of the F-4C/D. These guns carried about 1,000 rounds of 20mm ammunition. The primary difference in the two guns was in the way the weapon was powered. The F-4C did not have a lead computing gunsight, which was generally thought to be needed for air-to-air combat. In spite of that limitation, F-4C pilots used the jet's fixed gunsight to claim four MiG kills with the external gun. Six more were credited to pilots flying the F-4D, which was a highly upgraded aircraft in terms of computer-based electronics – the latter included a lead-computing optical sighting system that made accurate aerial gunnery appreciably easier.

About midway through my combat tour the F-4E with an internal gun arrived in the theater. With that tidbit on the gun described, let us continue the discussion of BFM.

After the "Fight's On" call, the defending pilot would start a defensive turn into the attacker, while the attacker would initiate a low speed "yo-yo" after initially pointing his jet at the defender. The low speed "yo-yo" was simply an acceleration maneuver accomplished by selecting full afterburner power and pushing the stick forward until approximately 0g was attained; 0g minimized the drag on the jet, expediting acceleration. As the attacker approached the defender to what would approximate a 2,000ft gun range (if the jet had a gun, that is!), the defender hardened his turn into the attacker to attempt to create an overshoot. If the attacker recognized the impending overshoot in time, he would roll wings near level and zoom vertically, executing a high-speed "yo-yo" to a position above and still behind the defender. At this point the defender executed a low-speed "yo-yo" and attempted to accelerate away from the attacker while the latter was still in a nose-high position. Recognizing the defender was about to get away from his overhead attack with "negative delta mach," the attacker used rudder to roll the aircraft back down, continuing his pursuit.

BFM never happened that perfectly, however, with the fight usually developing into a series of overshoots, reversals, scissors and vertical rolling scissors maneuvers, lag rolls and so on until one pilot achieved a gun firing position (if we had one), a stalemate became evident or the minimum hard deck height altitude for BFM was reached.

The scissors can best be visualized starting with both jets side-by-side several hundred feet apart. Each pilot is trying to get behind the other, and the technique is to pull hard into the vertical and roll toward the adversary. The jet with the highest nose position with each reversal of the scissors gradually works into a position behind the other jet. In similar-type aircraft, the winner of a scissor is the pilot with the best skill as the jets' performance potential is identical.

The lag roll is an interesting maneuver that was uniquely required due to the limitations of the early heat-seeking air-to-air missiles, which could not detect the heat of the defending jet from the inside of a turn. This mandated the attacking pilot maneuvering to a position directly behind the defender to allow the missile to "see" directly up the tail pipe of the engine(s) of the adversary jet. To accomplish this maneuver the attacking pilot rolled his fighter in the opposite direction of the defender's turn, and the resulting lag roll solved the angle off problem by putting the attacker in trail with the defender, instead of inside the defender's turn.

In spite of the apparent maneuvering at low altitude depicted in some movies (specifically *Top Gun*), 10,000ft above the terrain or the water is the normal minimum altitude for an air-to-air engagement in a training environment.

After BFM came ACM, wherein two fighters learned to operate as a pair against a third defender. That was the extent of our air-to-air training, and in ACM we flew as wingmen in a two-ship element. The wingman flew a formation known as fighting wing. That position was a 30-degree cone 1,500ft behind the element leader, who was the shooter. The wingman's role in life was to keep the bad guy shooters from gunning the leader while the latter was busy attempting to gun someone else. The IPs were always the leaders, and when the students asked them for details about what they did, the answers they received were vague and general.

When two elements operate as a four-ship, it is a formation called "fluid four," and we were trained as wingmen in "fluid four" formations. We didn't realize it at the time, but we were training for the last war – Korea. In Korea, it was gun-versus-gun. Vietnam was different following the introduction of the air-to-air missile and the notion, at the time, that the gun was obsolete in a fighter.

Our final air-to-air event was a live missile shoot. The way that worked was we fired an unguided five-inch Zuni rocket off our jet out in the Warning Area 168 range west of Tampa and then maneuvered to put our gunsight (pipper) on it. Having acquired a guidance tone, we fired an AIM-9B Sidewinder. Only about half the guys got that done, as I recall, before the five-inch rocket burned out and the AIM-9B was unable to get a heat signature. This was our first experience with the challenge of real-time switchology, and we learned that it was hard to do.

After air-to-air, we started learning about ground attack – dive-bombing, rocketry, skip bombing and strafing (with an externally mounted gun). With the USAF never ready to give up the nuclear role, we also learned two primary nuclear weapons delivery attacks, namely Level and Low-Angle Drogue Delivery (LADD), which used both visual and radar modes for ordnance delivery. All of this training was conducted on the Avon Park ranges in roughly the center of Florida.

These combat tools weren't taught one at a time. Instead, an SUU-16 external 20mm cannon and two 370-gallon external fuel tanks were loaded on the F-4 (SUU-16 on the centerline station and a single tank on the outboard wing stations). On one of the inboard pylons we had a weapons dispenser called an SUU-21 that featured bomb-bay doors. This had the capacity to carry six training bombs. On the other opposing inboard pylon was an LAU rocket pod containing two or three 2.75in. folding-fin aerial rockets (FFARs).

Four of the weapons carried in the SUU-21 were blue BDU-33 slick bombs, simulating the family of 500 to 2,000lb general-purpose Mk 82 and Mk 84 bombs. The remaining two were Mk 106 bombs that simulated nuclear weapons – we called the latter "beer cans" because of their flat front, which supposedly provided ballistics similar to a "nuke" fitted with a retard parachute. The SUU-21's bomb-bay doors were operated by the aircraft's circuitry via a nuclear control panel called a DCU-94 installed in the rear cockpit of the F-4.

The first two passes at the range were simulated nuclear deliveries to get rid of the "beer cans"; then the flight, usually of four aircraft, would cross the range scoring tower and call "Up for rockets, dive, skip and strafe." Two or three 30-degree dive angle rocket passes were duly made, followed by two 45-degree dive-bombing passes and two very low altitude-level or slightly descending skip-bombing passes – the latter were flown mainly to simulate napalm delivery. That emptied our bomb dispenser. There was significant switchology involved in changing from bombs to rockets, back to bombs, and then to the gun. Strafing was the final event on the controlled range, and we usually made five passes, expending 100 rounds of 20mm ammunition from our gun pods. The guns had a rounds limiter that could be set before takeoff. If set to 100, the gun would stop firing after expending 100 rounds.

On the approach to the range the flight lead would contact the range officer, who would give precise instructions on which range and the appropriate traffic pattern to be used. As noted in the illustration opposite, each range consisted of a circular nuke target, two circular conventional targets for rockets and dive-bombing, a long skinny target that looked like a rectangle on the ground for skip bombing, and cloth panels strung between two poles for strafing. The range officer was located in the center tower with a spotter, while another spotter manned at least one of the remaining two scoring towers. The conventional ranges were referred to as right range and left range. So as to avoid having to point a "hot" gun at the range officer's tower, the right range would use left traffic and vice versa for the left range.

So, the radio call between the flight lead and the range officer usually went as follows: "'Charlie' Range, 'Sporty'

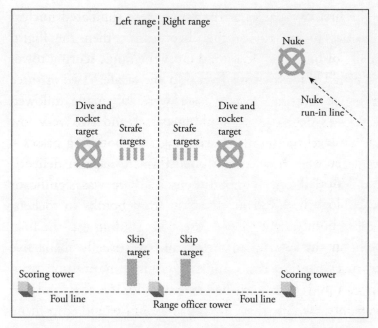

Diagram of a typical controlled air-to-ground gunnery range. Fighters could be directed to either fly "Right range, left traffic" or "Left range, right traffic." The range officer in the center tower and an assistant in either the left or right scoring tower triangulated bomb and rocket impacts on the nuke target or the dive and rocket targets, passing the score to the pilot.

with a flight of four for two nukes and rockets, dive, skip and strafe."

The range officer replied with, "Roger, 'Sporty,' you are cleared onto 'Charlie' Range for two nuke passes, followed by right range, left traffic for rockets, dive, skip and strafe. Call departing the nuke IP [Initial Point]."

"Roger, 'Sporty' Lead is departing the IP."

Each wingman would follow with briefed spacing between the jets. At the completion of the second nuke pass "Sporty" would join up his four-ship and then fly by the range tower at low altitude with the flight in echelon formation. The

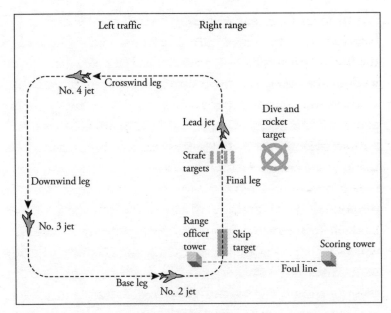

Diagram illustrating the flightpath of the fighters when cleared to drop on the right range with left traffic.

gunnery pattern at the range was similar to a traffic pattern for aircraft. Those positions are referred to above as Final, Base, Downwind and Crosswind.

Pitching up in a closed traffic pattern, the flight lead would contact the range officer with the call, "'Sporty' is up for dive." Each flight member then followed him down, with spacing that meant after the first pass the lead was on final, pulling out of the dive-bombing pass, with the No. 2 jet on base leg about to roll in, the No. 3 established on the downwind leg and the No. 4 on the crosswind leg.

The nuclear deliveries on the controlled range were flown at low altitude (typically at 1,000ft for radar deliveries and 500ft for visual deliveries). The approach to the target was along what was called a nuke run-in line – a straight line several miles long that was bladed out of the central Florida landscape by a bulldozer. One end of the line was known as the initial point, which was where the nuke delivery started, while at the other end of the run-in line was the target.

There were several different modes for level nuclear bomb delivery. One example made use of the aircraft's radar and a timer system. The radar was commanded into a mapping mode call MAP PPI. In this mode, the radar presentation took the form of a sweep that resembled a piece of pie, with the point of the pie at the bottom of the radar scope. The point represented the delivery aircraft. The outer part of the sweep, which depicted the radar's range, was selected by the aircrew with switchology. As the radar swept back and forth up to 60 degrees on either side of the nose of the aircraft, a strobe was illuminated at precisely five nautical miles directly in front of the jet. Appropriately, this was known as the five-mile bomb strobe.

A radar reflector at the center of the target was oriented to the run-in line to assist the F-4 backseater in finding the target with the radar. As the jet approached the target along the run-in line, the radar return of the reflector moved from the top of the scope down toward the five-mile bomb strobe. When the two coincided, the backseater would push and hold the pickle button (a red button located on the top of the control stick just to the left of the trim button) until the bomb came off the jet. With proper switchology on the nuclear control panel, pushing and holding the button while in nuclear lay-down mode started a timer that ultimately released the simulated nuke (a Mk 106 "beer can") when the appropriate bomb range was reached.

In a level delivery the bomb range was determined by the delivery altitude of the jet above the ground, as well as the aircraft's airspeed. All these numbers were calculated on the ground as part of the mission planning and then written by the pilot and/or backseater on their kneeboards.

The second nuke pass mode used by F-4 crews was LADD. This delivery could also incorporate the radar and the five-mile bomb strobe, or various other options. With LADD selected, the timer would command a climb at approximately 40 degrees. A climb needle on the attitude directional indicator (ADI) provided precise pitch control to the pilot. At the correct time for the appropriate bomb range, the weapon would come off the jet in what could be described as a toss maneuver. The range officer (and his assistants) in the scoring tower then triangulated where the bomb hit the ground via the smoke puff generated by the weapon on impact. He would pass the score to the aircrew via UHF radio, using a feet and a clock position reference. A gross bomb short (or long) would be communicated to the aircrew over the radio with the call "unscorable at six [or twelve]." A bullseye was called a "shack" and other impacts might be scored as "100 [feet] at 2 [o'clock]," etc.

Once the nuke Mk 106 bombs were expended, the flight of four repositioned for the conventional (versus nuke) deliveries of the two or three rockets and the four bombs. These deliveries were followed by multiple strafing passes with the 20mm gun.

Rockets were delivered from a 30-degree dive at an altitude that would permit a minimum height above ground level (AGL) of 1,000ft after a 5g recovery from the dive. I always found rockets tricky to deliver accurately with any consistency. The jet needed to be precisely at the g-loading corresponding to a trigonometry function (cosine, as I recall) of the dive angle with the gunsight pipper on the target.

I just wasn't as good at hitting those parameters as I wanted to be. I was better at dive-bombing, and a whole lot better at strafing.

We were trained to dive bomb at an angle of 45 degrees, releasing the bomb at a precise altitude above the ground exactly at the planned airspeed and, of course, with the dive angle nailed at exactly 45 degrees. As with a rocket attack, the planning of these parameters permitted the 1,000ft AGL recovery after a 5g pull-out from the dive. We also dropped bombs from a very low altitude near level delivery to simulate an attack with napalm. Referred to as skip bombing, the minimum altitude for such runs was 50ft AGL for a level delivery or 100ft for a slight dive of five to ten degrees.

Strafing was the most fun. Point the jet at the strafe target and "let 'er rip," being careful to cease firing before crossing the foul line between the scoring towers. The gun fired 100 rounds a second, and we normally expended very short bursts so as to permit four or five passes before consuming the 100 rounds allocated for each sortie. Limiting each sortie for training to 100 rounds permitted several gun sorties to be flown before the gun had to be reloaded. When the last member of the flight called "Winchester," indicating that all allocated rounds had been fired, the flight leader would call for a join up and the four-ship formation would return to MacDill.

The debriefings were important, but seemingly less important than the tally of the scores for each of the air-to-ground ordnance delivery events! Bets were made ahead of time on each of the best scores, and many quarters changed hands among the pilots as the wagers were settled. Little did we know at that point about how things would change in combat. Much higher release altitudes to stay above the enemy's small-arms fire was one thing. Another was the bet on a combat mission was not for quarters.

After we became acquainted with the delivery of weapons during daylight on the controlled range at Avon Park, we had to learn to do it at night. That was a thrill for sure. Then we got to go to the tactical range and expend actual inert and then live ordnance using combat release altitudes and other appropriate high-threat-area tactics. Finally, we were done, with only memories of "gunnery school," as it was called, coupled with a faint recall of the rowdy evenings in the "Stag Bar."

"STAG BAR" SHENANIGANS

At MacDill, the "Stag Bar" was a detached component of the Officers' Club, being located in a facility on overwater stilts along the shore of Hillsborough Bay. The building had previously been the dock and admin area for the crash boats that supported flight operations, these vessels having now been replaced by helicopters. It was a nifty single room building, with a bar down one side of the room. No women were allowed, and the behavior of those present was often bad, bordering on outrageous.

The flightsuits that are worn by aircrew have a small pocket on the inboard side of the left thigh. The purpose of the pocket is to house an orange two-bladed knife, with a pop-open blade on one end and a U-shaped blade on the other end. The knife goes into the pocket with the U end down but open, and the blade end up and folded like a pocket knife. The knife attaches to a ring in the pocket cover via a nylon cord, thus permitting quick retrieval if it is dropped when being used. The purpose of the U-shaped blade is to provide aircrew with a tool for cutting lines on a parachute to make it steerable. The modification is called a four-line cut, and when the marked parachute shroud lines are severed, air is spilled out of the canopy on the side opposite the direction the aircrewman is facing. This spillage gives the 'chute forward motion, and by pulling parachute risers on the left or right side the 'chute becomes steerable.

Fighter pilots wear an anti-g suit when flying to help them cope with the high-g loads experienced in combat aircraft operations, and the knife pocket is sewed onto the anti-g suit in approximately the same location as the pocket on the flightsuit. As a result, the original pocket is redundant, and therefore not used. Indeed, fighter pilots have the pocket removed from their flightsuits, keeping the knife in the anti-g suit pocket instead. Removal of the flightsuit pocket can be achieved in various ways, including it being ripped off by another fighter pilot. The technique employed is sometimes sudden and violent, with the attacker grabbing and ripping open the pocket cover, and then using it as a "handle" to rip the pocket itself from the flightsuit. Done well, the cover comes off neatly, leaving only traces of thread on the otherwise undamaged flightsuit. Done poorly, the leg of the flightsuit sometimes comes off with the pocket, and this usually results in a fight breaking out.

The so-called "pecker pocket" fights usually erupted when a new F-4 trainee showed up at the "Stag Bar" for the first time with an "unmodified" flightsuit. Other victims were transient personnel who wandered into "our house." On one such occasion, and under the judgment-inhibiting influence of several Beefeater gin-on-the rocks, it fell to me to modify an inappropriate flightsuit. The abuser of our rule on flightsuit "pecker pockets" took exception to the modification and a pretty good non-fist-fight tussle resulted. When it was over, my flightsuit was also in shreds, with the front zipper ripped out, along with both legs. My underwear was also missing. Thinking that it was time to call it a night, we disengaged and I mounted my trusty motor scooter for the half-mile ride to my house along Bayshore Boulevard. Along the way the last threads holding the legs of my flightsuit gave way, and I continued down the road with it flailing behind me like a cape, with not much else on underneath. I got home and realized I was locked out, and therefore had to ring the doorbell to get Jeannie to open the door. Her expression was welded into my memory cells, and the soft-spoken young woman who rarely uttered a profanity greeted me with, "You've gotta be shitting me!"

Beer is proof that God loves us and wants us to be happy.*

We also partied a lot with our wives and girlfriends – usually a few drinks, some food, more drinks and then sometimes there were games. I got a pretty good picture one night when the guys decided to dress in women's clothing.

Our assignments eventually came, and most of us learned that we were going straight to the Vietnam War. Then things changed, and several of us were held over for more training, with a follow-on assignment to the Vietnam War. The added top-off training was a short academic and flight training course in the employment of the AGM-62 Walleye glide bomb. Walleye was an electro-optically guided smart bomb that was developed for the US Navy. The National Museum of the Air Force describes the Walleye as follows:

Although designated an air-to-ground missile, the Walleye was actually an unpowered glide bomb with a nose-mounted

---

*Attributed to Ben Franklin.

television camera to guide it to the target. The Walleye's camera sent an image of the target to the pilot's television screen. Once the pilot "locked" onto the target, he launched the weapon. The Walleye's onboard guidance system independently compared the locked image with the current image and made course corrections. Since the pilot did not have to control the bomb all the way to the target, the Walleye was known as a "fire and forget" weapon.

Starting in 1967, USAF F-4s and US Navy A-4 and A-7 aircraft used the Walleyes, but they saw only limited use by the USAF. Walleyes worked well if a target stood out from the surrounding area, but they had trouble if there was not enough contrast. Also, the weapon's light weight made it ineffective against targets like bridges. The Walleye II, a larger version with extended range, was used in Operation *Desert Storm* in 1991, before being retired from service.

Technical Notes
Weight: 1,100lb
Range: 16 miles
Warhead: 825lb Mk 58 linear shaped-charge*

So, in 1968, our class at MacDill was the leading edge of Walleye combat employment training for the USAF. We learned academically that Walleye was essentially an edge tracker, which meant it was most capable of tracking the edge of an object. This could be either good or bad. In the latter case, if Walleye's TV optics were locked onto a bridge, for example, the absence of a corner allowed its tracker to run down the structure's beam, jump to a railing to the shoreline and then run along the edge of the land/water contrast until it acquired a corner that was big enough for the optics to hold

*https://www.nationalmuseum.af.mil/Visit/Museum-Exhibits/Fact-Sheets/Display/Article/195663/martin-marietta-agm-62-walleye-i/

steady and track. On a positive note, once it found a corner that was big enough to track, the optics did a good job of holding onto the lock.

Mechanically, the image the pilot or WSO in the F-4 viewed was that of a shades-of-gray video picture that was reasonably high resolution. There were two vertical and two horizontal lines that formed a small square in the center of the image. The square "looked" straight ahead unless the aircrew pulled the trigger on the control stick. When the trigger was pulled, the TV camera optics unlocked from their straight ahead view and the Walleye tracker locked onto whatever edge was in the square. The target was tracked from that point on.

Our academic task was to ascertain how the system worked and then to learn how to plan for a mission using Walleye against a particular target type. The angle of the sun, and resulting shadows in some cases, mandated the direction that had to be flown to optimize the tracker's ability to hold the lock-on until the weapon could reach the target. Then, the Walleye glided on its own to the target without further input from the aircrew. With proper switchology, the Walleye could be unlocked to track a target from either cockpit's control stick trigger. In combat it would also be released from the launching aircraft if either crewmember pressed the bomb release button on the control stick. In training, the release capability was disabled, allowing us to roam around southern Florida and practice locking up targets.

Then, after proper target attack planning, the task on our training sorties was to learn how to work as a coordinated flight crew. The aircraft commander would set the depressible gunsight to a mil (milliradian) setting that corresponded to where the little square in the Walleye seeker was looking. Thus, when the pilot pointed the jet so that his gunsight pipper lined up with a tree, bridge, building or other object on the ground, the "GIB" would then see the exact same tree, bridge, building or other object by looking at the radar scope in his cockpit. With proper switchology, the radar scope now acted as a television receiver.

Getting good at doing this took a lot of practice, and during the course of a 90-minute sortie crews would make multiple attempts at achieving the levels of coordination that the task required for it to be undertaken both quickly and precisely. Once a target was acquired and the seeker was unlocked with a trigger squeeze, the pilot flew the jet on a flightpath as if it were the Walleye. By simulating the release of the weapon, it permitted the aircrew to observe how well the tracker would hang on to the target after the bomb was released. This was done repeatedly until proficiency was achieved and the crew coordination was perfect. Once the fundamentals were mastered the mindset changed to a combat environment using the tactics we had previously learned.

Two of our instructors were Bill "Big Daddy" Dowell and Arleigh McRae. They had both received Walleye training either at Nellis AFB or some other location and now were passing on their knowledge to those of us that were about to take this smart weapon into combat. For Walleye training, we changed squadrons at MacDill from the 45th to the 46th TFS. As our tuition on the weapon training was coming to an end, one day* as I was leaving the squadron building, "Big Daddy" and Arleigh were heading in my direction on the short walk from the flightline. They were wearing their parachute harnesses and anti-g suits and carrying their helmets in the AF helmet bags. They had been instructors in the same F-4 on a two-ship training

*Editor's Note: June 27, 1968.

mission with two of our classmates, Capt Marvin Guthrie and 1Lt Calvin Stitcher. Both "Marv" and "Cal" were excellent pilots that had done well in training. "Marv" was a bachelor and "Cal" was married to a lovely Georgia girl named Donna. The Stitchers had two very small children, Dawn and Shane.

As the instructors got closer to me I could see that their expressions were ashen and they were in an intense conversation using their hands to demonstrate flightpaths. When we were within speaking distance, in words that I have erased from my memory, I realized they were telling me that Marvin and Calvin had crashed and that there were no parachutes, and thus no chance of survival.

The world stopped!

Jeannie and I were really close to the Stitchers, and my next memory was being at the front door of Donna's apartment with our squadron leadership team, the chaplain and a flight surgeon standing behind Jeannie and me. I rang the doorbell and after a moment Donna opened the door. She took one look at all of us and knew instantly that this was not going to be good news. I said something like, "Donna, we had an accident and we have lost Calvin." Both children were hanging on her legs by this time and all exploded into tears as the reality of the situation sank in. The children were too young to understand what had happened and their tears were in response to Donna's reaction. The rest of that event is a fog in my memory. Several of us did go to Atlanta with Donna and her children to be with her parents and sibling. Then, we went to Athens, Georgia, to be with Calvin's parents and his brothers. It was a tough start to the combat tour that was now so imminent. But somehow we got through this tragedy and moved on.

To War

Jeannie's dad Jack Hilger had retired as an Air Force brigadier general by this time and had settled in Las Vegas. As I previously noted, "General Jack" had been Jimmy Doolittle's vice commander on the famous raid against Japan. When he and his crew bailed out over China at the end of the attack he suffered combat injuries. As a result, "General Jack" was eligible under the combat disability law in effect at the time to retire, collect his full retirement pay and also go to work for the US government as a civil servant. "General Jack" had a mechanical engineering degree from Texas A&M, and upon his retirement he landed a great job with the Atomic Energy Commission in Las Vegas. A big shot involved with the underground nuclear weapons test program in Nevada, he directed the nuclear detonations at Pahute Mesa and also in Alaska.

"General Jack" and his wife Virginia bought a beautiful house at 1918 Bannies Lane in what is now known as the highly desirable Scotch 80s area of Las Vegas. It is located southeast of the corner of Rancho and Charleston Boulevards – a very ritzy part of town, both then and now. In fact, the roads are now blocked and the area is gated. It wasn't gated in 1968.

Jeannie wanted to live in Las Vegas close to her parents, and that made sense to me. So, after completing my time with the Replacement Training Unit at MacDill, we hocked everything we had, took a loan out against the value of my life insurance and bought a house at 6232 Casada Way in Las Vegas. Located a block or two north of Charleston Boulevard in the area of Torrey Pines, it was a little three-bedroom house that had had its one-car garage converted into a family room – that was a popular way to go in Vegas at the time. I later owned another house in Las Vegas at 724 Delta Way that was very similar, except it had air conditioning and a swimming pool. Casada relied on a swamp cooler, which chilled a house in very dry desert conditions by blowing air over water-wetted pads. That air was then forced into the house's ventilation ducts in a similar way to how a refrigerated air system functioned. The swamp coolers worked fine as long as the outside humidity wasn't too high. The house had a big cottonwood tree in the backyard along the fence line. Cottonwood trees are relatively fragile and have been known to blow down during Las Vegas's summer thunderstorm microbursts. I think power lines ran down the property line and through the branches of that tree. It always worried me, but as far as I know the tree is still standing.

So it was. We moved in and started to get settled as the date of my port call for departure to Thailand approached. There was so much to do and so little time left to get things done. The clock ran out and I had to leave. Jeannie was left with all of the unfinished projects. Many years later, I read and transcribed digitally all the letters that flowed back and forth between us in the following year. I was shocked at the magnitude of her task, which ranged from getting a fence repaired to managing the disposition of a pile of gravel in the yard that was left over from a previous project. I don't remember exactly how we worked the finances, but I think I left her with the family checkbook. I in turn relied on a fairly small monthly allowance that was augmented somewhat by the less than generous $100 a month combat pay. I don't know how, but we made it work.

THE "STRETCH 8"

God, it was a long trip from the West Coast of the USA to the Philippines in the four-engined aluminum tube known as the Douglas DC-8. There were no first or business class seats. Just six seats per row, divided by a center aisle that could have been mistaken for a lane of a bowling alley! The stewardesses were lovely young women that worked hard to ease our war anticipation anxieties with small talk as they brought us airline food. But the volume of male testosterone that clamored for their attention was overwhelming. Most of the "stews" had seen this act before and, eventually, mostly fell silent. As time passed the weary future warriors settled into a doze, wake up, get up, go pee, walk around routine that seemed like it was going to last forever.

Fuel stops in Hawaii, Wake Island and Guam were simply teasing events because we knew that another endless leg of flight across the vast Pacific Ocean lay just ahead of us. One of the guys nearly got thrown off the jet in Hawaii over his behavior, although by the time we got to Wake Island he had "run out of gas." The crew of the jet changed at each stop, but we continued. Finally, it was over. We were exhausted, but eager to find our billets and get some sleep. All were fighting not only the long trip in terms of fatigue, but also the many time zones that we had crossed. It was a mind-numbing combination of jet lag and sleep deprivation.

Eventually, we were in-processed and arrived at the Clark AB billeting office, only to find out that the on-base billets were full. That was no real surprise as Clark was choked with American humanity all either on its way to war in Vietnam or in support of those headed in that direction. The billeting clerks told us that there were contract quarters available off base in Angeles City, and that we would be billeted in one of those hotels. At least there was a prospect of a bed and some sleep. Time passed glacially but without drama or other events, and I was pleased to find an adequate hotel room with air conditioning. Sleep came quickly.

A few minutes after waking up I noticed that it appeared that my belongings had been searched as items were not as I remembered leaving them in my suitcase. I frantically attempted to account for the valuables, only to realize that my passport and wallet were gone. That meant I was without an identification card and without a checkbook and money. Further, I had no way to prove who I was or why I was there. A frantic visit to the security police office on base triggered an investigation, and almost immediately led to a new ID card, some cash and a plan to get a new passport. Helluva start! Steve Mosier also had his brand new Canon camera stolen – he had just bought it at the Clark AB Exchange.

The hotel floorshow that we witnessed on out first night in the Philippines soon saw us forget about the thefts, however. Called an Exhibition, it featured women and well-endowed animals all engaging in various forms of sexual activity. Amazing!

The following day I was able to go to the Clark AB Exchange and purchase my own self-winding Seiko wrist watch. These had become a rite of passage for the combat fighter pilot, and without a Seiko, you were just one of millions who had not participated in my generation's war. A Seiko on your wrist for all to see revealed to anyone who was in the know that you were a combat veteran – or, in my case, almost a combat veteran.

My acquisition of a Seiko seamlessly leads me into another story of questionable truth, but attention getting nevertheless. Students were about halfway through their jungle survival school training deep in the Philippine jungle in the vicinity of the volcano Mount Pinatubo when, while trying to sleep in a hammock hung in a jungle tree several feet above the ground, a shot rang out. The buzz of the jungle critters fell silent for a moment and the Negrito instructors lit up the surrounding area with lanterns, before rushing out to investigate the unexpected ear-shattering blast. They discovered that a trainee had shot his Seiko watch in the middle of the night with his 0.38-caliber Smith & Wesson revolver when he thought that the glow of the florescent watch face was a snake. He had hung his new watch on a tree branch right above his head, and upon waking in the pitch blackness in the middle of the night his misidentification and subsequent decisive action had mortally wounded his watch.

Steve Mosier doesn't remember the story the same way, and he makes a good point when he questions whether a bunch of trainees would have had live ammunition out in the jungle. Instead, he remembers the frightened officer ruining his watch with a machete. It doesn't matter. There were no injuries other than a bruised ego. I imagine he got a new watch at the Clark AB Exchange after he completed the jungle survival course.

UBON AND "D. J." ALBERTS

We continued our journey, and the next stop after the Philippines was the military side of the Don Mueang International Airport in Bangkok, Thailand.

Once here, we quickly learned that we had reached the end of commercial airline service. The final leg of our trip to Ubon would be via a C-130 Hercules intratheater airlift aircraft with the call-sign "Klong." Someone educated us to the fact that Klong was the Thai word, or nickname, for the muddy and polluted rivers in Thailand.

The tropical air in Southeast Asia can only be described as heavy, being a combination of a daily temperature close to 100°F and near 100 percent humidity. It was under that blanket of air in the military terminal that we waited for the arrival of "Klong." When the airplane arrived we realized that from this point on we were our own baggage handlers! The flight to Ubon only took an hour or so, and was uneventful except for the heat, humidity and bumpy air. After we landed, and as we taxied into the parking area, the tailgate of the C-130 was lowered, giving us fresh air and our first look at Ubon RTAFB.

Capt "D. J." Alberts found me milling about with the others as we rounded up our luggage. "D. J." was a battle-hardened young captain who was getting close to finishing his combat tour. The old guys, I soon discovered, were really happy to have new guys arrive. Slight in build with thinning blond hair, blazing blue eyes and dressed in a sweat-soaked flightsuit and green baseball cap, "D. J." could have been a combat fighter pilot poster boy. I was impressed and he was incredibly gracious and helpful, carefully and thoughtfully answering my unending questions. "D. J." had "borrowed" squadron commander Lt Col Ralph "Hoot" Gibson's jeep, and he helped me load my gear and luggage. We went straight to the squadron area, with "D. J." explaining to me en route that I had been assigned to the F-4D-equipped 433rd TFS, nicknamed "Satan's Angels." The squadron color was green, explaining "D. J.'s" green baseball cap with his rank embroidered in white on the front above the bill and his nickname on the back. He was very proud of the 433rd, and the fact that he had been assigned to the squadron for his combat tour. He assured me I would also soon share in that pride.

Once at the squadron, I unpacked my helmet and anti-g suit and followed "D. J." into the unit's life support section to drop off my gear. There, I met several of the NCO life support specialists that would be maintaining my equipment. I was assigned a position on a rack that would hold my helmet, anti-g suit, parachute harness and survival vest. Later, I would be issued with a pair of spare two-way survival radios and a 0.38-caliber Smith & Wesson revolver that would fit snugly in the holster sewed into my survival vest. Then, after a short tour of the squadron area, where I met some of the pilots for the first time, "D. J." took me to the "hooch" area where the unit was billeted.

COMBAT

At Ubon there were four fighter squadrons. One, the 25th TFS "Assam Dragons" (the nickname derived from the unit's World War II heritage), was assigned the *Igloo White* mission which saw its crews using the long range navigation (LORAN) D equipment in their specially modified F-4Ds to precisely place listening sensors along the Ho Chi Minh Trail in Laos. The theory was that we would be able to react to the truck traffic on the trail when the sensors detected noise. The latter was passed to Task Force Alpha (TFA), a communication center at Nakhon Phanom (NKP) in Thailand, and from there quick reaction forces could, theoretically, be diverted from a fragged mission to attack the trucks.

I personally never saw any measureable indications that *Igloo White* accomplished anything. On the other hand, I was a "slick-winged" (junior pilot) captain with no need to know. Perhaps the sensors were serving as pointers for the B-52 *Arc Light* raids during which they rained bombs on the jungle, sometimes coming so close to us that we could see the bombs falling as we worked on other nearby targets.

Additionally, the 8th TFW included the 433rd and the 435th TFSs, again both equipped with the F-4D. These were day-fighter squadrons that eventually became specialists in smart bomb delivery. The 433rd gave up its air superiority mission, dropped a few Walleyes while doing a lot of night flying and then specialized in the combat introduction of laser-guided bombs in a program called Paveway I. The 435th specialized in electro-optical or TV-guided weapons in a program then known as Paveway II. The fourth squadron was the 497th TFS "Night Owls," which handled nocturnal combat for the 8th TFW at Ubon.

Initially, there were a lot of administrative things to take care of. Medical and dental records were taken to the clinic and my Form 5 was dropped off at the flight records office. This document contains an individual pilot's entire flight history, sortie by sortie, and is carried by the officer from base to base with each new assignment. Each base has a flight records office that keeps the pilot's Form 5 up to date during the assignment. After each flight the pilot fills out a Form 781 in the aircraft forms book noting the flight duration, day/night conditions, instrument time flown and the mission symbol for the type of sortie flown. The Form 781 for all the flights of the day is removed once flying has ceased and is taken to the Form 5 section for formal recording. Now that we were in the combat theater, sorties to North Vietnam would be categorized with the mission symbol 01A, while flights to Laos were coded 01B. Every ten missions to North Vietnam resulted in the automatic award of an Air Medal, with 20 missions to Laos being required for the same decoration. Personnel records were given to the administrators at the Consolidated Base Personnel Office, and we also completed a veritable checklist of other appointments and briefings, the details of which are long since forgotten.

Then we started "new guy school." This was several days of intense training that, among other things, brought us up to speed on the Rules of Engagement (RoE) for combat operations. These included details on who had the authority to give us clearance for an attack, off-limits areas and conditions, and an entire host of rules regarding air-to-air combat and operations with a Forward Air Controller (FAC). The FACs typically flew small, slow aircraft and directed our attacks, marking targets with smoke rockets and other devices like incendiaries called "logs," which provided us with a helpful visual reference for attacking a target at night.

We learned about the differences between operations in North Vietnam and Laos. In North Vietnam, we could only go to Route Packages I and II – the areas just north of the DMZ. All points further north were, at that time, restricted by the direct order of President Lyndon Johnson. We were told that we would not have slow-mover FACs available in North Vietnam, but occasionally we might get to work with the F-100 high-speed FACs that operated with the call-sign

"Misty." We were briefed by the intelligence section and created personal search and rescue (SAR) identification cards. These were kept on file, and pulled out if an aircrew was shot down and a SAR was initiated. The cards contained several questions and answers used as authenticators to make sure the survivor using a flare or radio to coordinate a recovery was not a Viet Cong or North Vietnamese soldier setting up a flak trap for the rescue force. Other techniques of authentication were also taught. Steve Mosier, in his stories contained within this book, refers to "Mother over Father" etc., as examples of inputs into an authentication wheel.

We learned local area procedures with respect to Ubon RTAFB's traffic patterns and ground-controlled approach (GCA) procedures for instrument landings during the heavy rain of the monsoon season. There was an emphasis on the relationship pilots had with "Lion," our local radar or GCI controllers. They were vital when it came to our ability to find and join up with pre-strike aerial refueling tankers. We were told that we refueled outbound on almost all combat missions. We also learned that for most missions our tankers would be on an orbit called the "Cherry Anchor" at an altitude of about 20,000ft mean sea level (MSL). A tanker would also be on this station to provide us with fuel on the way home in case we were running short or were expecting bad weather at Ubon for our recovery. In the event we were unable to land at Ubon, we required enough fuel to divert to another Thai airfield, or return to the tanker.

We were briefed about the other USAF wings in Thailand, and their locations, procedures, missions and air-to-air refueling tanker tracks. The air war from Thailand was exclusive to North Vietnam and Laos. Later, Cambodia also became a part of the area of responsibility. The US Navy conducted combat operations into North Vietnam with "fast movers" from the aircraft carriers on *Yankee Station* in the Gulf of Tonkin. The air war in South Vietnam included US Army fixed wing and helicopter operations in support of its troops on the ground. The "fast mover" combat was mostly prosecuted by USAF and US Marine Corps units stationed in South Vietnam, and they used an entirely different set of procedures and RoE. Combat operations in South Vietnam were referred to as the "in-country" war.

We had exhaustive refresher information presented to us by the wing's Weapons Officers, who covered subjects including the preflight briefing, fuse settings and delivery options for the bombs, rockets, cluster bombs, napalm and missiles that we would carry.

Let's pause for a moment and take another look at dive-bombing. In addition to a review of switchology, we learned details about another word – parameters. This can have many meanings. Simply stated, in the air-to-ground world of a fighter or attack pilot, parameters are the conditions that must be met for the accurate delivery of bombs or other weapons dropped off or fired from an aircraft using a manual (non-computer assisted) release. The key to the accurate delivery of a bomb is to release it at the exact range to the target for the parameters chosen. This bomb range will vary depending on both the ballistics of the weapon, which are always the same for a specific bomb, and the release parameters. The latter consist of the dive-bomb angle, the release airspeed of the aircraft dropping the bomb and its altitude above the target.

In order to hit the target, the planned parameters must be achieved with the sight on the target. We didn't actually refer to the Phantom II's sight as a bombsight. Instead, it was generally called a gunsight, even though we didn't have an

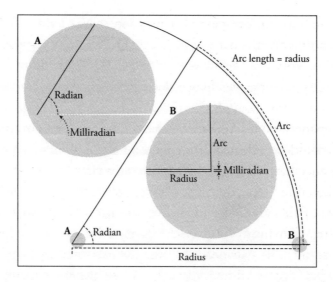

internal gun in the F-4D. The jet's sight had to be adjusted manually by the pilot when in the air-to-ground mode. The depression angle was measured in milliradians, abbreviated to mils. Since a radian is mathematically defined as the angle formed when the length of a circular arc equals the radius of the circle, a milliradian is the angle formed when the length of a circular arc equals 1/1000th of the radius of the circle.

The sight was calibrated at 0 mils when the gunsight reference mark or pipper was pointed directly ahead of the aircraft. The pipper projected onto what was called a combining glass directly in front of the pilot. As mils of depression were added, the gunsight moved down toward the nose of the aircraft. The mil setting for strafing with either the external SUU-16 or SUU-23 gun pods on the F-4C/D or the internal gun in the F-4E was approximately 35 mils. Rockets required more depression as an aim point. As I recall, the mil setting for rockets was in the neighborhood of 47 mils. Dive-bombing required even more mils of depression – usually 100+ mils, depending on the dive angle, release altitude and airspeed.

Gunsights have evolved over time. In World War I, the biplane gunsights were generally a fixed metal circle around a metal cruciform or "plus" symbol. As bombing became better understood, tables were developed for every type of ordnance that could be released from the aircraft. Different types of ordnance have different ballistic characteristics.

Therefore, separate tables were provided to the fighter pilots of the Vietnam era for each weapon. The tables were ordered first by weapon type and then by combinations of release altitude, airspeed at release and dive angle. Huge tables existed for the pilots to search for the desired weapon parameters. Typically, the starting point was to locate the table for the ordnance scheduled to be carried on a given mission. Then, the desired release altitude was selected. This was critical because of the effectiveness of the enemy's AAA defenses. We considered 4,500ft AGL as the "real-time envelope" for AAA. This meant that the time of flight of a projectile fired from a gun on the ground at an aircraft flying at this altitude was essentially zero, or at least so quick that the attacking pilot did not have time to weave or jink to defeat the AAA gunner's firing solution. So, while we had accepted much lower recovery altitudes in training, combat changed the rules.

In order to remain at 4,500ft AGL, a pilot flying at 450 knots and recovering from a 45-degree dive angle had to release his weapons and then dramatically increase back pressure on the control stick to obtain at least 5g in two seconds. This was clearly unachievable in an F-4D if your release height was also 4,500ft AGL, as there was insufficient altitude to allow a jet to safely effect a dive recovery. I don't remember exact release altitudes, but 6,000 to 7,000ft AGL were not unusual selections.

The next parameter was the dive angle. The steeper the dive angle the more recovery altitude was needed to stay above the 4,500ft minimum altitude. We typically used 45-degree dive attacks in the daytime and 30 degrees at night. We also had to consider the weather. Crews always carried the combination of depression settings, dive angle and release altitudes for lower angle attacks, should we be forced to operate under a ceiling that precluded the optimum high-angle release. If we were scheduled to operate in northern Laos as part of Operation *Barrel Roll*, the terrain elevation was much higher. Often, we had to use 30-degree dive angles because a fully loaded F-4 simply did not perform well at the higher altitudes mandated for the 45-degree attacks.

This manual dive-bombing sounds really complicated, and it was. That is why I have always said dive-bombing is an exact science, and executing an accurate dive-bombing pass is an art. The illustration opposite attempts to provide a picture of the bombing challenge we had to master over and over again. In training, a bomb accuracy of about 130ft was considered to be adequate. In combat, we learned that a bomb accuracy of 0ft was needed. Anything else was a miss.

Adding to the bombing complexity challenge was the uncertainty of the topography of enemy territory and a general lack of accurate target elevations. This was especially true when missions were flown against targets of opportunity under the direction of a FAC. These sorties did not have the benefit of careful advance target area planning and study that would have reduced or eliminated the local elevation uncertainty. The F-4D did, however, have a radar and computer-aided attack system called "dive toss." An experienced and well-trained aircrew

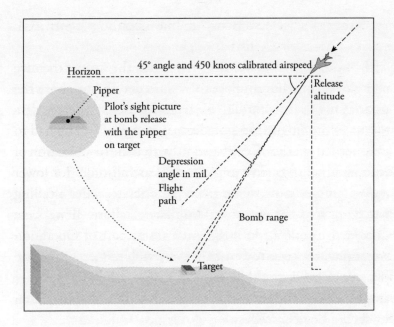

generally improved accuracy with dive toss, particularly when compared with the preferred manual dive-bombing mode of attack. Most pilots were neither well trained nor experienced with dive toss, which meant that few aircrew used it in combat.

I had only carried live munitions on one or two training missions prior to reaching Ubon. The new (to us) attack parameters also included the minimum release altitudes to ensure bombs didn't dud because of inadequate time to arm the fuses. We reviewed and noted the different attack parameters like roll-in altitudes and mil settings of sight depression for delivering the weapons. We took a lot of notes that were later transformed into checklist-like items on a 5x7in. card we carried in the cockpit on a kneeboard as a memory reference. New guy school was very detailed and comprehensive. We were expected to master the fundamentals. Actual application would follow with "on the job training."

Next was a follow-up trip to the squadron life support section. Most of us had brought our personal equipment with us, and this included a helmet, anti-g suit, flightsuits and gloves. The life support specialists covered up the white exterior of our helmets with green and black camouflage tape, tightened up our anti-g suits, issued new flightsuits to those that needed them and outfitted us with combat vests and the equipment to be carried in them. This included UHF survival radios (usually two); spare radio batteries; personal marking flare guns for sending a signal up through a heavy jungle tree canopy to enable a SAR helicopter to spot us in a shootdown situation; and a tree-lowering device (which could reach more than 100ft) that could be used to lower oneself from a high tree canopy to the ground in the event a parachute was hung up in the branches. We were also issued with a sophisticated compass, a 0.38-caliber revolver and plenty of ammunition. Most aircrew also carried a large knife or machete. Some of the guys, including Grant Stewart, had brought their own handgun, and they were allowed to take them instead of the government-issued 0.38.

We also were given plastic maps to assist us in overland navigation in case we were shot down and forced to evade capture while attempting to return to friendly control. Aircrew also had blood chits that promised help from the US government in the event that the local populace helped us hide from the enemy in a survival scenario. The blood chit was made of fabric and included an American flag and the promise written in several different languages.

Water, a whistle and some rations typically rounded out the vest content. Every crewmember could choose what to carry and which survival vest pocket to stow it in. Some guys carried additional water, flares or a radio or battery in their custom-tailored, calf-located, anti-g suit pockets. Someone mentioned that in the event of an ejection, the added weight in the pocket during either the ejection itself or when the parachute abruptly opened moments later would rip a hole in the pocket, spilling the contents. Soon thereafter, anti-g suits were spotted with heavy leather reinforcements to those pockets.

Finally, we flew a local area orientation mission that began with a general look at the countryside around our air base, along with significant landmarks. We then navigated west about 100 miles to the Royal Thai Air Force's Chandy air-to-ground bombing range and contacted the range officer, just as we had done at Avon Park a few months earlier during our training. We fired rockets and dropped bombs from the combat altitudes we would soon be using for real. In our training in Florida we had used 1,000ft AGL as the minimum altitude for high-angle dive-bombing and rocketry. That was deemed too dangerous in the combat theater, so the minimum altitude was jacked up to 4,500ft AGL.

As previously noted in this chapter, but worth repeating here, the area below 4,500ft was described to us by our instructors as the real-time envelope of the AAA gunners that would be trying to kill us. We needed to operate higher so as to be able to foil the gunners' lead. We did that by making almost continuous climbing and diving turns, holding a given attitude or turn for only a few seconds before reversing or hardening the turn, climb or dive. This was called jinking. Having a good jinking technique was the key to life for a combat fighter pilot during the Vietnam War, as the guns posed the greatest threat to us in 1968–69. Jinking was especially important when recovering from a high-angle dive-bombing attack, or at any time when operating at low altitude.

Dropping bombs from an altitude 3,500ft higher than we had ever done before turned out to be a real challenge. Our roll-in attack altitude also had to be increased by 3,500ft, and we later learned that the F-4 with a full bomb load struggled to cope with that seemingly small increase in height. This was especially true in the area of northern Laos known as the Plaine des Jarres (Plain of Jars), where we usually carried out our *Barrel Roll* missions. Targets in southern Laos were hit as part of Operation *Steel Tiger*, and although the ground elevations there varied greatly, they were typically 1,000 to 1,500ft MSL. The ground elevation during *Barrel Roll* missions was typically around 5,000ft MSL. This in turn meant that a fully loaded F-4 required afterburners to get high enough to make a 45-degree dive-bombing attack. We didn't carry sufficient quantities of fuel to use afterburner like that, so we were forced to use a 30-degree dive angle instead. This went against the fighter pilot's mantra of "the steeper the better" – a steeper dive angle makes it more difficult for the AAA gunner to accurately target you during your attack run.

The primary point of the flight to the Chandy range was to give the new guys one final opportunity to experience the higher release altitudes synonymous with the combat missions they were about to fly, and all the attendant challenges created by this change in an operational environment.

INTO COMBAT AT LAST

I was scheduled to fly my first combat mission against a target in southern Laos, and my "life guard" for this sortie was a highly experienced and respected backseater by the name of Ed "Fast Eddie" Cobleigh. Ed and I were also initially roommates. Over the years that followed we became close friends, both of us serving as FWS instructors at Nellis after Ed's second tour in combat as an F-4 aircraft commander.

That first mission was totally unremarkable, and my only memory of it is more of an impression of the combat arena as Ed played tour guide and pointed out the various target areas such as Tchepone, Mu Gia Pass and the "Dog's Head" – the latter was simply a bend in the river southwest of the Mu Gia Pass on the Laos side of the country's border with North Vietnam. The "Dog's Head" had been so badly bombed by then that, in an area otherwise covered in thick jungle, there were no trees at all over a substantial area. We expended our ordnance on the assigned target in the "Dog's Head" area and returned to Ubon. That was that. Mission no. 1 in Laos was complete!

A part of the new guy orientation included a tour of downtown Ubon, including its bath houses, jewelers and, most importantly, Raja Wongse's tailor shop. An Indian by birth, he made our party suits, "Howdy Hats," custom flightsuits and casual embroidered shirts. When we went downtown the goal was usually to borrow the squadron commander's jeep or the Operations Officer's covered pick-up truck for the trip from the hooch area to the main gate. Otherwise, it was a long walk. We weren't allowed to take the jeep or truck off base, but we could park it at the gate and hire samlor transportation just outside.

The samlor is a bicycle-powered device similar to a rickshaw. The bicycle is attached to a single-person seat about the size of a wheelchair, and with wheels on either side of roughly the same size. Some had a canopy-like cover for protection against the hot Thai sun and periodic drenching rain. The boys that drove the samlors loved to pick us up, as we usually had a wager going as to who would reach downtown first.

A race almost always ensued, which was great fun as we made our way to Ubon.

At his tailor shop on the main drag, Raja would greet each newcomer with a sincere smile and words of welcome. A bear of a man and a Sikh through and through, I never saw him without his Dastaar headpiece. After enjoying a beer – usually a Thai Singha – he took measurements and an order for a casual shirt with the new guy's name on it, along with the squadron emblem. We all had party suits that went with our squadron color – green for the 433rd TFS, red for the 435th, black for the 497th and gold or yellow for the 25th.

By the time Raja had finished measuring you up for your order, his assistants had finished an individual "Howdy Hat" with your name on it for you to take home after your first visit. The hat was a floppy piece of head gear, similar to a US Navy sailor's cap, but with the brim folded down. It was made out of camouflage material for sun protection and, ostensibly, help downed aircrew blend in with the jungle. It would not have been overly effective since we were wearing the classic solid green Air Force K2B flightsuits most of the time. The "Howdy Hat" was only worn while walking to the aircraft from the squadron life support section at the start of a mission, and then again upon returning from the flight. It could easily be tucked into the anti-g suit pocket during the mission, as per tradition. I came home under nontraditional circumstances and have no idea what happened to my "Howdy Hat."

I have often wondered what happened to Raja in the days that followed the end of the Vietnam War. We were certainly his cash cow during that time.

A trip to the Sabiathong (phonetic spelling) bathhouse usually followed for a rub and a scrub. Upon entering, a Singha beer was usually the first item of interest. We joked that it was made with formaldehyde, and this statement may have had an element of truth in it judging by the headache that usually followed the next day. The Thai girls at the bathhouse all wore white uniforms and sat behind a one-way glass wall reading, knitting or otherwise occupying themselves. We could see them from our side but they only saw a mirror when looking toward us. Each girl had a number and, after a lengthy and thoughtful study, you identified the girl of your choice by number and the management would call her out and introduce her to you.

At that point she became the guide leading the customer to a small neat and clean room that contained both a massage table and a large bathtub. A nifty bath followed and then came the total body massage. Sometimes the smaller girls would even walk on the back of the customer. These massages were absolutely great, and, upon their completion, with a little dab of Brill Cream applied in the proper place, a "happy ending" was offered as a final courtesy, whether accepted or not! The girls remained fully clothed throughout.

A few days after placing my order for a casual shirt, I made a return trip downtown, whereupon Raja's merchandise was exchanged for a few baht (the Thai currency). Following this incredibly good deal, another trip to the bathhouse inevitably followed.

Early on, our more experienced fellow warriors informed us that it would be prudent to have some "war hero" photographs taken to return home with – I don't remember the details that led to my shots being taken, some of which are included in this book. My favorite was one of me sitting in the jet.

We had a young Thai man that worked as one of the bartenders at the Officers' Club. He was a nice-looking man, thin in stature with jet black hair and long pork chop sideburns. Thus, we nicknamed him "Sideburns," and he seemed to enjoy responding to our moniker. It turned out that "Sideburns" was a talented pencil artist, and for US$5 he would turn one of our 8x10in. war hero photos into a large pencil drawing of incredible detail and quality. I happily surrendered my cockpit photo and was totally satisfied with his work. When I asked for the picture back, he reluctantly complied, and I gained some insight into his technique. My glossy 8x10in. print had been turned into a matrix of horizontal and vertical lines, and a resulting series of small squares. "Sideburns" had thus created a model and was able to replicate each of the small squares on the photo into the full-sized drawing. It was miraculous in detail, and in all the years it has hung in my "I love me" room at home, no one has initially believed it was a pencil drawing. It is truly a treasure.

DAY AND NIGHT MISSIONS
TO NORTH VIETNAM

North Vietnam, for the purposes of our combat missions, was divided up geographically into six numbered route packages. Route Package I was just north of the DMZ, with the remaining five progressively north from there. The area around Hanoi and Haiphong was designated Route Package VI, and it was in turn divided into two parts, VIA and VIB. The USAF conducted operations in the western sector of Route Package VI (VIA), while carrier-based US Navy units hit targets in the eastern coastal area of Route Package VI (VIB).

The air war in North Vietnam was managed from Saigon in a command post with the call-sign of "Blue Chip."

It issued the daily Air Tasking Order (ATO) to each of the USAF units that conducted operations in North Vietnam. Naval operations were run in broadly the same way. Each base received the ATO in a document called the "frag" because its responsibility was only a fragment of the overall daily ATO. Each base had a group of officers that worked in what was called the "frag shop." Here, the missions assigned to that specific wing were broken out of the ATO and then distributed to its squadrons. I never directly participated in this process, except when being in receipt of a particular combat line number, with associated target, tanker etc.

Each day, the pilots would check the schedule and find out when they were tasked with flying and against what target areas. Early in my combat experience the desired targets were in North Vietnam, as the primary goal for a fighter pilot was to complete 100 missions "up north." When American involvement in the conflict escalated in 1965, the completion of 100 missions to North Vietnam signaled the completion of a combat tour. By August 1968, when I arrived at Ubon, the 100-mission marker was no longer a milestone that signaled an end to combat operations. Instead, pilots had to complete a full year in-theater before they could return home. Nevertheless, "100 North" was still a coveted goal.

Scheduling for a combat mission commenced shortly after the tasking had been extricated from the ATO. Weather and intelligence briefings would take place prior to the actual flight briefing for the aircrew. Pilots then made sure that they had completed the walkaround of their fully armed and fueled jets well in advance of their briefed takeoff time. Once aloft, they typically proceeded directly to a KC-135 tanker track or "anchor." The closest track to Ubon was "Cherry Anchor," which roughly followed the Mekong River between southeastern Thailand and Laos. There were other air refueling tracks further north in the Vientiane area of Laos just north of Udorn RTAFB, but "Cherry Anchor" was the track that we most often used for missions out of Ubon.

While classified at the time, combat missions were also being flown into both northern and southern Laos in campaigns known as *Barrel Roll* (north) and *Steel Tiger* (south).

After refueling, the flight lead would call one of the EC-130E ABCCC aircraft from the 7th Airborne Command and Control Squadron for confirmation of the fragged mission and clearance to either enter the route package target area of North Vietnam or to contact a FAC in Laos at a specific Delta Point. The aircrew carried a little card that listed the latter's geographic coordinates. The backseater in the F-4 could dial these coordinates into the aircraft's INS, which would then provide the pilot in the front seat with a compass heading to use as steering information, along with a digital readout of the distance to the Delta Point in nautical miles. For the most part, that is how we navigated around Southeast Asia, especially at night and when the weather conditions precluded the use of visual references on the ground for orientation.

The missions to North Vietnam were referred to by the pilots as "counters," with reference to the historic 100 missions north "Go Home" upon completion rule. When a counter was flown, the pilot logged a 10A mission. As previously mentioned, ten 10A missions also merited an Air Medal. Non-counters were flown into Laos and were logged as 10Bs. It took 20 10B sorties to earn an Air Medal.

The call-signs for the ABCCC C-130 depended on geography and time of day. Daytime call-signs were "Hillsboro" and "Cricket," while at night these changed to "Moonbeam" and "Alleycat." "Hillsboro" and "Moonbeam"

C-130s orbited about 100 nautical miles southeast of Udorn along the Mekong River, while "Cricket" and "Alleycat" operated about 100 nautical miles northeast of Udorn over Laos. These aircraft flew 12-hour shifts from 1730 to 0530 hrs and 0530 to 1730 hrs, plus transient time to and from their home base at Udorn.* Much effort was made by flight leads to snivel counters from ABCCC, even if they weren't scheduled into North Vietnam. Usually it didn't work, but sometimes it did.

*http://www.mofak.com/ABCCC_Flying_in_Vietnam_War.htm

3

The Night the Lights Went Out
in Route Pack II

Steve Mosier was my regular "GIB" at Ubon, and he has kindly provided me with a brief insight into his war during our time in-theater:

We had four fighter squadrons at Ubon in 1968–69. The 497th "Night Owls" flew almost exclusively after dark. The bellies of their Phantom IIs were painted black and their cockpit instrumentation was taped over in a unique way so as to reduce glare from the dials, thus preserving the crew's all-important night vision. This in turn meant that the aircraft commander and the "GIB" needed to practice very close collaboration in order to maintain spatial orientation in a darkened cockpit at night. The 25th "Assam Dragons" primarily flew *Igloo White* missions, taking off before sunrise and delivering their sensors from unique dispensers and pods with the precision their LORAN D-equipped jets allowed. The 433rd "Satan's Angels" mostly flew daylight missions, its crews pioneering laser-guided bomb (LGB) operations with the AVQ-9 Pave Light "Zot box" system – the unit also performed four to eight sorties on the early night schedule. Then there was the 435th. No one knew what they did, and no one really cared!

For a period of several months in 1968 I flew night missions with the 433rd. We were a pretty small group working this mission. We called ourselves the "Sewer Doers" and had a special patch showing a scrawny rat peeking out of a sewer main, graphically depicting our views on mucking about in bad weather after dark over Laos and North Vietnam. Our weapons loads consisted of CBU-24/49s, Mk 82s with and without fuse extenders, and, in most cases, one bird in a two-ship had SUU-25 flare dispensers. We worked with O-2 "Nail" FACs and C-130 "Blind Bats" that used starlight scopes to pick out "lucrative targets" along the trails. Sometimes, we had pre-fragged targets that we sought out and bombed on our own, using visual cues illuminated by the moon or by our own flares. If it was a good night, we hit some trucks, fuel and POL [Petroleum, Oil, Lubricants] dumps and aroused the gunners, creating other targets for their 23mm, 37mm, 57mm and, sometimes, 85mm guns.

Some nights we just moved dirt and trees. "D. J." [Dave Jarrett], one of the "Night Owls" and a pilot training classmate of mine, sent a "suggestion" to Seventh Air Force HQ that we fill our external tanks and all of the napalm cans with wet concrete and drop them in the choke points at Mu Gia Pass and Ban Karai. They noted that concrete was harder to move than bomb craters were to fill, and at the end of the day we'd have some neat pedestals to install war memorials on – funnily enough, we never received a response to our suggestion.

I remember one special evening when Hal – one of the "Sewer Doers" who had contacts in Seventh Air Force HQ and had also developed a penchant for doing his own target assessment – divined that there was a juicy target on the

Ho Chi Minh Trail just north of Mu Gia Pass in Route Pack II. This was one of the areas allocated to the Navy, but beyond the combat radius of their carrier-based strike force operating from *Yankee Station* off the coast of North Vietnam. Hal was adamant that the NVA (North Vietnamese Army) was using this seemingly unreachable sanctuary to marshal supplies before the push into Laos through *Steel Tiger* and on to South Vietnam.

I was never sure whether we had permission to go into Route Pack II, but we checked in with "Moonbeam" nevertheless and pressed on to the area Hal was desperate to check out. We made low passes with varying angles and offsets, and were pretty sure we saw supplies, including POL pipes along the road. At first we drew no reaction from the NVA, so the flare bird dropped a string across the road – holy shit, there was indeed shit everywhere! I vaguely remember that one of our Phantom IIs was carrying CBU-2s on this sortie, but maybe I am mistaken. In any case, we dropped everything we had on several passes and the fires we started were massive. So was the AAA in response. "Winchester," we climbed out and checked back to see blazes at least 200ft high, secondary explosions and lots of visual AAA.

We called "Moonbeam" and informed them that there were some REAL lucrative targets, and gave coordinates. There was a pause at the other end to check the coordinates of the location again – it was maybe, just maybe, somewhere we should not have been! Regardless, "Moonbeam" diverted the night's action to where we had just departed, and they kept the pot stirred for the daylight go too, which continued to pound the area with great success for another 12 hours or so. Checking out with "Bruce" onboard "Moonbeam" (if you'd have flown over Laos in 1968–69 you'd know who Bruce was – a distinctive and familiar voice for the nightfighters), he congratulated us on "good work." It *was* good work, and we were proud of Hal for being the best intel/targeteer we knew. We were also happy that the A-4s from the carriers had left us a sweet spot for that one night. Beer at 2230 hrs, chili-cheese omelets in the Officers' Club dining room, in the rack by 0130 hrs and out till the next afternoon, before undertaking another trip to the "Sewer."

4

Walleye Targets and Other Adventures

When scheduled or cleared into North Vietnam, we roamed the area looking for lucrative targets for our ordnance. By this point in the war there weren't many, and I recall wasting a Walleye on a pier near the mouth of a river that emptied into the Gulf of Tonkin. On another occasion we plonked a Walleye into the entrance to a long-abandoned railroad tunnel along a river in North Vietnam. The rails no longer existed but the tunnel through a piece of karst that came to the banks of the river was still in place, and seemed like a fair target that day.

We had heard from our intelligence folks that the enemy had mastered the art of floating supplies down the rivers at night and then unloading them into sanctuaries of one sort or another to protect the cargo from us during daylight hours. They also "sank" the barges carrying the supplies so they would not be attacked from the air. The next night they would refloat the temporarily sunken barges and continue on their way south. It seemed to me that the karst tunnel along the river could be one such sanctuary. So, we attacked. The tunnel ran roughly east-west along the south bank of the river. Our attack was also made from east to west, which in retrospect wasn't very smart because if we had taken battle damage requiring ejection, we would have been headed toward more than 100 miles of "bad guy land," instead of in the direction of the Gulf of Tonkin, and relative safety.

The Walleye attack was textbook from the days prowling around south Florida practicing locking onto targets of opportunity and perfecting the crew coordination required to make a quick successful lock-on and weapon release. I rolled the F-4 into a bank, letting the nose drop below the horizon into a shallow dive angle. As the nose of the jet approached a point near the tunnel entrance I rolled the F-4 out of the bank, with the gunsight pipper on the tunnel entrance. My backseater called "locked" and I glanced down into my radar scope to verify the tracking of the Walleye and then pressed the bomb release button on the stick.

The glide bomb released and the jet bucked with the sudden change in gross weight. I immediately pulled hard back on the stick, looking for the feel of about 5g, unloaded and rolled right and then reset 5g. Holding this for two or three seconds, I then unloaded again and rolled to the left. The nose was now above the horizon. I jinked two more times and then held the jet in a left turn while I looked back at the target just in time to see an impact explosion at the mouth of the tunnel. Seconds later, I jinked right, followed by a roll-reversal to the left for another look. I saw the other end of the tunnel explode like a roman candle. It was spectacular. We realized at that moment that we had done our job, having really messed up the "bad guys'" day – at least for those that happened to be in or around that tunnel.

We flew home without incident, landed and taxied the aircraft back into the revetment at Ubon. Feeling pretty good about things, I climbed down the ladder to be met by the crew chief, who told me we had taken a hit. I told him no way and he "marched" me over to the left main landing gear and pointed at the tire. It was still fully inflated, but had a clear and distinct groove the full length of the sidewall. We chatted briefly about how that could have happened and then looked further and found a small bullet hole in the aft part of the landing gear door. We looked further at that hole and the following trajectory of the round that had grazed the tire. Realizing that the landing gear was up at the time, we looked at the up and locked position of the tire in the gear well and, sure enough, there was another hole through the front of the gear well panel forward of where the tire had been. We searched and could find no exit hole, so we dropped the panel on the bottom of the wing and an almost undamaged bullet fell out onto the tarmac.

The slug was a little bigger than a 30-06 round, but not as big as a 0.50-caliber shell. Analysis suggested it was an armor-piercing round with an ablative covering, but with no other explosive. The shooter had probably fired it at us, and the round was at the peak of its trajectory when we flew through the bullet's arc. The slug made an almost glancing blow, with just enough energy to penetrate the belly of the aircraft and the forward gear well, grazing the tire on its journey to a final resting place in out jet. It was the only mission I flew where my F-4 suffered battle damage, and it didn't amount to much. I carried that round in my pocket for over a year until one day I lost it. I think it came out of my pocket while on a US commercial airliner after I got home – probably generated a lot of unanswered questions from whoever found it. Not many people have the opportunity to carry, like a trophy, the bullet that was shot at them.

The squadron awards and decorations team got excited about this, and the bomb damage assessment (BDA) that followed, and I was duly awarded my first Distinguished Flying Cross (DFC). This medal was presented for achievement and not heroism, which I guess was appropriate.

FOGGED UP AT BAN PHANOP

The F-4 did not have a great cockpit heating and cooling system. The pilot had a rheostat on the right panel that was supposedly a temperature selector. Cold was fully left and hot was fully right. Theoretically, the cabin temperature could be set by this rheostat. There was also a lever a few inches outboard of the rheostat. Fully forward selected maximum airflow through ducts at the base of the windscreen that were pointed up and aft. Fully aft reduced the airflow to almost nil. Sounds good, but the problem was that there wasn't a moisture separator and remover in the system. As a result, moisture caused by humidity always created a problem. If hot air wasn't selected before climbing to high altitude, moisture could form on the inside of the canopy and windscreen and actually freeze, given that the temperature of the atmosphere at 30,000ft and higher is well below zero. This problem followed us down to lower altitudes, wherein we often experienced a "rainstorm" in the cockpit if the heat wasn't hot enough and the flow lever was too far forward.

Now take this situation to Southeast Asia – a tropical location that seemed to have rocket exhaust temperatures and near 100 percent humidity much of the time. The solution in hot and humid climates was always to keep the temperature rheostat up and the airflow reduced to almost nil so as to avoid the rainstorm. When flying at mid to high altitude, the pilot had to preheat the canopy before descending by turning the rheostat up to hot and the lever forward to a high flow position to dry out the system. Failure to do so added to the risk of a fog cloud forming in the cockpit and heavy dew-like moisture coating the inside of the canopy and the windshield.

It was one of those days in the target area near the Mu Gia Pass on the Laos side of the border with North Vietnam. It was very hot, with near 100 percent humidity. I don't remember why I had a lapse that day, but for some reason I did not heat up the cockpit and canopy in order to dry out the heating/cooling system prior to descending to attack the target near the "Dog's Head." We were carrying 500lb Mk 82s, and planned to drop them in bombs single mode during the course of several passes. I set up the switches for bombs single, armed nose and tail and selected master arm "On." I had the mil setting on my kneeboard for a 45-degree dive-bombing pass that would permit a 5g recovery while keeping the jet above 4,500ft AGL. I planned to drop and then pull and jink, unloading and jinking in a non-repeating pattern until safely back at a higher altitude.

The "bad guys" were firing seven-round clips of 37mm AAA at us while we were in orbit above the target and at my squadronmate attacking ahead of me. I think I must have been No. 4 in a flight of four. I noticed the muzzle flashes on the ground as the 37mm guns fired. Then, the rounds were invisible until exploding, each one erupting in a white puff. Although I don't remember being afraid as I set up for my pass, something distracted me to the point that I didn't preheat the cockpit and the canopy. That could have been a fatal mistake, except for good luck.

I rolled in to make my first pass, and simultaneously remembered I hadn't preheated. I quickly reached over and twirled the rheostat to full hot and slammed the lever forward in an attempt to correct my error. Moments later my eyeballs were at the center of a cloud in the cockpit that was so thick I could not see the instrument panel. By feel and experience I knew I was at pickle altitude, so I pressed the bomb release button and simultaneously leaned as far forward as my shoulder harness would permit and pulled hard on the stick. I could not see anything except the shape of my ADI on the instrument panel. It was totally obscured by moisture.

While continuing to pull, unload and trying to jink, I reached with my throttle hand and attempted to wipe the moisture off the ADI. I was flying blind at this point, not sure which way was up or where I was in my jink pattern. I got enough of an image on the ADI to start flying on instruments while continuing to wipe the moisture off the dials. I jinked on instruments, quietly praying I wouldn't hit the ground in my semi-disorientation. It seemed like time stopped for a long instant, but soon I realized that I was okay and climbing. The fog in the cockpit cleared and life was good again. Better to be lucky than good – again.

MAIL

Years after I retired I read through every letter that went back and forth between me and my loved ones at home while I was in Thailand. Then, I transcribed the letters and digitized them on a spreadsheet so that I could sort them out properly. There was a common thread in both my writings and Jeannie's. The mail service was terrible. It is hard to believe in this day and age of e-mails, texts, Skype and generally instant communications worldwide that we would go for days and sometimes even weeks without receiving mail, even though

Jeannie and I were writing to each other almost every day. Many times I remember receiving five or six letters in one day and then not getting any more for a depressingly long time. And the lag time made it hard to remember what had been written, and even harder to understand or interpret the answer to a question that had been asked.

We were also tantalized with the prospect of making a phone call home. Such a call was said to be possible through the Military Affiliated Radio System (MARS). We had to sign up to make a MARS call weeks in advance, and then when the time came, as often as not, the high frequency radio that was used would be unable to establish communications with the target radio in the United States. Sometimes this was due to higher priority communications that made even the attempt impossible due to the limits on the capacity of the MARS. Other times it was atmospheric conditions that prevented the link.

Once contact with the US was established, the operator at home had to make a long-distance telephone call to the number in the States. There were issues when all the circuits were busy or, worst case, no one answered the home phone. We tried to let wives and parents know when to expect a call, but it never seemed to happen on time, resulting in frustration reigning on both sides of the world. And adding fuel to the fire was a half-world of time zones. Add daylight savings time – or not – and establishing contact with home became even harder.

If we did get through there was the hassle of a non-duplex system, meaning that we could not talk to each other at the same time. Instead, at the completion of every sentence or thought, one had to say "Over," signaling to the person on the other end that they could now talk. That was hard enough for experienced aviators and nearly impossible for an untrained spouse or, worse still, a child. Most of us gave up on MARS and went back to waiting out the letters.

ROGER JOHNSON'S MEETING

Upon my arrival at Ubon I had been assigned to "C" Flight of the 433rd TFS, with Maj Roger Johnson as my flight commander. I had finished new guy school and completed my orientation trip to Chandy range over by Takhli RTAFB, after which I then progressed from my first combat mission through my checkout as a wingman during sorties into Laos and the southern route packages of North Vietnam. There had been ups and downs and at least one great mission. I felt like things were going pretty well.

One day, Maj Johnson called a "C" Flight meeting in the screened-off lounge area of our hooch. All the aircraft commanders and pilots were present. He started the meeting by explaining that our daily schedule was built based on the ATO issued from Saigon and Seventh Air Force's "Blue Chip" command center. The entire battle plan for the next day was put together by the planners and then issued to the fighter wings as the ATO. Maj Johnson continued briefing us on things we already knew – the frag pertaining to the 8th TFW was received at the wing level and the wing "frag shop" broke out the tasking and assigned the combat missions to the four squadrons. The latter actually got to choose the missions they wanted, and the order of choice rotated on a daily basis.

One of our squadrons was the 497th TFS "Night Owls," this unit flying almost exclusively at night. Maj Johnson continued by explaining that the portion of the frag dedicated to night flying had exceeded the 497th's capacity to man all the night missions it was being assigned for some time and, therefore, other units in the 8th TFW had been pitching in to fill the rest of the night sorties. I was only vaguely aware that we had night flyers in the 433rd, and this revelation came as something of a surprise to me. The "powers that be" had decided it was time to select additional aircrews to fill that requirement because the current pilots and WSOs would soon finish their year of combat and rotate on to their next assignments. Usually, night flying was followed by a couple of months of day combat prior to the completion of an operational tour and rotation back to the States for the next assignment.

At this point Maj Johnson asked for a captain aircraft commander to volunteer to become a dedicated night flyer. I looked around the room and realized that I was the only captain aircraft commander in "C" Flight. It thus occurred to me that I would either volunteer or be volunteered, based on the captain aircraft commander selection criteria. So it was. I became a night flyer and was assigned as Maj Brian McMahon's wingman for my night checkout. I was further informed that my backseater would also be a new guy. I was thrilled to learn that I would be crewed with 1Lt Steve Mosier, who had been in my F-4 training class at MacDill. Steve and I weren't close friends at that point, but we knew each other and I held him in high regard. I think the same was true for him.

Maj McMahon's dedicated backseater was Dickie Dull, and Steve and I soon learned that we would be flying with an experienced nightfighter at the beginning of our training. Dickie Dull would man up my back seat and Steve Mosier would go in Brian's back seat until the experienced night flyers determined that we were safe enough to fly together as a new crew. Those early missions went quickly, and soon Steve and I were routinely flying together. We both liked the idea of being a dedicated crew that always flew together – that was a really good idea, for night flying could be very challenging.

Soon, I was informed that Brian would check me out as a two-ship flight lead. All of our night missions were flown as two-ships, while the day flyers normally went as flights of four. The night checkout as a flight lead went quite well thanks to my previous ATC experience as both a flight lead and a night flyer.

On one of those night checkout missions I showed up for the flight briefing with Brian and Dickie. Typically, the flight lead would get the tasking, determine the game plan for the night and then brief the wingman on the mission. It took me back when I heard Brian McMahon mutter, "You've gotta be shitting me!" as he looked at the frag for our mission. He ranted, "What kind of idiot schedules F-4s for a night mission on the 'Trail' with napalm?" It was a rhetorical question aimed at no one in the "frag shop" in particular. Instead, it was simply disbelief that the writers of the ATO could have so little understanding of weaponeering. Brian continued, "Holy shit, it's finned nape. So, tonight we go to Laos and dive bomb napalm. Incredible!"

By that point I was getting the picture that this wasn't going to be a mission soon forgotten. I was a new guy and Brian McMahon and Dickie Dull were still checking me and Steve Mosier out as nightfighters. Dickie was still flying with me and Steve was still flying with Brian. Thus, the writing was on the wall. I was a nightfighter long before the age of night vision goggles!

There was quite a ritual I was about to experience about learning to fly night combat. Our F-4s were not that old, but they had seen a lot of combat and were showing signs of wear and tear where pilots got in and out of the cockpits and maintenance personnel had dropped tools that caused a lot of scuffs to the paint. At night, when the cockpit lights were turned on, every one of those nicks in the cockpit glowed red. Even with the light rheostat turned to the minimum setting, they cast reflections on the inside of the canopy. This wasn't noticeable during daytime operations, but at night it was vital that the reflections be eliminated. Failure to clean up the cockpit led to distractions and could result in incorrect actions being taken by the crew. The simple act of turning one's head could create the illusion of AAA coming at you.

So, step one of learning to night fly was taping up the cockpit. We would take several feet of duct tape with us in strip form, temporarily stuck to our anti-g suits, and once in the cockpit we would turn the lights up and start taping over every speck of leaked light. The goal was a totally black cockpit, with only the faint red glow of a single light illuminating the ADI. The latter was the key to mission success at night. It also played a crucial role in keeping the crew alive, as it kept you oriented as to the location of both the sky and the ground. Once the cockpit was prepared, we were ready to go.

That night, our jets armed with finned napalm, we prepared mil settings of depression for the gunsight matching the release altitudes chosen for a 30-degree dive angle. It was determined through experience that any dive angle steeper than 30 degrees at night increased the risk of vertigo during the subsequent 4–5g dive recovery. That night our call-sign was "Pintail" and our target was a ferry crossing a stream known to the pilots as Hu Hung. There was also a very active AAA site nearby, manned by a gunner who had been labeled the "Mad Gunner of Hu Hung Ferry."

Off we went into the pitch black in single aircraft takeoffs. As soon as Brian pulled his engines out of afterburner I lost sight of him, but Dickie, operating our radar, got a lock on and steered me into close formation. Meanwhile, Brian commanded us to change radio frequencies from Ubon control tower to "Lion," our local area GCI controller. After checking me in on the new radio frequency, Brian called for a vector to "Cherry Anchor."

"'Lion,' 'Pintail' airborne with two looking for the 'Cherry Anchor' tanker."

"Lion" quickly replied, "Roger 'Pintail,' 'Lion' has radar contact. Turn left heading 340 degrees and look for your tanker on the nose for 26 miles."

In almost the same breath the controller transmitted, "'Boat 26,' turn left heading 340 degrees. Your chicks are now 20 miles on your nose and closing with a nice offset."

Dickie almost immediately had a radar contact on the tanker, and confirmed the perfect geometry for the rendezvous. He admonished me as I started to make a contact call on the radio. "That's lead's job, so shut the fuck up unless he asks for help." "Roger that," was about all I could get out in response. Simultaneously, from the lead aircraft, Brian radioed "Pintail" with the radar contact call "Judy." This was the brevity code radioed to the GCI controller confirming that the flight lead was now assuming control of the intercept, and that the GCI had done his job.

I joined up on Brian in close formation with a scant four or five feet spacing between wingtips and awaited his visual signal to loosen the formation slightly. The signal came in the form of Brian moving the rudder on his Phantom II enough for me to see it, instructing me to reposition my jet two to three wingspans away from him. I could still fly formation from this position, while also looking around for the tanker. Suddenly, there was the giant shadow-like presence of the KC-135 tanker – a variant of the famous Boeing 707 commercial airliner – nearby. Noting that Brian was going straight to the air refueling pre-contact position, I moved up into formation on the left wing of the tanker.

Brian's approach was swift, and at the correct moment he stabilized the Phantom II in a perfect position for the boomer to insert the air refueling boom into the spine-located receptacle on the F-4. Not a word was said between fighter and tanker, and when Brian's jet was topped off he pressed the disconnect button on the control stick and the boom immediately separated, with a slight vapor wisp of fuel that disappeared instantly. He moved his jet up and onto the right wing of the tanker and I dropped to the pre-contact position, before inching forward. I already had my air refueling door open and the boomer coaxed me forward by tapping his light system. Slightly forward, up slowly, steady, contact, and the light on my canopy bow told me instantly that I was getting fuel.

The position lights on the belly of the KC-135 provided guidance to the fighter. There were five or six pairs of lights. The center pair were green, and when illuminated, they indicated a perfect position fore and aft, as well as vertically. The lights on either side of the green ones were amber, while the outer lights were red. The goal was to always have the green lights on. They resembled captain's bars, and were called thus by fighter pilots.

With the refueling behind us, we headed east toward our Hu Hung ferry target area. I knew there were other fighters in the area, even though they were unseen in the total darkness. Numerous times, a bright explosion on the ground would indicate that a fighter pilot had dropped a bomb, and as often as not the bright tracers of AAA pawed the sky in an effort to kill the attacker. The 37mm rounds typically came up in clips of five to seven rounds, followed by a flash of light as the round exploded. The ZSU-23-4 23mm guns looked more like a fire hose as the rounds ripped through the sky. The level of activity was amazing.

As previously noted, "Moonbeam" and "Alleycat" were the two nighttime ABCCC EC-130E aircraft responsible for the management of the "out country war" at night, which was divided into north and south sectors. Tonight, we were fragged to "Moonbeam" in the south. Upon checking in, "Pintail" was cleared as fragged and directed to contact "Nail 46" – a FAC flying an O-2 Skymaster – for target identification. The O-2 was a twin-engined high-wing Cessna with one puller prop and one pusher prop, along with twin boom tails. The civilian version was designated the Cessna 337 Super Skymaster, and the USAF acquired no fewer than 532 of them. Some 178 of these were lost during the Vietnam War.

The "Nail" FACs liked to mark targets with devices we called logs. The FAC would drop them in the target area, and as a part of its arming sequence the log would ignite, creating a pinpoint of light on the ground.

As we approached the target area another radio frequency change put us into voice contact with our FAC. He had already dropped his log and the light on the ground was clearly evident. Brian commanded me to go trail, which meant dropping back a couple of miles behind him. We had briefed that we would attack out of a "wheel" centered on the target area. An important part of that brief was whether the wheel would initially be right hand or left hand. We wanted to follow each other around the circle and not meet head on. Between each attack we sometimes reversed the wheel as a part of our tactics to avoid the AAA.

Everything was on track. The FAC told us the target was approximately 100 meters north of the burning log and that we were cleared to attack under flight leader control. Then, as so often happened, we flew into clouds, which were not visible at night. Brian made the radio call that he was descending to get below the cloud layer and for me to stay high for the moment. In the meantime, we were maintaining our trail formation with reference to the radar. The call came, "Two, lead is in the clear below 8,000ft so come on down and we'll get to work. That is going to put us about 4,000ft above ground level." The lower altitude mandated a shallower dive angle for our attacks than had been planned, and that became critical on my final attack. We each dropped a finned napalm weapon, estimating the location of the ferry, but nothing caught on fire on the ground after the initial impact.

Brian had called in hot out of "Miami," and after his release he jinked his F-4 to reduce his vulnerability to the ground fire that was squirting up at him. The gunner was shooting at noise so the risk was minimal. The "Miami" reference was the code word used to indicate that he was attacking from the southeast. We had long ago determined that our handle on geography was probably better than the defenders', and we therefore used a mental picture of the continental United States to indicate where we were in the sky in relation to the target, rather than referring to actual directions that could be heard by eavesdropping gunners. As Brian pulled off he called "Lead is off left toward Frisco." By this time I was over "Houston" in our wheel, and announced that I was in from "Houston" to "Chicago." I was spooked by the decreasing weather ceiling and the attendant visibility. I was passing in and out of the ragged cloud bottoms, encountering pounding rain every few seconds. The storm developed above us and lightning added to the drama.

On my last pass I knew my dive angle was shallow and, therefore, I needed to delay pickling my napalm beyond the normal release altitude. Dickie was keeping me informed of our altitude, and my job was to get the aircraft's gunsight pipper onto the target. I pickled off the last can of finned nape and started my jinking recovery, making an appropriate radio call so that Brian would have some sense of where I was. The nape hit long. In fact, I missed the entire narrow valley and had dive-bombed the plateau beyond the valley by a few hundred meters. Rather fortuitously, my misdirected napalm canister hit an ammo dump. Things started exploding, illuminating the night sky and the bottoms of the overcast from the spectacular secondary explosions. It was an incredible sight.

Brian thought I had hit the ground, and called on the radio, "Two, are you there?" I quickly replied, "You bet," and I wanted to add – but didn't – "Nifty hit wouldn't you say?" His response was a very matter of fact, "Join up and let's find a tanker for our trip home." As we cleared the frequency the FAC announced that we had done a nice job, and could expect paperwork to reflect the success (even though it was totally accidental). The "Mad Gunner of Hu Hung Ferry" continued to light up the sky with AAA to no avail as if to dispatch us on our way back to Ubon.

Although my performance over Hu Hung that night had not been "heroic," evidently it had been "meritorious" according to the Awards and Decorations team, hence my receipt of a second DFC.

Soon I was a night-flight lead, and Brian completed his combat tour and rotated home. My new nocturnal partner was an experienced F-104 pilot from the Tennessee Air National Guard (ANG) by the name of Norman Fogg. Drawing inspiration from his unusual surname, we quickly nicknamed him "Phineas" for the main protagonist in the Jules Verne novel *Around the World in Eighty Days* – although Verne's character was actually called "Phileas," we stuck with "Phineas," for we were both young and ignorant in those days! Norm was a great pilot, a cooperative wingman during his checkout, a gifted singer of the bar room ballads and just a really good guy in general. He quickly checked out both at night and as a flight lead. From that point on we took turns leading during the remainder of our night escapades. We all thoroughly enjoyed the aircrew comradery between the four of us who flew a lot of combat as a team. Some moments were more memorable than others.

My favorite thing to do with "Phineas" was night BFM over Ubon after the completion of a combat mission. This routine had commenced when Norm was flying as my night-flight lead. He would take us to the "Cherry Anchor" tanker track and beg for enough fuel to fill up our internal tanks. Then, we would play. I learned more about BFM from these missions than in any formal course of instruction. Our rules were simple, as were our scenarios. The fundamental rule was engines in at least minimum afterburner so we could see each other. The scenarios we played out were always perch attacks, where one jet is the target and the other is the attacker.

In a perch attack, the attacker takes a position several thousand feet behind and a thousand feet above the defender, making sure that he is offset to one side or the other. At the command "Fight's On," the defender turns one way or the other defensively and the attacker pushes the stick forward to about 0g and rolls toward the defender in an effort to accelerate and obtain either a gun-firing position inside the defender's turn or a rolling maneuver into pure trail behind his opponent. Pure trail was the only place in those days that an IR missile like a Sidewinder or a Falcon could track a heat target. As already noted, we didn't have an internal gun on the F-4D. This came later with the F-4E – in my opinion, largely thanks to the advocacy of famous ace and former 8th TFW CO at Ubon, Col Robin Olds.

The defender in a perch attack sometimes hardened the turn to create defensive angles for the attacker to deal with or, alternatively, unloaded to 0g and attempted to dive away while turning the defending jet just enough to keep the attacker out of that lethal trail position where the IR missile of the day was effective.

We did this over and over, exchanging the positions of attacker and defender until we reached our bingo fuel and had to "knock it off," taking spacing for a "safe" straight-in GCA or instrument landing system recovery to Ubon. It seemed ironic that after the maneuvering we had just been doing, both in combat and playing overhead afterwards, we had to recover with a straight-in approach and landing at night. We would have preferred to report initial with a flight or two for a (daytime) overhead traffic pattern.

CBU-2 UP THE BEACH AT NIGHT

President Johnson eventually called off the air war in North Vietnam (codenamed Operation *Rolling Thunder*), effective November 1, 1968 – the offensive had started on March 2, 1965. My birthday is October 31, and I flew a combat mission that night. It was my 36th trip "up North." Prior to the end of "our war" in North Vietnam I had been cleared to undertake combat missions, trained to fly operational sorties at night, become a night-flight lead and checked out

"Phineas" Fogg as a replacement for Brian McMahon as the other F-4 aircraft commander in our night team.

One night "Phineas" and I were scheduled for a mission into North Vietnam with our jets carrying ordnance that neither of us had previously used, namely the CBU-2. We were academically trained in the weapon's employment, but not actually experienced in its use. The CBU-2 was designed for low-altitude delivery, its weaponry taking the form of bomblets dropped horizontally from a dispenser. The latter was loaded on the outboard stations of the F-4, and each of 19 tubes (70mm in diameter) mounted horizontally within the SUU-7 dispenser were filled with bomblets – each canister could carry up to 600 BLU/BDU-designated bomblets, depending on the variant being used. Each time the pilot pressed the pickle or bomb release button on the control stick, several of the bomblets were ejected aft out of the dispenser tubes. The dispenser itself was not dropped until all the bomblets were gone.

Some guys were afraid of these weapons because the bomblets had a nasty tendency to hang up as they were exiting the tube. The fear was that the bomblet would explode either while still in the dispenser hanging on the launching aircraft or explode close enough to the jet to cause irreparable damage.

When employing the CBU-2, the idea was to fly at low altitude along a road or waterway looking ahead for targets – personnel, trucks, boats, etc. – and when they were observed, the pilot flew directly at the target. At the appropriate time he would press the bomb release button, which resulted in a stream of bomblets falling away behind the dispenser tubes. The resulting carpet of bomblets were then spun armed as they rained down on the target.

We weren't too keen about going out after dark into North Vietnam and using a weapon with which neither of us had personal experience. At night, a CBU-2 attack would come from a two-ship in trail formation, searching, in our case, the coastal road that generally ran north-to-south in the southern route packages of North Vietnam. The lead aircraft (on this occasion flown by "Phineas" and Dickie Dull) carried flares and the wingman's jet (me and Steve Mosier) was armed with the CBU-2 munitions. If the lead pilot spotted a potential target he put out a flare, illuminating the scene for the wingman, who would then acquire the target and lay down a carpet of bomblets. Great concept, but one that was extremely dangerous, and difficult to accomplish.

We launched out of Ubon and found our "Cherry Anchor" tanker without incident. Full of fuel, we headed east, gaining clearance from "Alleycat" ABCCC to proceed into North Vietnam for armed reconnaissance as fragged. The weather deteriorated, and soon we were forced to fly close formation as we navigated out over the Gulf of Tonkin. Once clear of the landmass below, which was hidden by heavy clouds, we began a descent in the weather over water, relying on our radar altimeter to precisely measure our height above the Gulf of Tonkin. Meanwhile, our pilots in the back seat were working the radar in a ground map mode to break out the coastline of North Vietnam. The plan was to positively identify an inlet with the radar that would permit us to safely proceed overland and pick up the coastal highway visually.

Our descent was slow and cautious as we let down through the clouds, seeking clear air between the base of the clouds and the pitch black Gulf of Tonkin below. As we made our way toward the shoreline, we finally broke out of the clouds at several hundred feet above the water as measured by our radar altimeters. At this point the lead continued inbound and, as the wingman, I took up my position several miles back, using the airborne radar to keep track of the leader. This was a challenge for the pilot in the back seat due to the ground clutter picked up by our pulse radar, but we managed.

Then, up the coast we proceeded until we reached the northern limit of our target area authority. We saw nothing, dispensed no flares and dropped no bomblets. We were exhausted from this hair-raising 20-minute experience, and thus we climbed back out over the water in the safety of the clouds, still keeping track of "Phineas" in the lead aircraft with the radar. Eventually, we got on top of the weather, jettisoned our unexpended ordnance and joined up. Heading home, we later confessed to each other that we had been quietly promising ourselves that we would never ever do that again!

These challenging night missions seemed to fuel Norm, and he never ran out of ideas on how to tweak the system with a prank. Here, Steve Mosier eloquently recalls the details of a "funeral" that took place at Ubon, with Norm amongst the mourners:

A "Funeral" in Ubon

Most USAF fighter wings have three squadrons. Unusually, the 8th TFW at Ubon had five in 1968–69, the fifth being an AC-130 unit (16th Special Operations Squadron). Actually, technically, it had six if you counted the B-57G unit (13th Bombardment Squadron) on base from October 1970, but we F-4 guys never did. Don't get me wrong, they were combat units, taking their lumps on patrols over the trails of Laos and in the route packages of North Vietnam with the rest of us, but we didn't count them. We just didn't.

There were four we did count – the 433rd "Satan's Angels," the 435th "Eagles," the 497th "Night Owls" and the 25th "Assam Dragons." "Satan's Angels" were MiG killers, had the LGB commitment and flew night missions. The 435th had an electro-optically guided bomb mission and carried "iron" to the target. The 497th flew almost exclusively at night – so much so that the bellies of their Phantom IIs were painted matt black, not glossy white (to reflect the effect of a nuclear blast we were told – sure) as per almost every other Phantom II in service, and their cockpits were essentially permanently taped over for blacked-out night ops, thus reducing the chances of instrument glow illuminating the canopies and causing night blindness. The 25th flew specially modified LORAN D jets boasting the most accurate navigation system in-theater at the time. The "Assam Dragons" were principally tasked with delivering sensors along the Ho Chi Minh Trail during regular early (I mean really early) morning missions.

But when it came down to it, we felt there was only one fighter squadron on the base – the "Satan's Angels." We had the class leaders – Ralph "Hoot" Gibson (former lead pilot of the Thunderbirds air demonstration squadron and a Korean War ace), Dick O'Leary, with his Robin Olds knock off moustache, Jack Bennett (a heck of an aviator whose career included an F-8 tour with the US Navy), and Ray Battle, the first "Pappa Wolf." We had the missions. On deck for MiG hunting if the north opened up and the first to use LGBs that became a game changer in air-to-ground warfare – we also had a minority stake in the night mission. The 433rd mostly had friendly rivalry with the "Night Owls," and we didn't much care what the other two squadrons were up to.

The rivalry between us and the 497th extended to our mascots too. We had a great dog in the form of a classic Thai Sabre Tail that hung out in the squadron and hooch areas. On occasion, the "Night Owls" would kidnap our dog, dye him forest green and then give him back to us. They never hurt him and, frankly, he kind of enjoyed the attention. The "Night Owls" also routinely stole our samlor that we used for the ceremonial ride back to the squadron building for crews completing their tour. The samlor was often found *on top* of our building. We knew how to get it down, and duly retrieved it, repaired any damage and then put it back to work. This was a game we routinely played with the 497th.

Now, although I have already mentioned our highly esteemed leaders, we had one that was not on the roster with a title, despite him being our secret weapon. Norm "Phineas" Fogg was a Northeaster by birth, Tennessean by way of duty in that state's ANG and prankster by nature. He was able to function (mostly) with a low profile and develop our retaliation plans. I must add that he was aided in his task by his close relationship with, and respect for, the squadron "GIBs." Indeed, it was from within their ranks that he gathered the manpower for dirty jobs. His top cover was provided by Lt Col Bill "Padre" Strand, another squadron leader we counted on for receiving forgiveness from after the act had been performed.

So, we endured several pranks from our "Owl" comrades, but with Norm's counsel and restraint we waited for his decision on when to mount a strategic retaliatory strike. Suddenly, there was an opportunity – a change of command for the "Night Owls." Lt Col Jack Trabucco was moving on and Lt Col Carl Cathey was coming over from the "Assam Dragons" to take control of the unit. Any time a squadron change of command takes place it is a big deal, and this only amplifies in magnitude when it is a combat squadron turning over. High Profile – High Risk – High Reward. Just what Norm was looking for!

The "Night Owls'" prize possession was a gift from a Special Operator [almost certainly from the Central Intelligence Agency (CIA)] they'd supported in Laos – an owl from the area. It was an impressive bird, being fierce looking and very attentive to anyone in proximity to its cage, which was kept in an honored place within the squadron operations building. This made it a high-value target for retaliation. Firstly, I must qualify that no harm was ever meant to be inflicted on the owl, and none actually took place. But that didn't eradicate the fact that potentially serious consequences awaited the perpetrators of the events that followed if anything went awry. Norm, one of the "Satan's Angels'" "Sewer Doers" – AKA nightfighters – went into planning mode, regardless of the risks to his career.

He eventually settled on the following operation: 1) kidnap and hide the owl; 2) plan a wake for the deceased bird; and 3) hold the ceremony at a significant time and place – namely, the forthcoming change of command ceremony. I was not privy to the kidnap plans, but suffice to say there might have been some inside help, and the fact that the squadron was virtually unoccupied during the late morning time, reflecting its nocturnal schedule of night combat ops. The owl was soon in "Satan's Angels'" hands, secure and safe in an off-base location.

The schedule for the change of command was in the public domain. It was to be held in the Ubon Officers' Club in an afternoon ceremony. Presiding officer would be either Col Charles C. "Buck" Pattillo, commander of the 8th TFW, or his vice-commander. The presence of a senior officer only upped the ante as far as Norm and his team were concerned. The next phase of his plan centered on the logistics. Norm needed a high-quality casket for the owl, the religious accruements required for a proper wake, someone to preside over the wake, pall bearers willing to become high-visibility participants and, of course, an owl, but not *the* owl, for the casket.

The casket was easy. Thailand abounds with teak and carpenters and silk and tailors. A few days and a few baht later, and it was ready for the somber occasion. Norm also called on his connections within the base chapel (religious garb and incense to burn were acquired), and although their contribution was probably not officially endorsed, it was made willingly. The conductor of the event was, of course, Norm, and his pall bearers came from his close-knit cadre of "GIB" lieutenants. As for the owl, it was not an owl at all, but some form of fowl. Plucked, cooked and stripped to the bones, which were bleached white, it certainly looked the part lying in a quality casket.

Now for the ceremony. The schedule of events was well known, and a time after the opening of the main event but before the actual change of command took place was selected. The wake participants and the owl were assembled in a room adjoining the ceremony. A sentry guarded the door from unintended intruders, and he was also instructed to keep track of progress of the change of command. At the proper time, "Chaplain Norm" and his entourage entered the room and proceeded down the aisle toward the front of the room. Norm was swinging the burning incense and chanting his own memorial for the owl. It went something like, "Yo, the owl is dead. He was a great bird, loved and feared. The owl is among us" – you get the picture. The crowd was quiet, surprised and speechless. The casket was delivered to the front of the room, appropriate (or not) last rites were delivered and the chaplain and the pall bearers left the room and the Officers' Club, both quietly and rapidly.

I am told that participants and the audience remained pretty quiet for a short period of time, before eventually removing the casket and proceeding with the change of command ceremony. Since it was mainly a "Night Owl" crowd, there was little levity, although some of the senior officers from the wing and other units in attendance did manage some suppressed smiles for a short time. Meanwhile, the owl was returned to base and restored to the 497th's Operations Building before any retaliatory action could take place. Another chapter in the rivalry between two groups of warriors had been written.

Later, on my tour in Tactical Air Command (TAC) Headquarters, I worked for then Maj Gen Cathey in the Requirements Directorate. On an informal occasion I reminded him of the owl's funeral. Maj Gen Cathey was a great guy, and he was also easy to read. In this case it was really easy – his face sort of clouded up with a frown, then transitioned to a somewhat forced smile, and he replied, "it was a pretty good trick, wasn't it?"

Mike "Ghost" Davison recalled that Norm used the incense gag another time too. "Ghost" recalled a drunken night when Norm strolled through the banquet room of the Officers' Club during a party that he was not a part of. Dressed like a priest, Norm was waving an incense burner and chanting "Battle damage. No Hydraulic Power. Generators offline. Leaking fuel. Pilot Error. Pilot Error."

T. R. AND ESTELLE GRAY

Shortly after arriving at Ubon, and after getting used to the daily routine of flying combat, I got swept up with a group of fellow 433rd TFS pilots that were invited downtown to the "Grays' home." I had no idea who the Grays were or why we were going to their home. I went with the group, nevertheless. That evening, I was introduced to two of the most gracious and caring Americans that I had ever met. T. R. Gray and his wife Estelle lived in downtown Ubon in a stunning house that could only be described as a villa or perhaps a chalet. Young Thai domestic help abounded, making hosting a group of pilots a reasonably easy event for T. R. and Estelle.

We were met at the door with a handshake from T. R. and a hug from Estelle. T. R. was employed by the United States Agency for International Development (AID). I don't know how long they had been in Ubon, but it was long enough to adopt the pilots of the 433rd TFS, and as a group we were blessed by this relationship.

Through the evening both of the Grays spent extra time getting to know the several of us that were FNGs ("fucking new guys"). The sincerity and warmth of these conversations was overwhelming. I initially really hit it off with Estelle. I would guess at that point in her life she was in her early 50s. I was 27, and her attention was almost motherly. I never heard her express fear or worry about our combat activity over the nearly year that followed, even though we lost a few squadronmates. She was just magic in her relationship with each one of us.

One night, weeks later, while at her house with a small group of "Satan's Angels," she asked me what I was doing the following day. By that time in the evening I knew I wasn't on the flying schedule, and thus said, "Not much, I'm not flying. Guess I'll be catching up on paperwork at the squadron." She replied, "Can you get away for a couple hours and play nine holes of golf with me?" I was stunned. Firstly, I'm such a terrible golfer I should never be allowed on a course, and secondly, I had no idea there was a golf course in the Thai town of Ubon Ratchathani. We went golfing and had a great morning, even though my game was so bad I was embarrassed. In her way she put that aside, enjoyed the light conversation and the time together one-on-one getting better acquainted. She wanted to know about my family at home and she shared details of hers. It was a delightful experience in the middle of a war.

BBQ AT THE HOOCH

Our backseaters were always up to something. Some were pilots and others highly experienced navigators mostly from either bombers in SAC or F-101 Voodoo fighters of ADC. We also had an increasing number of "GIBs" fresh out of navigator school. One of the more memorable "events" organized by the group during my time in-theater was a roasted pig BBQ in our squadron area next to the "Inferno." The latter was a "private" bar that was built totally by personnel from the 433rd in their spare time. It became a favorite hangout as a worthwhile alternative to the main bar in the Officers' Club. We were able to purchase liquor and beer on base for extraordinarily low prices, so the bar was soon fully equipped.

The Thai girls that worked in the Officers' Club were also permitted to come to the "Inferno," along with the American secretaries and nurses employed on-base and, of course, our special off-base American civilian friends like the Grays. The "Inferno" became a very popular hangout, and the other squadrons soon followed suit with bars of their own.

I have no idea where the pig came from or where the guys got the charcoal. There are pictures of the fire pit with the pig rotating on a forked stick-supported spit. Of course it takes a long time to roast a pig, so many cans of beer were consumed in the meantime, with the empties piled high into a pyramid that blocked one of the sidewalks in the party hooch area. The pyramid became a challenge to the former track athletes among us, with many vaulting it between beers and while waiting for the pig to cook. Again, there are pictures to prove it. In one of these photos are two of the officers we lost in combat, Wendell Keller and "Jeb" Stewart.

The BBQ was a huge success, and other similar events certainly continued long after I had completed my combat tour.

END OF *ROLLING THUNDER*

I was scheduled for a night mission on October 31, 1968. That Halloween was also my 28th birthday. The details of the mission have faded from memory except for two things. Firstly, not a shot was fired at us in North Vietnam that night and there was not a visible light on the ground anywhere north of the border with Laos. And, secondly, that mission was flown on the last day of *Rolling Thunder*, President Johnson having called off the air war against North Vietnam. Now, we were to focus exclusively on interdicting the jungle trails through Laos that paralleled the border with North Vietnam.

A few weeks later, North Vietnam was bright with lights at night, the country no longer being targeted by our nocturnal fighter-bombers. We could see convoys of vehicles with their headlights fully on driving along roads toward the Mu Gia and Ban Karai passes, which led directly into Laos. At the border, the trucks' headlights went off and Laos became as dark as North Vietnam had been before the bombing halt. It would remain this way for the remainder of my year in-theater.

On May 9, 1972, newly elected President Richard Nixon unleashed the "dogs of war" against North Vietnam with the decisive *Linebacker I/II* campaigns. *Linebacker* brought an end to US hostilities in Vietnam and the return of the American PoWs that had been held captive for so long. Sadly, in spite of the terms of the subsequent peace agreement that brought a halt to *Linebacker II*, North Vietnam resumed the war against South Vietnam. By then, Americans were thoroughly sick of their nation's involvement in the conflict, and for a variety of political reasons, US forces did not re-engage. Finally, on April 30, 1975, South Vietnam fell to the overwhelming strength of the NVA. By then, President Nixon had already resigned from the presidency over the Watergate scandal.

CHRISTMAS 1968

I flew a combat mission on the morning of December 25, 1968. It was kind of a crazy day, as "Phineas" and I had our picture taken in front of Ubon's Tactical Operations Center (TOC), which had a festive "Peace on Earth" sign hung out front acknowledging the Christmas season. We found that ironic. After we debriefed from the mission, we changed clothes and went to the Grays' for Christmas dinner. Estelle served turkey with all the trimmings.

A few weeks later I learned that I was eligible for a week of leave, so I decided to try to get home. The plan came together and I had a wonderful time with my family in Las Vegas. We enjoyed a late Christmas and simply treasured the time together. We took the children sledding up on Mount Charleston, just west of Las Vegas, and had a ball with the kids in the snow. And, one night, we got a babysitter and Jeannie's parents took us to a dinner show at the Tropicana. We were drinking pretty heavily that evening, and while cutting a piece of steak my serrated knife slipped and I severely cut my right index finger at the middle knuckle. Fortunately, the tendons were spared, and by the time I got back to Ubon it had pretty well healed up. The trip back to Ubon was tedious and full of the typical drama associated with space-available travel for a journey halfway around the world. But, I finally made it back to the 433rd, and no one was particularly upset that I was a few days late arriving.

STRAFING UNDER FLARES AT NIGHT

After the bombing halt against North Vietnam commenced on November 1, 1968, our night combat was exclusively conducted in the *Steel Tiger* area of southern Laos. The missions varied, but they were all challenging, and included working with O-2 "Nail" FACs, each of whom had a unique pilot number. The "Nails" (assigned to the 23rd Tactical Air

Support Squadron) had a detachment at Ubon, and after missions we often gathered in the bar at the Officers' Club, drank heavily, relived missions we had flown together and frequently engaged in games of "sockey," or was it "hocker"? The games involved two sides, typically "Nails" versus the fighter pilots, a scrunched beer can that looked something like a hockey puck and a few pitchers of beer spilled on the floor just to make the footing unsteady and to add to the drama of the drunken event. We never agreed on a name for the game, some preferring "sockey" and others "hocker." The club barmaids and the bartender were the cheerleaders and there were no referees.

I remember one night we were in the middle of such a game, with bodies hitting the floor as we tried to kick the beer can soccer-style though the opponent's hockey-like goal – which consisted of a chair – when, through the club's main entrance, came a "full bird" colonel. I don't remember whether he was a base support "weenie" or part of the FAC or gunship leadership cadre. He took a quick assessment of the situation, turned around and exited the same way he had come in. Moments later, we saw him enter the Officers' Club restaurant area through an alternate door on the far side of the bar area. Good judgment. I don't remember any senior officer ever trying to control the drunken bar room antics of the late night combat pilot crowd that congregated in the Officers' Club every night.

As often as not, one of our squadronmates named Al Turin would stroll through the carnage in the middle of one of the games and mount a table. Al was a big guy, and he had very Italian features that kind of went along with his name. Once in place on the table, all the "Satan's Angels" present would stop playing and yell "Guinea, Guinea, Guinea." Without missing a beat, "Big Al" would respond with "Wop, Wop, Wop." We were later totally disenchanted when we learned he was of Armenian descent and not Italian at all. What a great fighter pilot he was! Al and I later served together as instructors at MacDill after our combat tours. The "Wop, Wop, Wop" tradition followed "Big Al" to the halls of MacDill's "Stag Bar."

Night missions also included the escort of AC-130 Spectre gunships from the 16th Special Operations Squadron. On these missions, we generally orbited above the gunship and attacked any AAA sites that opened up on the Hercules. The results claimed by the gunships amazed us, as we generally saw nothing from our vantage point above them. Later, we were privileged to see the IR images from the gunship's sensors, and were stunned with the accuracy and lethality of this modern combat weapon.

We kept track of the gunships below us by visually monitoring a red beacon that was mounted on top of the AC-130 about where the wings attached to the fuselage. The beacon was not visible to the gunners on the ground below.

On other missions, we worked with unarmed C-130s that carried flares. Their call-sign was "Blind Bat," and sometimes there was also a "Nail" O-2 FAC nearby directing traffic, pointing out targets and calling for flares. Attacking targets at night under flares was especially challenging. We treasured our night vision, which was instantly destroyed when a flare was illuminated. But, under the flare light, we could actually see targets on the ground instead of relying on white phosphorous rocket impacts or burning logs put out by the "Nail" FACs. When the flares burned out, our night vision slowly came back. Timing good night vision was always a challenge because when you needed it, you *really* needed it, and to be surprised by a flare illuminating at a critical time in an attack could make things "really ugly" for the F-4 crew.

One night, Steve and I were carrying a gun pod and we were strafing some fires in pitch blackness that a previous flight had managed to get started on the ground. The target was in a long, narrow valley. The light from the moon and stars was such that I could make out the ridge lines on either side of the valley. I rolled in on the target area, and just as I commenced firing a "Blind Bat" C-130 kicked out a flare that totally illuminated the ridges, the valley and Steve and me in our F-4. We were below the elevation of the ridges on either side. Instantly, the gunners on both sides of the ridges opened fire on us, shooting *down* at us from their positions above our F-4. Although I was initially blinded, I was quickly able to regain vision and a view of the ground below, as well as laterally above us on both sides.

I pulled back hard on the stick and attempted to roll the jet to the right, knowing that most fighter pilots roll left. The stick would not go to the right, and for a split second I thought we had been hit. I unloaded, rolled back left, and then attempted to roll right again. By this time we were above the height of the ridges and the illumination of the flare in pitch black sky. I was thinking, "Holy shit, what's with the jet? Did we take a hit?" I was still trying to force the stick to the right, but to no avail. Then, Steve yelled at me, "Lighten up boss – you're about to break my leg." I replied, "What the fuck are you talking about?" He calmly informed me that when the flare illuminated, his clipboard had, under the forces of my sudden jink, slipped off his right thigh and was now wedged between his leg and the stick. I cut him some slack with the stick, he reclaimed his clipboard and we just about died laughing at the situation.

We decided that we had had enough "fun" for one night, so I gave him the jet and Steve sucked up a little fuel from the "Cherry Anchor" tanker and then flew us home, making a picture-perfect night back seat landing, We were still giggling a little as we rolled to a stop on the ramp.

PRASIT AND THE SNAKE

Mornings in Thailand often have a special glow about them, the tropical air being heavy with the humidity, the sky an azure blue with a faint hint of haze in the air and the dew making the grass glisten. That was the setting one morning when I headed out on my short walk to the flightline, and a new day. We lived in long, low buildings that we called hooches. One side had a long porch wide enough to accommodate chairs and still enable passage. The roof of the hooches overlapped the porch significantly, providing some shelter from what could be driving rain. Four or five aircrew rooms opened onto the porch. In the middle of the hooch was the bathroom and shower area, and adjacent was a screened room suitable for meetings and other gatherings. On the other side of the screened room the porch continued, with another four or five aircrew rooms leading off it.

The aircrew rooms were modest in size, and they boasted two clothes lockers and two single beds. At the end of the room opposite the entry door was a window air conditioning unit between the two twin beds. The entry door was on one side of the room, and on the other side was a sink suitable for shaving, etc. The clothes lockers were typically set up as a barrier between the entry door, the sink area and the beds. The generous width of the room permitted easy passage between the lockers, with their doors facing the room entrance and the sink. Such was our home for a year. Roommates changed with some frequency as people departed and arrived and/ or friends made arrangements to switch roommates so as to bunk together. Some guys set up shelves between the lockers and their beds for their newly acquired tape decks, turntables, amplifiers and speakers.

I don't remember how many hooches there were but there were enough to house aviators for four fighter squadrons. There were green grass areas in between the hooches, and this was where outdoor functions such as BBQs and other social gatherings took place.

The hooches were all in a row perpendicular to a street and joined by a short concrete path to the sidewalk that ran parallel to the street. There was a lot of grass. Across the street were larger buildings that housed the enlisted force. In amongst those buildings were bunkers made of sandbags and steel that could have been used in the event of an attack on the airfield. Attacks were almost nonexistent during my time at Ubon and I never entered one of the bunkers.

To look after us, each hooch had a houseboy. We had Prasit, who took care of whatever we needed when it came to keeping the place clean and tidy. He also took care of our washing. We used to joke that the houseboys took our flightsuits and underwear down to the river, where the women washed the clothes. That was a fact. The joke was that they had a special machine down on the riverbank that ripped out the metal snaps (stud buttons) from our underwear and then shot them through our t-shirts. How else did almost every new t-shirt we acquired get so "holey" so quickly?

On one of those clear mornings, with the dew still on the grass and the air so thick with humidity and tropical heat that you felt like you needed a knife to cut your way through it, I was running a little late and stepped off our porch and took a shortcut across the grass to the sidewalk. What happened next was a blur for me. One minute I was strolling along minding my own business traipsing through the short grassy area and the next thing I knew I was flat on my back. I looked around and there was our houseboy Prasit picking himself up. He pointed at an object that I didn't immediately recognize. Then, reality hit! Prasit had bodily blocked me in order to prevent me from stepping on a deadly bamboo viper – an extremely poisonous snake whose color had blended in perfectly with the grass. Another save. Better to be lucky than good, especially when luck involves a close call with a deadly snake.

While brave and loyal Prasit protected us in our hooch, the guardians of the hooch bathrooms were little Thai geckos that looked remarkably similar to a famous TV insurance lizard. Our geckos could talk too, even though their vocabulary was limited to just a couple of words. The little guys would start their expressive call of the wild with little chirps, which increased in frequency and volume until they started yelling "Fuck You, Fuck You, Fuck You." Naturally, they were lovingly referred to as the "Fuck You" lizards.

Squadronmate Dickie Dull, who, at the time was still an F-4 WSO – he later upgraded to the front seat of the Phantom II, completed a second distinguished combat tour and attended FWS – was gifted with an insatiable curiosity about everything, including the "Fuck You" lizards. To learn more about them, Dickie set out to catch one of the little guys. And he did. The details of the capture are long since forgotten, but the aftermath is indelibly etched in memory. Once a captive, the little lizard took great exception to its new state of existence and, while Dickie was sort of playing with it, its mouth opened and chomped down on the end of Dickie's finger. He reacted, offering the lizard a chance to escape. However, the taste of revenge was so sweet for the little guy that he held on tight to the digit of his captor. Perhaps the lizard intended to eat Dickie starting with the finger.

Very soon, the entire scenario turned from funny to worrisome because the lizard defied all efforts to force open its mouth, thus freeing Dickie's finger. There are different memories about how the issue was resolved, including the decapitation of the gecko. No one could have a clearer memory of the finger extraction than Dickie. And his story is that fellow pilot John McBroome came to the rescue, prying open the mouth of the lizard with a spoon and freeing Dickie's finger. Such were some of the antics and experiences accrued in between combat missions in-theater. Nobody remembers what happened to the lizard. He, or she, may still be "on point" guarding a hooch bathroom.

5

"Wolf" FAC

About halfway through my year flying combat I began to hear stories about an F-4 FAC program, whose crews used the call-sign "Stormy," that was gaining traction at Da Nang AB in South Vietnam. I believe it was patterned after the F-100 "Fast FAC" program (call-sign "Misty") that had also enjoyed success in South Vietnam, Laos and just north of the DMZ in the area of North Vietnam we called "Tally Ho." Rumor soon gave way to fact, and the program was established at Ubon with the call-sign "Wolf," inspired by the nickname of the 8th TFW. Ray Battle was the founder and first commander of the "Wolf" FAC flight, and my nocturnal backseater, Steve Mosier, soon joined. He is quoted on the "Wolf" FAC website as being the author of the flight's credo: "Respect the elders; teach the young; cooperate with the pack; play when you can; hunt when you must; rest in between; share your affections; voice your feelings; leave your mark."

The pilots that flew the "Wolf" FAC mission generated war stories at a rate that was impressive. Some of the tales had a happy ending and others didn't. Let's start with one of Steve Mosier's personal stories from his time flying as "Wolf 05":

Unaccounted for but not Forgotten
It was late in the afternoon, near twilight on a spring Laotian day. "Wolf 05" was getting ready to depart for a post-strike tanker and head home. "Owl" FACs from the 497th TFS and Spectre AC-130 gunships would soon be headed out to stalk the trail, the latter armed with the 105mm howitzer and, for the day, a sophisticated sensor suite. All of a sudden, an emergency beeper began its foreboding howl on Guard. Not good news for some American aviator. Soon, a radio call came in from a wingman announcing a Thunderchief was down.* A rough location was given – a Delta Point just west of the Ban Karai Pass (a major crossing point on the Ho Chi Minh Trail from North Vietnam to Laos).

We checked our gas and made contact with "Cricket" ABCCC, telling them that we had F-105s working that very area and that there was gas available on a "Cherry Tanker" so we could extend our play time to assist at the front end of what we hoped would be a Combat SAR (CSAR). We authenticated who we were by using our coded wheel and radioing "set Mother over Father" or "Richard over Elizabeth." The ABCCC controller immediately confirmed the downing of an aircraft and gave us a good cut on the location. We then headed northeast for the general location of where we hoped the survivor had come down.

The terrain around the Ban Karai Pass was noted for its switchback roads. These were always targets for bombs and delayed-fuse mines that were used to interdict vehicle traffic

---

*Editor's Note: The aircraft in question was the F-105D of Capt John M. Brucher of the Korat-based 34th TFS/388th TFW, its tail having been blown off by AAA while bombing a POL storage site on February 18, 1969. The pilot reported to his wingman via his emergency radio that he was hung up in a tree, and that he had a dislocated shoulder. Brucher was not heard from again.

carrying troops, ammunition and supplies for NVA regulars and their Viet Cong brothers down south. One of the most sought after targets were the infamous bulldozers used to keep the roads navigable. A bulldozer was in some ways a tougher target than a tank or armored personnel carrier. It was easy for the crew (of one) to abandon a bulldozer when under attack. Not only that, bulldozers proved to be stubbornly durable. A 500lb Mk 82 could hit the ground just ten meters away and merely move the bulldozer sideways or perhaps tip it over, inflicting little damage. The introduction of the 2,000lb Mk 84 LGB was a game changer, however. When it exploded within ten meters of a bulldozer, the results were far more devastating.

Being a key supply route, the Ban Karai Pass was one of the most defended areas in Laos. Its proximity to the sanctuary of North Vietnam following the bombing halt meant AAA could be moved in and out of the area as required. We were particularly familiar with this area, having been there only a couple of days earlier. Having arrived on scene ahead of other friendly assets, we were forced to wait for additional fighter support. In hindsight, orbiting overhead the pass in the "high teens" at a less-than-smart tactical airspeed made little sense. After making a few laps, our casual, careless state was interrupted by a flash of light over the aircraft, followed by a dirty blossom of smoke visible in the mirrors. Our assessment was a "big gun" – an 85mm at least or perhaps even a 100mm piece – had taken a shot at some lazy aviators. We had given the "gomers" a predictable target at a "sweet" altitude, allowing them ample time to take a shot at us. The shell had detonated close to us, but it hadn't done any damage. Nevertheless, it was a reminder that a lazy dog will get kicked!

During the course of this mission we came in low and fast – much lower and faster than I had ever previously flown in-theater – hoping to get the attention of the survivor from the downed F-105. No luck. The rescue beeper had gone silent, so we did a fast visual survey of our best guess of where the crash site or survivor might be. We were engaged by both 23mm and 37mm guns, each type distinctive by their burst lengths and smoke residue from the exploding rounds. No luck, then we saw what we thought was a 'chute – another pass, and we could verify it was indeed a 'chute, mostly deflated, but hanging in a tree. A few more passes, some more AAA, but nothing else – no colored smoke, no mirror flashes, no pen gun flares.

The light was fading, and we were in the last few minutes of being able to see things on the ground. Now, anyone that has flown at 300–500ft AGL and 500 knots while "keeping it moving" (jinking) knows it is not easy to find and identify things on the ground. Those same guys (and now girls) will tell you it is an acquired taste, and when you see something standing out, you know it. What we saw creeping along the side of a road, in the shadows, was what I still remember as being an open car – not a jeep – but a car like Field Marshal Rommel rode in when he was raging through the Ardennes or along the roads of the Libyan desert when the Wehrmacht was the scourge of Western civilization. In it were two bodies in the driver and shotgun seats, and a lone person in the back. This staff car was headed northeast toward the Laotian/North Vietnamese boarder. We'll never know, but I am convinced it was a "Thud" pilot, probably injured from his ejection and capture, bundled into the back seat and on his way to interrogation and incarceration.

The CSAR never got started – light was gone, and although we had some 20mm rounds in the external gun pod fitted to our F-4, there was no viable target for it. There was activity indicating a survivor was on the ground, but the forces were not in proximity to get the CSAR going. We left there with an ugly feeling in the pit of our stomachs. In our hearts we knew there was a survivor – we also knew in our hearts he was captured. We went and tanked and went home to Ubon for a debrief.

In the tradition of the US military, we committed to a return the next morning, with a CSAR package ready for business – "King" for Command and Control, standby tanking, "Sandy" A-1s for close escort and defense suppression, and the Jolly Greens, both high and low, for the pick-up and extraction. F-4 assets would also be airborne and available for diversion to take on the guns around the Ban Karai Pass with CBU and Paveway LGBs if needed.

That night, preparing for a possible CSAR the following day, working with the "Wolf" team was a model for intel/ops integration. We were up to mandatory crew rest – and plus some – but we kept on planning for "what ifs" should a rescue be possible. The primary "what ifs" centered on locating the AAA that had so stoutly defended the area and brought the F-105 down. We also needed to work out where the alternate positions were – on both sides of the border – for the weapons. When we finally left the TOC it was for a quick dinner and then off to bed. Sleep wasn't easy – it was hard not to think about one of "us" in a bad way. The alarm went off early and we then rushed back to the ops center for an up-to-date review of the situation and a briefing on the plan for the morning.

The listeners at NKP and elsewhere had monitored the situation throughout the night. An RF-4C from Udorn was out early on a photo and sensor scan of the area, and "Wolf 06" was airborne before sun up and in the target area to search for any contact from the survivor, visual or otherwise. As light became available we searched the area for evidence to justify launching a CSAR package. It wasn't there – we wished it had been, but it wasn't. It hurts to lose an airman, and his cohorts are willing to risk it all if a rescue is even remotely possible, regardless of the odds for success. In some ways it hurts more to know when you can't try. We finished our "Wolf Cycle" and headed home, not feeling good.

I watched the news relating to PoWs being released for years after the war and never saw the name of the "Thud driver" we knew had gone down around Ban Karai Pass that afternoon. Even today, nearly 50 years later, it hurts to know an American airman remains unaccounted for.

CRIPPLED F-4

Another one of our squadronmates, Lt Col Ray Battle, also joined the "Wolf" FAC team as its commander – he quickly became known as "Pappa Wolf." On November 18, 1968, Ray and his "GIB," 1Lt Kenny Boone, were off performing the "Wolf" mission searching for targets in a heavily gun-defended part of Laos near Tchepone. I don't think I ever knew further details of their sortie that day except for the conclusion. They took a massive hit from AAA. In fact, the hit was so terrific that the nose of the aircraft* was shot off just forward of the cockpit. Kenny either chose to eject, or was ejected, from the aircraft while Ray struggled to regain control.

Two separate stories resulted. In Kenny's case, he parachuted into the jungle and became the subject of a SAR mission. The details of why the first SAR attempt was aborted are lost, but it was probably because the rescue could not be completed before darkness fell. Thus Kenny spent the night in the jungle before being rescued the next day.

Ray regained control of the F-4 and was able to fly back to Ubon and land, although that event was not without

*Editor's Note: the aircraft was F 4D 66-0249, which had been the first D-model credited with a MiG kill on June 5, 1967.

its excitement as the jet had no nose cone, the back seat canopy was missing and the cockpit was empty. The seat was guided up and clear of the aircraft during ejection by an expandable boom or rod that was several inches in diameter and, when extended, was clearly visible, with the upper end several feet above the aircraft. So, picture this crippled F-4 with the nose shot off leaving jagged metal edges protruding into the airstream just in front of the pilot, and with this boom sticking up into the air from the rear cockpit (see the plates section for a photograph of this aircraft).

The runway at Ubon was quite narrow, and it had a crest to it so the torrential rain could more easily run off to the sides adjacent to the tarmac. This sounds good, but the runway was only 125ft wide, which was narrow by fighter standards. It also had grooves across it to further facilitate rainwater runoff. Since the photographs of the jet taken by a chase aircraft show the tail hook down, I imagine Ray intended to take an approach end barrier, with his tail hook engaging a wire much like during a carrier landing. The main landing gear was disabled, probably as a result of the AAA hit. It doesn't really matter because the point is that the jet did not engage the wire and instead skidded along on its belly and eventually departed the runway in a huge cloud of dust and dirt before finally coming to a stop. Nobody got seriously hurt, so that is a "Wolf" FAC war story with a happy ending.*

---

*Editor's Note: Capt Battle's 66-0249 was subsequently repaired and returned to service with the 8th TFW in June 1971. The veteran fighter was eventually lost in a non-fatal crash caused by an engine fire on March 22, 1985, the Phantom II plunging into the Gulf of Mexico shortly after taking off from Tyndall AFB.

On July 12, 1969, squadronmates and close friends Maj Paul Bannon and "GIB" 1Lt Peter Pike took off from Ubon on a "Wolf" FAC mission. Peter was a last-minute substitution for a pilot originally scheduled who got sick and was grounded – this was his first FAC sortie. They accomplished the routine pre-strike refueling and then headed into their assigned target area to search out the enemy. They were never heard from again. Both Paul and Peter and their aircraft were still missing at the end of my tour. They were highly respected and competent aviators, but their lives were lost to an unknown, unhappy ending.

No one on "our side" knows what happened to these men. There may be people on the "other side" who know, but the US government has been unable to learn details of their fate. As a result, there has been a lot of speculation without conclusive findings. The speculation ranges from Internet reports to books on the subject, to readings on The Virtual Wall® – an online Vietnam War memorial that opened in March 1997. I have included some of this material, just to emphasize the gravity of the situation when families and colleagues don't know the final fate of their loved ones. The following is a report from The Virtual Wall®:

A Note from The Virtual Wall
On July 12, 1969, then-Maj Paul Bannon and then-1Lt Peter Pike launched from Ubon RTAFB in F-4D 66-7697 [of the 433rd TFS/8th TFW] on a "Wolf" FAC mission over the northern part of the Ho Chi Minh Trail in the Laotian panhandle. The target area was covered with low cloud. Maj Bannon, finding it impossible to operate below the overcast, advised the airborne control post that he was going to find a hole to climb through en route to an area with better weather conditions. However, his radio transmission stopped

in mid-sentence and the radar return from the Phantom II disappeared from the controller's radar scope.

The aircraft was known to have gone down in a mountainous area south of Ban Nathon, but SAR efforts were severely hampered by bad weather. The SAR forces were unable to locate the wreckage of the F-4, nor was voice contact established with either crewman. When the formal SAR effort was terminated both men were classed as Missing in Action [MIA], since there was no firm evidence of their deaths.

The two men remained in MIA status (and were promoted while MIA) until the Secretary of the Air Force approved Presumptive Findings of Death for them, Col Bannon on January 22, 1979 and Capt Pike on May 28, 1974. As of June 29, 2006, their remains have not been repatriated.*

Paul Wedlake Bannon
ON THE WALL: Panel W21 Line 105
This page © 1997–2018 www.VirtualWall.org Ltd.
PERSONAL DATA:
Home of Record: Hueytown, AL
Date of birth: 10/15/1934
MILITARY DATA:
Service Branch: US Air Force
Grade at loss: O4
Rank: Promoted while in MIA status
Promotion Note: None
ID No: 417449746
MOS: 1115F: Pilot, Tactical Fighter
                      (F-4 Phantom II, various models)
Length Service: **

---

*Text © Kenneth J. Davis, CDR USN (Ret.), first published on The Virtual Wall®, here: Ami Partin, Dr. Vernon P. Wagner Lt Col, USAF (Ret.), Jan Takac, Antoinette Zelig et al. "Paul Wedlake Bannon." The Virtual Wall®. 04 Nov. 2007. www.VirtualWall.org, Ltd. 29 June 2018. http://www.virtualwall.org/db/BannonPW01a.htm. Reproduced by kind permission of Kenneth J. Davis.

Unit: HQ SQDN, 8TH TAC FTR
                         WING, 7TH AF
CASUALTY DATA:
Start Tour: 01/31/1969
Incident Date: 07/12/1969
Casualty Date: 01/22/1979
Status Date: Not Applicable
Status Change: Not Applicable
Age at Loss: 44 (based on date declared dead)
Location: Laos
Remains: Body not recovered
Repatriated: Not Applicable
Identified: Not Applicable
Casualty Type: Hostile, died while missing
Casualty Reason: Fixed Wing – Pilot
Casualty Detail: Air loss or crash over land
URL: www.VirtualWall.org/db/BannonPW01a.htm
Data accessed: 8/31/2018

THE VIRTUAL WALL® www.VirtualWall.org*

From *On The Wall*, Panel 21W Line 105:

PIKE, PETER XAVIER
Name: Peter Xavier Pike
Rank/Branch: Captain/US Air Force
Unit: 433rd Tactical Fighter Squadron
                         8th Tactical Fighter Wing
                         Ubon Airfield, Thailand
Date of Birth: June 15, 1943
Home of Record: New York, NY

*Text © The Virtual Wall®, same source link as previous reference, "full profile"
section. http://www.virtualwall.org/js/Profile.htm. Reproduced by kind permission
of The Virtual Wall®.

Date of Loss:	July 12, 1969
Country of Loss:	Laos
Loss Coordinates:	180400N 1051300E
Status in 1973:	Missing In Action
Category:	4
Aircraft/Vehicle/Ground:	F-4D Phantom II
Other Personnel in Incident:	Paul W. Bannon (missing)

REMARKS:
SYNOPSIS: The McDonnell Douglas F-4 Phantom II, used by Air Force, Marine and Navy air wings, served a multitude of functions including fighter/bomber, interceptor, photo/electronic surveillance, and reconnaissance. The two-man aircraft was extremely fast (Mach 2) and had a long range – 900–2,300 miles, depending on stores and mission type. The F-4 was also extremely maneuverable and handled well at low and high altitudes. It was selected for a number of state-of-the-art electronics conversions, which improved radar intercept and computer bombing capabilities enormously. Most pilots considered it one of the "hottest" planes around.

On July 12, 1969, Maj Paul W. Bannon, pilot, and then-1Lt Peter X. Pike, WSO, comprised the crew of an F-4D aircraft, call-sign "Wolf 04," on a FAC visual reconnaissance mission. Their mission area included extremely rugged jungle-covered mountains, known to be under the control of the NVA, located approximately ten miles southwest of the Laos/North Vietnamese border and 38 miles southwest of the major North Vietnamese city of Vinh. Further, this area of eastern Laos (Khammouane Province) was considered a major artery of the infamous Ho Chi Minh Trail.

When North Vietnam began to increase its military strength in South Vietnam, NVA and Viet Cong troops again intruded into neutral Laos for sanctuary, as the Viet Minh had done during the war with the French some years before. This border road was used by the Communists to transport weapons, supplies and troops from North Vietnam into South Vietnam, and was frequently no more than a path cut through the jungle-covered mountains. US forces used all assets available to them to stop this flow of men and supplies from moving south into the war zone.

At 0845 hrs [on July 12, 1969], Maj Bannon accomplished an air refueling and returned to his assigned area to continue their mission. By 0950 hrs he notified a radar controller who was monitoring the flight that they were going to try to find a hole in the clouds to climb above them because of the poor weather conditions, with broken to overcast cloud layers. At that time the cloud tops were at approximately 4,300ft, with 5,830ft peaks in the surrounding area. Their last known position placed them 55 kilometers southeast of Khamkeut, 30 kilometers southeast of Ban Lakxao and 12 kilometers northeast of Ban Songkhone [all in Laos].

There was no indication of problems with the Phantom II. However, during the last radio transmission, the conversation ended abruptly and their image disappeared from the radarscope. Because of the bad weather, no formal search and recovery operation was possible. A C-130 already in the area orbited the loss location for two hours trying to make contact with the downed aircrew. During that time no emergency beepers were heard and no voice contact was established. The search effort by the C-130 was terminated at 1240 hrs the same day. Both Paul Bannon and Peter Pike were immediately listed as MIA.

[According to a later report from the same reference,] after 1975, when all US involvement ceased in Southeast Asia, reports kept trickling into the CIA's Bangkok station that Americans had been seen among the prisoners working on Laotian road and irrigation projects. In 1979, a Lao informant for the Defense Intelligence Agency claimed that 18 Americans had been moved to a cave north of Nammarath, in Laos. He identified one of them as "Lt Col Paul W. Mercland," but no Mercland was listed as missing. Pentagon intelligence analysts suspected that Mercland was a garbled version of an American name, and erroneously assumed it to be the officer's last name. Based on their extensive evaluation of all the known data about this group of prisoners, and of all records of PoW/MIAs, they believed that Mercland was possibly Paul W. Bannon. The source passed a polygraph test, while satellite photos analyzed in the Pentagon confirmed the cave's location.

In November 1980 US intelligence sources provided solid information about approximately 30 American pilots working as a road gang near the central Laotian town of Nammarath. These source reports were supported by a spy satellite photo confirming that a prison camp had recently been built near the town. This camp was later nicknamed "Fort Apache" by the US intelligence community. Two months later, the Pentagon began preparing Operation *Pocket Change*, a top-secret plan to retrieve these American captives. It was the only post-war rescue the US government ever considered in Southeast Asia. Never before had photographic, electronic and human intelligence all pointed to one site where American PoWs might very well be alive. Spy satellites continued to watch the camp 24 hours a day, while the CIA and Joint Special Operations Command planned and practiced to rescue the PoWs.

On March 18, 1981, because the Joint Chiefs of Staff did not want to run the risk of being accused of keeping too many key government officials uninformed, members of the congressional PoW Task Force were given a classified briefing. The result was a flood of media leaks about Operation *Pocket Change*, and the need for the head of the Pentagon's news division to convince news agencies to sit on the story.

On March 29, 1981, a 13-man CIA indigenous team crossed the Mekong River into Laos to confirm the existence of the camp, and that US servicemen were being held there. This team did not include any Americans as originally planned. It immediately ran into trouble in crossing the 40-mile distance to Nammarath. When they finally returned to Thailand on May 13, the extent of its failure to properly photograph and visually examine the camp was slow to unravel. In the end, the news media believed the US government was intentionally dragging its feet about the raid to rescue PoWs, and on May 21, 1981 the first news stories about this mission were aired. The end result was Operation *Pocket Change* was canceled and the PoWs were once again abandoned.

Was Paul W. Bannon one of some 30 American PoWs who could have been liberated in 1981 as was believed by US intelligence analysts? Could Peter Pike have also been among these prisoners? These questions, along with many others, remain unanswered. What is known, however, is that in February 1994 the Laotian government finally allowed a Pentagon team into the country to inspect the Nammarath prison. Americans in the party say nervous Laotian officials rushed them through their tour of the camp and gave them little time to read the prisoner logs. Further, no photographs were allowed to be taken. Investigators were allowed to interview only two elderly villagers from Nammarath who claimed they never saw PoWs. With that, the team was forced to report back that there was "no evidence" Americans had been held there.

Paul Bannon and Peter Pike are among nearly 600 Americans who disappeared in Laos. Many of these men were known to be alive on the ground. The Laotians admitted holding "tens of tens" of American PoWs, but these men were never negotiated for either by direct negotiation between the US and Laos or through the Paris Peace Accords which ended the war in Vietnam since Laos was not a party to that agreement. Since the end of the Vietnam War, well over 21,000 reports of American prisoners, missing and otherwise unaccounted for, have been received by the US government. Many of these reports document LIVE America PoWs remaining captive throughout Southeast Asia TODAY.

Fighter pilots in Vietnam and Laos were called upon to fly in many dangerous circumstances, and they were prepared to be wounded, killed or captured. It probably never occurred to them that they could be abandoned by the country they so proudly served.*

An Internet search or other research might yield more information or a different slant to the interested reader in respect to the loss of Maj Paul W. Bannon and 1Lt Peter X. Pike. My grief for their loss precludes my further research. Good friends went, did their job and paid the price.

---

*Profile and text taken from http://taskforceomegainc.org/P080.htm. Reproduced by kind permission of Task Force Omega, Inc.

6

R&R and Other Escapades

An opportunity for a little R&R (rest and relaxation), or was it I&I (intoxication and intercourse), came up whenever a squadron crew was required to take a Phantom II to the Nationalist Chinese island of Taiwan for major maintenance by Air Asia*. The F-4D's AN/APQ-109A radar was classified at the time, and therefore it had to be removed from the aircraft prior to the trip to Taiwan. This created a huge "cargo-carrying space" in the nose of the Phantom II.

On one such trip the crew initially flew the jet to Clark AB, where it was quickly refueled, after which they continued on to the Taiwanese joint civil/military airfield of Tainan – also home to Air Asia's maintenance facility. The trip was uneventful and the hospitality shown by the Nationalist Chinese and American Consulate was overwhelming. At an evening function held after the crew arrived, a grand party was held complete with abundant food and drink and lovely young Chinese female hostesses. As the evening progressed,

*Editor's Note: Air Asia was originally formed to service CIA aircraft flown in the region by Air America.

the aircraft commander paired up with an especially lovely and friendly young woman and they soon disappeared for the night. Later, the pilot had to borrow money from his backseater in order to pay off the young woman, who turned out to be a pro!

Without the classified radar in the nose of the F-4, it was like an SUV in respect to the space it had available for cargo hauling. In Taiwan, there were either no music/publishing copyright laws or they were unenforced. In either case, these trips became the perfect opportunity for the clandestine airlift back to Thailand of really cheap long-play vinyl records and full sets of encyclopedias, all purchased locally in Tainan City for a fraction of the list price.

The Thai women were young, slim and pretty, with an easy laugh and a great, sweet personality. Many of the younger backseaters were single, and over the course of time they acquired Thai girlfriends, or "tealots." Many of these acquaintances developed from contact in the Officers' Club, where the women worked as waitresses, barmaids and bartenders. Some of the officers even arranged to have flats or apartments downtown for their "tealot," while others shared accommodations off base that were used as party houses for aircrew. A few used their "off base housing" as more or less private getaways. While I, of course, went to a few parties off base at these houses, I didn't partake in the favors some of the ladies were offering.

RIVER RUN ON THE MEKONG

After a mission we sometimes "played" in our F-4s if we had the fuel available or were able to snivel a few hundred pounds from the "Cherry Anchor" KC-135 aerial tanker.

An idle power descent from a refueling altitude of about 20,000ft permitted a low-altitude level off and the chance to go screaming down the Mekong River at 100ft and 500 knots just for fun because we could. It was a true thrill, and we did it every now and then. The river was wide, with little islands and lush jungle right down to its banks. The blanket of foliage that ramped up from the river into the rolling hills was beautifully green in varying shades.

Sometimes we would pass over a small boat, with the sole occupant being clearly visible standing up with a paddle. I always wondered what happened to the "skipper" after we flew by him in an ear-shattering burst of noise. I imagine some had to dry their clothes after a sudden dip in the river.

EXTRA DUTIES

So, what else did we do when we weren't flying, planning to fly or debriefing from flying? The answer is performing our extra duties. Squadron Duty Officer (SDO) was a common detail. Every few days, when we were not on the flying schedule, squadron schedulers would duly assign us to one rotating task or another. SDO was one of those tasks. This was a heavy load, and it fell mostly on the backseaters, who came to call it "Duty Pig."

Anytime we were flying we had at least one officer and a more senior supervisor on duty at the squadron at what we called the duty desk. The latter was a bar-like structure in that it stood roughly chest high, was a couple of feet wide and had a foot rail. The duty desk did not run wall to wall, and, therefore, there was room to go around either end in order to get behind it. The back side had a desk-like structure at normal desk height, along with chairs on rollers. It was essentially the squadron communications center, with several telephones for landline communication and at least one UHF radio, which was tuned to a squadron-common frequency, permitting aircrew within range of the radio to communicate directly with the squadron, even when airborne. The landline telephones were a combination of dial-up phones and hotlines. The hotlines connected the squadron to the command post, which was the 8th TFW nerve center, as well as to maintenance control, which managed the weapons loading and other flight preparation of our squadron aircraft. When the receiver for the hotline phone was picked up at the duty desk, it immediately rang at maintenance control or the wing command post. There may have been other hotlines and there were probably multiple dial-up phones.

Behind the duty desk was a large acetate plastic-covered scheduling board that listed the daily flying schedule, along with aircrew names, call-signs, mission numbers, ordnance and other pertinent information. It was the job of the SDO to manage and maintain the scheduling board using grease pencils to post the schedule and then make subsequent adjustments as things changed during the course of the flying, day and night. This was one of our rotating duties, usually assigned to the more junior officers in the squadron for the routine work, along with a supervisor to handle any major decisions.

Since our flying day was generally a 24-hour event, the SDO task was done in shifts, and therefore required several officers for the full daily manning. The SDOs were generally junior officers drawn from the ranks of the back seaters, as well as aircraft commanders. If there was a big mission in the works, then adult supervision (major and above) might be added to the SDO pool.

Meanwhile, there was another level of activity going on in the TOC through the late evening and into the wee hours of the morning – this was known as "breaking the frag." Before going over to "Wolf" FAC operations, Steve Mosier had an additional duty working in the TOC as a night "frag officer." There, he supervised a team of intelligence, weather and maintenance specialists getting the 8th TFW's daily flying schedule extracted from a many-page message from "Blue Chip" in Saigon. This message, known as the frag, contained detailed information on munitions and tankers, as well as times on target for fighters, recce, FAC, command and control and CSAR forces. It was disseminated nightly, tasking all Air Force units in-theater. Steve Mosier's pulled night "frag officer" duty a lot, and he offered the following insight into what was a very important task:

The Night Shift
Every big organization operating on a 24-hour basis has a night shift. The USAF is a big organization, and during the Vietnam War it was clearly operating a night shift – this allowed it to support allied forces engaged with the enemy in various parts of Southeast Asia. I spent some time on the night shift while I was stationed at Ubon, located in the eastern central part of Thailand. Part of that night shift was flying F-4Ds on strike missions with the 433rd TFS against targets in Laos and North Vietnam. That was the exciting part of the night shift, flying mostly two-ship sorties looking for trucks and other vehicles on the Ho Chi Minh Trail after dark, or supporting gunships and Special Forces teams as they conducted similar missions to interdict the flow of supplies (from the USSR and China) down the Trail to NVA and Viet Cong units in the south.

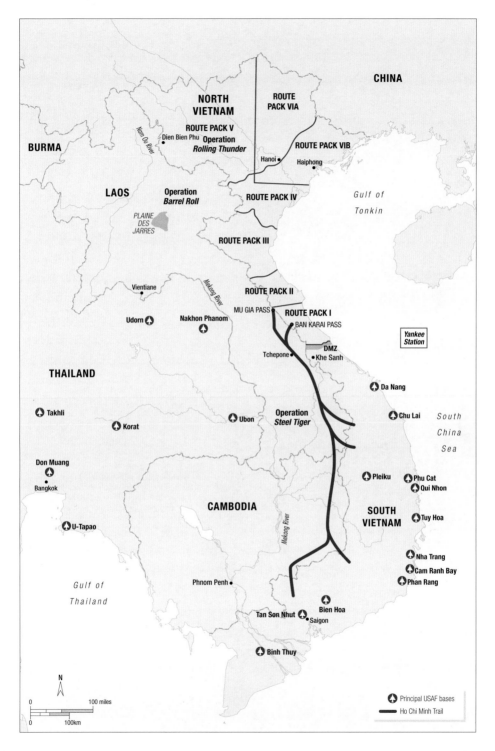

CHINA

NORTH VIETNAM

ROUTE PACK VIA

ROUTE PACK V

Dien Bien Phu

Nam Ou River

Operation *Rolling Thunder*

BURMA

ROUTE PACK VIB

Hanoi

Haiphong

LAOS

Operation *Barrel Roll*

ROUTE PACK IV

Gulf of Tonkin

PLAINE DES JARRES

ROUTE PACK III

Vientiane

Mekong River

ROUTE PACK II

MU GIA PASS

ROUTE PACK I

BAN KARAI PASS

Udorn

Nakhon Phanom

Yankee Station

DMZ

Tchepone

Khe Sanh

THAILAND

Da Nang

Takhli

Ubon

Operation *Steel Tiger*

Chu Lai

South China Sea

Korat

Don Muang

Pleiku

Phu Cat

Bangkok

Qui Nhon

CAMBODIA

Mekong River

SOUTH VIETNAM

Tuy Hoa

U-Tapao

Gulf of Thailand

Phnom Penh

Nha Trang

Cam Ranh Bay

Phan Rang

Tan Son Nhut

Bien Hoa

Saigon

Binh Thuy

N

0   100 miles

0   100km

⊕ Principal USAF bases

━━ Ho Chi Minh Trail

1

2

3

4

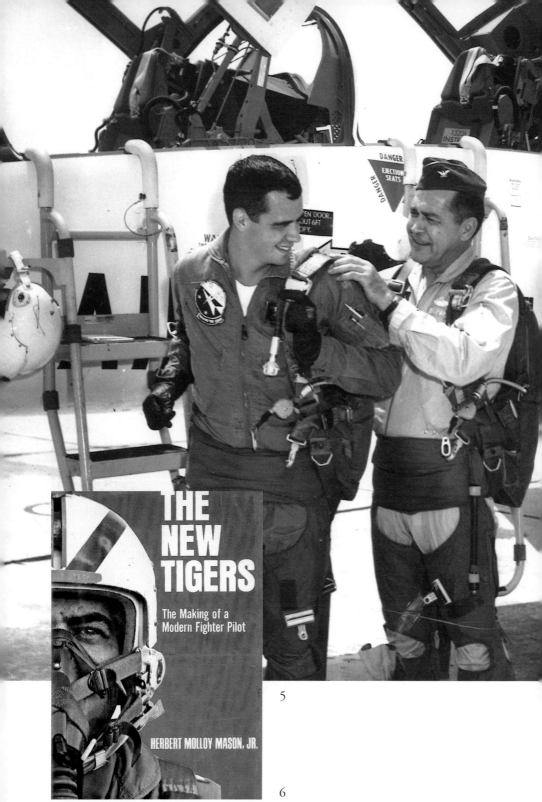

THE NEW TIGERS
The Making of a Modern Fighter Pilot

HERBERT MOLLOY MASON, JR.

5

6

7

8

9

10

11   12

433RD TAC FTR SQ.

★ Worlds greatest fighter pilots

★ Modest Heros

★ International Lovers

★ Masters of the calculated risk

Yea, though we fly through the valley of the Shadow
of Death, We will fear no evil, for We are the
toughest Sons of Bitches in the valley.

13

14

15

16

17

18

19

20

21

22

23

24

25

27

28

29

30

31

32

33

34

35

36

37

38

39

U.S. AIR FORCE T-38A NO·
A.F. SERIAL NO. 61-806λ

SERVICE THIS AIRCRAFT WITH GRADE
JP4 FUEL IF NOT AVAILABLE T.O. NO
42B11-1-14 WILL BE CONSULTED FOR
EMERGENCY ACTION

SUITABLE FOR USE OF AROMATIC FUEL

42

43

44

47

48

49

50

51

52

53

54

55

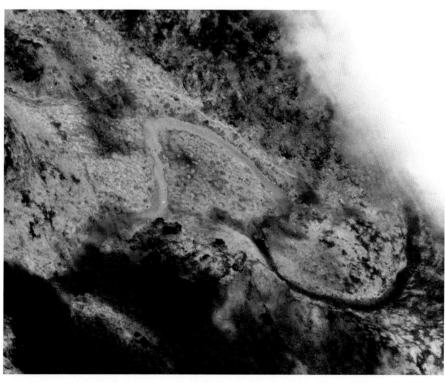

56

57

58

59

60

61

62

63

64

65

66

67

68

One of the mundane tasks of the night shift involved manning the "frag shop" from 2300 hrs to 0700 hrs (we used the term "zero-dark-thirty" long before the media began to throw it around over the past two or three years). A small group of aviators, intelligence personnel and some maintenance folks – all pretty much of the lieutenant variety – were responsible for taking the frag from Seventh Air Force in Saigon and parsing the information to work out what was required to fulfil the mission brief. The "frag shop" worked out how many sorties (aircraft) would need to be flown, what ordnance the jets would be loaded with, whether or not air refueling was needed, and where and when the flights would join their tankers, which squadrons would fly specific missions, and what the targets were and where they were located.

Once this information was digested, it would be provided to the four F-4 squadrons, where call-signs would be allocated and specific pilots assigned by position (leader and wingmen). Along the way, the frag team would do a logic check to see that weapons were appropriate for the target, review the threats in the area of operation (types, numbers and best estimate of the location of anti-aircraft systems in the area – guns, SAMs and the disposition of MiGs) and ensure that the tanker frag married up with the fighter tasking. It also performed several other quality control "scrubs" of the product Higher Headquarters had given the wing for the next flying day.

The frag was a time-constrained schedule, and what usually "broke" it was a last-minute change that caused a rework of the product and scurrying by lieutenants to get an approved plan out before the aircrews and day shift began to show up for mission prep and preflight actions. The latter normally took place from around 0330 hrs as the 25th TFS made ready for its usual pre-dawn launch as part of its *Igloo White* mission supporting the "McNamara Line" with sensor drops, the latter supposedly monitoring and targeting movement on the Trail.

You quickly learned that "frag shop" operations were never routine, with the squadron being tasked to support special one-off missions, emergency searches for downed pilots and support for Special Ops teams patrolling in Laos and North Vietnam. Frequently, a "well-oiled" frag operation could fall foul of vagaries in the weather, increased enemy threat levels, tanker availability and the whimsy of higher headquarters. Such hiccups usually meant that lots of changes had to be jammed into the frag right up to the time the aircrew actually stepped to their jets – normally 45 minutes or so before takeoff.

I vividly recall one night while I was working in the "frag shop" with 1Lt Mulder and SSgt "Radar," we were taking a break with Royal Crown Cola – our drink of choice because there was no Pepsi or Coke in-country, which meant that "RC" was the *only* choice – when we got a hotline call from the command post. "Head's up, the ADO (Assistant Deputy Commander for Operations) and a VIP are heading for the "frag shop"! We tidied up a bit and prepared for a brief "show and tell." Shortly thereafter the ADO and a congressman (whose name I don't think I ever got, and certainly don't remember) walked into the main briefing room where all of the crew briefs took place and all the annotated maps and photographs were displayed on boards around the room.

Now it is to be noted that ADOs traditionally never have much to do, which in turn means that they rarely have any important responsibilities. In fact, they are usually hoping to be elevated to Deputy Commander for Operations status if things go well for their Boss. This one was no different. He of course wanted to give the impression to the congressman that he was alert, informed and on top of his game, and he asked us to describe the night's missions. I grabbed the frag and Mulder went, with pointer, to the map. I described the missions on the board as follows, "Sir, 'Dipper' is working with Mk 36s near Mu Gia Pass, 'Pintail' has a mission with 'Covey 43' working a truck park just east of Tchepone, and 'Banyan' is escorting 'Spectre 06' working Route 7 where it enters Laos from Pack 1 – they have flares and CBUs." This was pretty good I thought, especially since Mulder was right with me with the pointer.

Well, I was WRONG. The ADO bristled and addressed me very sharply, "Lieutenant, in my wing we don't do anything that lacks precision – I didn't expect a brief sketch of the activity. I wanted exactness! Let's try again the 'Wolf Pack' way!" He glanced knowingly at the congressman and apologized for having his time wasted by my casual discussion of important information. I know he wanted to strike me with a glove – like Patton – to emphasize the gravity of my lack of appreciation for the situation. Regrettably, he had no glove! We rewound the tape.

"Sir, 'Pintail' is a flight of two F-4Ds. Each has six Mk 36 Destructor 500lb bombs with delayed fuses. Each is carrying an SUU-23 20mm cannon pod on the centerline. They will be placing their bombs on a section of road recently successfully cut with LGBs by the 433rd TFS in an attempt to keep the NVA road crews from repairing the road and moving supplies in this segment of the Trail tonight. The DMPI [designated mean point of impact] is WE336433 [these were map coordinates used to precisely reference a target location, common to ground troops and pilots, used before the precision of GPS became routine, and these weren't the *actual* coordinates for these targets – for you detail monsters, I am too lazy to find my old maps and give you the real coordinates. Rest assured the ADO and the congressman got the real ones in six-digit accuracy]."

"Much better," the ADO replied. "Now just where is WE366433?" Mulder responded by deftly moving the pointer. "Right here, near Mu Gia Pass, sir," which was pretty much where it had been moments earlier – no, not pretty much, exactly where Mulder had placed the pointer moments earlier. We proceeded to review the details of the remaining sorties in exhaustive depth, and *enjoyed* the opportunity for the ADO to demonstrate his mastery of lieutenants. After some other discussion highlighting both his limited knowledge and actual interest in doing anything other than talking in front of the congressman, he allowed us to come to attention as they departed for another adventure in the workings of a fighter wing at night.

Our RC Colas were warm by now, but we finished them anyway and prepared to turn over our work to the day shift and head to the club for a world famous chili-cheese omelet, proud that we had played our part in keeping our leadership happy and a VIP even slightly entertained on his Oriental "shopping trip." After eating, I then commenced crew rest so that I could get back on the flight schedule for the night shift's good gig!

This particular ADO was actually a "FADO," and I am not here making a reference to a genre of Portuguese music, but to the four-letter profanity that was prefixed to ADOs with little promise of ever rising higher in responsibility or rank. Our full colonels in the 8th TFW were either World War II aces, former Thunderbirds, or test pilots of "Century Series" fighters, and all thoroughly competent aviators and leaders. They made sure "FADOs" got their combat tours without ever actually harming anyone's livelihood or career and then quietly faded into jobs they deserved.

MOBILE OFFICER

Mobile, as we called it, was a small yellow facility adjacent to the approach end of the runway. Check out the photograph in the plates section. There was only room for one person inside, and the unit had a glass roof that allowed the Mobile officer to look out and observe aircraft preparing for takeoff and in the traffic pattern for landing. The unit was fitted with communications equipment that consisted of a dial-up phone and a UHF radio. With the former, the Mobile officer could talk to any of the squadron duty desks, various maintenance shops or the 8th TFW command post.

The primary job of the Mobile officer was to log the call-sign and the time for each takeoff and landing and then inform the respective squadron of that event. Another task was to visually watch each approach and ensure the pilot had lowered his wheels before landing. It was an important, but boring, task to sit there for hours logging takeoff and landing times and watching for gear-up landing attempts. I don't remember ever having to remind a pilot to lower his wheels!

My backseater Steve Mosier reminded me of a story witnessed by the Mobile officer one day:

We had a couple of staff officers that came to Ubon once a month to fly a combat mission with us. While great guys and able pilots, these fellows were not at a level of currency or proficiency to lead flights, and probably shouldn't even have been flying in combat as wingmen. Our squadron leadership worked hard to keep these pilots in the loop, but not in positions of authority during their visits. It usually worked. One day, however, things fell through the cracks and they were scheduled to fly a combat mission together as leader and wingman. The backseaters weren't aware of the squadron leadership's efforts to keep these two always as wingmen and to only send them to areas of low threat.

All went well during the briefing, engine start and taxi out to the runway. Their jets were armed and they were cleared for takeoff by Ubon tower. In the pre-takeoff checks, when the engines are run up, the lead aircraft vented a little fuel – not an uncommon event. However, the wingman, in a shrill radio call, told the lead he was leaking fuel. At that time the leader (one of our erstwhile staff officers) announced that he was aborting and proceeded to recite the boldfaced Abort emergency procedure over the radio:

1. THROTTLES – IDLE (BAD ENGINE OFF FOR FIRE)
2. CHUTE – DEPLOY
3. HOOK – DOWN

This procedure was designed for an aircraft on takeoff roll and not for one sitting statically on the runway before releasing brakes. As he recited the emergency procedure he took each step. And so there sat an F-4 on the runway with the drag 'chute flapping in the jet's exhaust and with the tail hook down. After recovering from a hysterical laughing fit, and a short but seemingly endless radio silence, the tower controller responded that "Banyon" Flight was "cleared to abort." The controller added a footnote suggesting that the lead pilot raise his hook so as not to engage the jet barrier wire stretched across the runway ahead of him.

With the drag 'chute and its accompanying drogue 'chute fluttering, the tail hook was finally raised and the mighty F-4 cleared the runway, much to the amusement of all. The Mobile officer later noted that both backseaters had their heads buried in their radar scopes in total embarrassment over the event.

We didn't see much more of these staff guys after that.

Steve Mosier also recalled the follow incidents in which staff officers – and rockets – played central roles:

Rockets
Rockets have been a part of aircraft armament since the early days. Biplanes in the Great War used them sparingly. In World War II, RAF Typhoons and USAAF Thunderbolts enjoyed great success with them against Wehrmacht columns

after the D-Day invasion. Luftwaffe fighters also used them to try to disrupt American heavy bomber streams targeting Germany. USAF Thunderjets and Mustangs and US Navy aircraft, again both propeller-driven and jet-powered, also fired rockets in massive quantities during the Korean War. Pilots of early USAF interceptors trained to use them to counter Soviet bombers in the 1950s, and rockets remained a key part of the Army, Navy and Air Force arsenal at the start of the Vietnam conflict. Indeed, basic fighter training in the USAF demanded proficiency with the 2.75in. unguided rocket. Pilots trained with them on ranges such as Avon Park, Cuddeback Lake [in California] and Gila Bend [in Arizona].

Initially, unguided rockets were used against point targets, specifically tanks and vehicles. Fired from close range, they were effectively little more than bullets with warheads. While used to firing single shots on controlled ranges during training, fighter pilots eventually graduated to employing pods of rockets that could unleash as many as 19 unguided projectiles at a time against area targets – troops, vehicle columns, supply and ammunition dumps and, in some cases, AAA sites. Airborne FACs used rockets equipped with white phosphorus warheads to designate ground targets for fighters. Dubbed "Willie Pete," these were typically fired singularly or in pairs to direct the eyes of crews in other fighter-bombers onto the enemy and/or away from the friendlies.

When I arrived at Ubon, rockets were often loaded and used on armed reconnaissance missions in the lower route packages of North Vietnam and Laos. While they could be useful against area targets, they also required a very "up close and personal" attack profile to be flown in order to ensure accuracy and effectiveness. Typically, we would close to within 4,000ft – sometimes even closer – of the target before firing, leaving us vulnerable to most crew-served AAA. With the exception of use by FACs, rockets had been pretty much taken off the frag and replaced by CBUs for area coverage and Paveway LGBs for precision by the late 1960s, these new generation weapons ensuring that damage was inflicted on the intended targets most of the time.

I had two "special" experiences with rockets while they were still in regular use. One involved a senior member of the 8th TFW staff. A flight of four 433rd TFS Phantom IIs was on armed recce in Route Pack I, our jets carrying 750lb M117 "iron bombs" and LAU-3 pods – each of the latter contained 19 unguided 2.75in. FFARs. The folding fin feature will become important later. We had dropped our bombs on some suspected supply dumps and made a couple of road cuts, but had found no targets appropriate for rockets. Lead got a bingo call from a wingman and directed return to base. Leaving the threat area, a rejoin was directed to allow each Phantom II to be checked over for battle damage and any hung bombs. He also made a fuel check and called to "safe 'em up," and started a gentle turn to effect the join-up.

Things were good until No. 2 accidently fired a pod of 19 rockets at lead! WTF – they flew straight toward an unsuspecting lead at such a rate there was no time to call for him to break left or right. The good news was No. 2 was pointed at lead in this stage of the rejoin – pure pursuit. The rockets passed well behind lead and, unknowingly, he was fat, dumb and safe. The rest of us had internal conversations within each jet (maybe not in No. 2) but the general comms frequency remained silent.

No. 2's F-4 had a KB-18 camera installed in the left front Sparrow well. This was one of those inventions that sounded good at Eglin but wasn't much use in combat. It was triggered whenever an armament release was initiated, using either the pickle button or the trigger. The camera only looked directly ahead at "twelve o'clock," however, which meant it was great for capturing weapons release and effects on a range and virtually useless when you were maneuvering against an enemy aircraft or jinking off target. It also worked well in pure pursuit, and when the film was developed back at Ubon it had captured the rocket release just fine. We now had proof of the switchology errors perpetrated by one of our bosses, and the incriminating film went directly into the 433rd TFS safe (or maybe it was destroyed – who really knew?). This was as good a "get out of jail" pass as any squadron could have.

My second experience involving rockets and a senior pilot occurred during a combat mission in the same area with a new member of the 433rd TFS. He had combat experience – in Korea flying unarmed photo-recce missions in RF-80s, which was no piece of cake due to marauding MiG-15s and the considerable AAA threat on every flight. Nevertheless, this was not a way to develop sound fighter tactics, and an extended staff tour and then a spell as an instructor on the faculty at Maxwell AFB didn't help much either. He was an eager aviator but lacking in air sense in many ways.

On the armed recce mission in question, lead spotted "lucrative targets," called for a left roll in for a rocket pass and went after it. No. 2 replied with one of the great calls of the day – "Me too." He pushed over into negative-g and salvoed two pods of 19 rockets. Now for the folding fin part. Each of the many FFARs had metal clips on the end that sprung loose when the projectiles left the tubes of the pod so the rockets had some stabilization. On a routine diving pass, the clips would be released well clear of the aircraft. Not so in a bunt or pushover. Around 160 metallic objects were now in the path of the firing jet – in fact, directly in front of it. It was like flying through a flock of metal wrens, and they hit the F-4 before any reaction was possible from the pilot. Fortunately, on this occasion, they only inflicted some nicks on the paint and on the face of the J79 engines, allowing the jet to be flown back to base. It wasn't long after this flight that the lieutenant colonel found a place in the wing staff where administration was important. I don't recall there being a going away party for him.

As FACs, we used the 2.75in. "Willie Pete" rockets much like a sniper would use his rifle – patient stalking of the target, a quick curvilinear roll-in for a snapshot of one or two rockets, with one for a mark, two to draw a reference line to work from when discussing target tactics with fighters and then a quick jinking out of the way of tracking or barrage AAA. On a few occasions "Wolf" FACs bartered cold beer for some five-inch High Velocity Aerial Rockets (Zunis I think) from Marine Corps A-4 "Playboy" FACs. They came in pods of four, were shot from greater ranges, flew true and, with a much larger warhead, were a pretty effective defense suppression weapon against gun position. But they weren't certified on USAF fighters. Thanks again, Eglin.

NEW GUY HOSTING

Another rotating extra duty was new guy hosting. When the squadron received information that an inbound pilot or navigator was being assigned to the 433rd TFS, the squadron leadership would assign a sponsor to contact the officer before arrival and assist the "bed down" of the new guy after arrival.

Each squadron within the 8th TFW was usually divided into four flights designated "A," "B," "C" and "D," with each flight being led by a senior officer, usually a major. All the pilots and navigators were assigned to one of these flight commanders. As people completed their combat tours and returned home or moved onto other subsequent assignments, "new guys" were allocated to fill the vacancies. It was the flight commander's duty to appoint an experienced flight member as the new guy's sponsor. Sometimes, the sponsor was able to contact the new guy before his arrival, or as was the case when I arrived at Ubon, my sponsor found me when I was gathering my belongings following my C-130 flight from Bangkok.

The sponsor arranged billeting for the new arrival, provided a general squadron tour and got the new arrival scheduled for "new guy school." And the sponsor was generally responsible for helping out as the new pilot or WSO settled into the groove of the squadron's combat operation.

There were other more permanent extra duties that lasted several weeks or months before being handed off to a fresh replacement. Among these was serving as a member of the awards and decorations staff. The latter was responsible for debriefing aircrew or, in some cases, the intelligence debriefers to learn of noteworthy combat accomplishments or achievements. Then the awards and decorations team prepared the paperwork nominating an individual or group for a combat decoration. Some were routine, as in the earning of an Air Medal for every ten combat missions to North Vietnam and every 20 missions to Laos. Others recognized a significant achievement, heroism or gallantry in the face of combat operation.

In another extra duty role, one officer was generally assigned to coordinate with the NCOs that were in charge of our personal equipment. In current times we call this life support. Our personal equipment included our helmets, oxygen masks, survival vests, parachute harnesses, firearm and anti-g suits. The most important of these in most officers' minds was the survival vest. It was a mesh vest with multiple zippered pockets. Each aircrew member was given the latitude to load up the pockets in the vest with the equipment the officer felt was most important. The jungle survival school we had attended in the Philippines while at Clark AB influenced these decisions. Each vest also had a tree-lowering device for use in case a survivor's parachute was hung up in the 100–300ft-high multiple-canopy jungle forest that covered parts of Laos and North Vietnam. Beyond these basics, aircrew carried at least one and usually two survival radios and multiple batteries. Many officers also had a sheath sewn into the back of their anti-g suits at calf level that was used for housing a machete-style knife that could potentially prove useful for hacking one's way out of a jungle thicket.

We also carried pen-flares that could be fired by hand from a device not much larger than a ballpoint pen. A flare cartridge was attached to the device and when activated with a thumb lever spring-loaded release, the flare was launched several hundred feet into the air to act as a visual aide to helicopter SAR crews attempting to locate a survivor.

Our parachutes were built into the Martin-Baker ejection seats and were maintained by the maintenance egress personnel. As stated earlier, our personal equipment harnesses had Koch fittings that attached to the parachute in the seat of the aircraft once the aircrew were sat in the cockpit.

Finally, we of course wore anti-g suits that were routinely tested by the personal equipment specialists. They also regularly tightened the laces that were an integral part of the suits, as time and events would cause them to loosen up. The anti-g suits were worn from the waist down in a similar fashion to the chaps traditionally used by cowboys. There were air bladders in the front at stomach level, and also on the front of each thigh. A zipper on the side of the waist was the primary attachment point, and each leg had a zipper down the inside to complete the donning. After boarding the jet, the anti-g suit hose attached at roughly the left hip was plugged into a quick disconnect fitting within the aircraft's cockpit.

The quick disconnect was important in the event of ejection. When airborne and pulling gs, high-pressure compressed air from the engine was metered through the hose. The more gs, the more compressed air inflated the bladders, squeezing the belly and upper legs.

The purpose of the anti-g suit is to prevent pooling of blood in the lower extremities of the body, depriving the eyes and brain of needed blood. Without an anti-g suit, and with increasing g, the vision of the aircrew starts to decrease from the peripheral edges in what is called gray-out. Increased g further degrades the vision until all that is left is a pinpoint of light, followed by total black-out. With vision blacked out, the pilot or WSO may still be conscious, but a continued increase in g will lead to unconsciousness. So, the proper fitting of the anti-g suit is vitally important, especially to a fighter pilot in combat.

There were myriad other admin duties that also needed to be performed, ranging from teaching new guy school to planning end-of-tour flightline receptions and parades (and partying after parades).

KAYTE BABY

About three months into my year of combat I became senior enough among the pilots to have one of the squadron's aircraft (F-4D 66-0750) assigned to me. That meant I got to christen the jet and have my name painted on the canopy rail. This was a big deal to me, and I thought long and hard about an appropriate name.

My oldest daughter is Katherine Adair, and we have always called her Kayte. The name came from Kay Briggs, the wife of Lt Gen James "Buster" Briggs. He had been the

Superintendent at the Air Force Academy while I was a cadet, and he was also the commander of ATC when Jeannie and I got married. Jeannie's father, Brig Gen Jack Hilger, was Briggs' Chief of Staff at Randolph AFB during those years. The Briggs family lived next door to the Hilgers at Randolph and were very close friends of Jeannie and her parents. *KAYTE BABY* therefore seemed appropriate, and several aircraft have been decorated with the name since that first Phantom II.

I had a model of the aircraft made at the shop known as F-37 in Angeles City, near Clark AB. Artist Joe Mike Pyle subsequently used the model decades later for the development of his painting that graced the cover of the Winter 04 issue of the *USAF Weapons Review* (AFPR 11-1 Issue 4, Vol LII). The original hangs in the 433rd Weapons Squadron building at Nellis AFB. A photo of the painting also appears in the plates section of this book.

7

Silver Star Mission

Stupidity sometimes reigns supreme and blind luck pulls you through.

On January 25, 1969, we were coming off the "Cherry Anchor" tanker on what I expected to be a fairly routine "dusk patrol" mission. "Dusk patrol" involved a daylight takeoff and air-refueling as nightfall approached. By the time the target area was reached it was either pitch black, with only star- and moonlight, or it was pretty dark on the ground but still daylight at 10,000–12,000ft AGL. That meant the aircrew were staring down at a dark earth while the gunners manning AAA sites on the ground were looking up and seeing clearly visible aircraft above them. This lighting circumstance gave all the advantages to the gunners.

I was leading, with Capt Jimmy Hoffman in my back seat. Maj Joel Rosensweig was the pilot in my wingman's aircraft and 1Lt "Little Mike" Meroney was in Joel's back seat.

I gave the command to switch radio frequencies from the tanker primary to the ABCCC EC-130E, call-sign "Moonbeam." Our backseaters changed the radio frequencies and after a couple seconds I checked Joel in on the new frequency. "'Pintail,' check!" He responded "2." My next transmission was "'Moonbeam,' 'Moonbeam,' 'Pintail' with a flight of two loaded with hard ordnance." The mission number followed. We were expecting "Moonbeam" to tell us to contact an O-2 "Nail" FAC on his frequency, with instructions to find him at one of the Delta Points – using a Delta Point code prevented the enemy from monitoring our frequency and anticipating our target area.

There are at least three different versions of what happened next – my memory, the account from the F-100 "Misty" FAC who wrote my wingman and me up for combat decorations and the lengthy and probably embellished version prepared by the squadron awards and decorations team. What follows is how I recall the mission panning out.

This was supposed to be a routine mission, but "Moonbeam's" reply was anything but routine. Instead of sending us to work our planned target area with a "Nail" FAC, "Moonbeam" instructed us to proceed to a Delta Point further south and contact "Misty 80." As explained earlier in this book, the "Misty" call-sign belonged to the famous F-100F FACs who normally operated in South Vietnam and the areas of North Vietnam just across the DMZ in an area we called "Tally Ho." We made radio contact with "Misty 80" and proceeded inbound to the target area.

The briefing the FAC gave us caused some confusion on my part. I thought there was a downed friendly aircraft and that the area was being defended by numerous AAA sites, most of which would be firing 37mm rounds. The "Misty 80" pilot, I later learned, was Capt Greg O. Parker. He asked about our ordnance and suggested we make one pass each and drop everything we had due to the extent of the defenses. "Misty 80" also stated that he would light his afterburner and feint a roll in on the target area. This would trigger the defenses to start shooting, thus giving both my wingman, Joel Rosensweig, and me a clear indication of exactly where the guns were located as the muzzle flashes would be clearly visible against the dark earth background.

Our F-4Ds were each carrying ten Mk 82 500lb bombs, with four on the centerline multiple ejector rack (MER) and three on each wing-mounted inboard triple ejector rack (TER). We were carrying a 370-gallon external fuel tank on each outboard station. Other reports indicated we were carrying rockets, although I don't remember us having such ordnance that day.

Given the circumstances I thought I understood, it made no sense to me to drop all ten bombs on one pass. I instructed Joel to set up his switches for "bombs single," with the plan being to make a pass and check out the defenses. I passed this info to "Misty 80" and he responded, "Your call," meaning that it was up to me as the attacking flight lead. I called, "Ready" and the F-100F pulled up slightly, the pilot lighting his afterburner and then rolling left, letting the nose of his aircraft drop toward the earth as if he were making a high-angle dive-bombing pass.

The guns on the ground opened up almost immediately and "Misty" aborted his pass, returning to the sunlit orbit above the target area. I called, "'Pintail' Lead is in," selecting afterburner and forcing the heavy and reluctant F-4 to turn toward a gun on the ground whose location I had mentally marked. As the nose of the jet dropped, the dive angle approached 45 degrees. Jimmy Hoffman started calling out altitudes over the intercom to help me with the timing of the release of our first bomb. When I heard the "Pickle" command from the back seat, I pressed the bomb release button on the stick and, almost simultaneously with the shudder of the aircraft becoming 500lb lighter due to the bomb release, I pulled hard back on the stick to 5g, added top rudder, unloaded the g and entered a roll to the right. Then, I unloaded the jet again and rolled back to the left in a jinking maneuver to hopefully defeat any AAA gunner's tracking solution. Then, I reset the 5g.

At the pickle altitude it had been dark, but as I climbed back up to our orbit I was suddenly in bright daylight again. I didn't see any guns shooting at me on that first pass until I was in the recovery from the dive. Then, looking left and behind my left wing, I could see tracers like a red fire hose arcing up toward my aircraft, but way behind us – ZSU-23-4 probably, and the gunner didn't lead us enough. The jink had worked.

Meanwhile, Joel Rosensweig was able to see the guns shooting at me due to their muzzle flashes against the dark earth, and he used those same flashes as an aiming reference for his bombing run. The tone of the "Misty" pilot's voice was ecstatic as he reported to us that we had both scored direct hits on the guns. I remember thinking, "That wasn't so bad." So, we did it again, using the "Misty" as bait. Although we had knocked out two guns on the first pass, there were many more, and they opened up on the F-100 and then us as we continued to make single bomb passes. On each pass the AAA came from different points on the ground, and the gunners were starting to figure out our tactics. So, we changed them, reversing the direction of our orbit and appearing to alter the sequence of the attacks.

We each made ten passes in total, and more than once after that initial "free" pass I saw the muzzle flashes on the ground through the gunsight, adjusted my aiming reference and pickled off the bomb. On these passes I visually tracked the red hot AAA rounds as they came up at us from the ground. Every time they passed either above the cockpit or off to one side or the other. I later thought, "Why did we do that?" I have no clear answer to that question except that it seemed like the right thing to do at the time.

Finally out of bombs, I radioed the "Misty" that we were "Winchester" and leaving the target area. Our trip home to Ubon included a post-strike aerial refueling from the "Cherry Anchor" tanker, followed by a night landing – both passed uneventfully. Not much was said in either cockpit on the way home, but our brains were racing as we each thought about what we had just done, and the luck we had had to live through it.

The intelligence debriefing followed our landing, and the debriefing officer commented that it looked like we had done some nice work. I replied, "We'll see. It was exciting." A debriefing with our squadron awards and decorations team came later. After reviewing the mission report, the awards and decorations debriefer said that this might be a Silver Star mission. He then clarified that it would have to go through "Col O" first. "Col O" was Lt Col Dick O'Leary, our squadron commander.

Time passed, and one day I got called to "Col O's" trailer – his billet. All the squadron commanders had their own trailers as living accommodation. "Col O" asked me to go over the mission. When I finished he showed me a report written by Capt Greg O. Parker that had been sent to Ubon by the "Misty" commander. The transmittal letter was signed by a captain who later became the Chief of Staff of the Air Force, four-star Gen Ronald Fogelman.

More time passed, and eventually someone gave me a copy of the awards and decorations package that had been sent to higher headquarters for consideration. When I reviewed it I remember wondering about, and admiring, the journalistic talents of the awards and decorations staff. Their goal was to get "gongs for the guys," as our Operations Officer, Bill Strand, once said. We later learned that Silver Star decorations had been approved for the aircraft commanders, but that the backseaters had only been submitted for DFCs. That didn't sit well with me, as the "GIBs" were with us every step of the way and were deserving of equal treatment. The award didn't sit well with the backseaters either, I later learned, but it wasn't my call.

My award was presented at a military parade at MacDill AFB – my next operational duty station. It made the base paper there too, but otherwise the event was pretty low key. There were a lot of true heroes in the Vietnam War like Merlyn Dethlefsen, Leo Thorsness, Jerry Hoblit, Billy Sparks, Steve Ritchie, Mike Francisco and many others. While honored by the receipt of the award, I still don't feel like I was in the same category as these brave warriors.

My wingman and I made ten diving-bombing passes against guns that were shooting at us as we came down the "chute" in every attack. We had won the gun fight. And, "Misty" FAC Greg O. Parker duly took note, wrote us up and Joel Rosensweig and I were awarded Silver Stars for Gallantry in Action. The citation that accompanied this award is reproduced in full in the Appendices.

8

"Sherman Lead"

Partway through my tour a very young captain named James David ("J. D.") Allen showed up for duty in the 433rd TFS as an aircraft commander. Over the years that followed "J. D." was a classmate of mine at the FWS, and he then did a second combat tour during *Linebacker*, before returning to Nellis as a fellow FWS instructor. We have been great friends for about 50 years!

On March 1, 1969, a little over halfway through my year-long assignment, I was scheduled to fly another night mission with Maj Wendell Keller and 1Lt Mike Meroney because their regular wingman, "J. D." Allen, was in Bangkok for a few days of R&R. Wendell was the flight lead for the mission, call-sign "Sherman 1," and he and Mike didn't come home that night.

We had briefed for a two-ship night interdiction mission on the "Trail" in the *Steel Tiger* region of Laos. We were armed with some hard ordnance, probably Mk 82 500lb bombs and pods of 2.75in. FFARs. It was an idiotic night load because the blast of light from the rockets when they ignited revealed the launch aircraft's position to every AAA gunner within range, and also had the undesirable effect of temporarily destroying night vision. We finished the briefing, got our intelligence code words for radio comms and received a quick weather update, after which we headed for our jets. Taping up the cockpit took longer than I had remembered, but I got it done to minimize the reflections from any outside light like stars or fires on the ground, or from un-taped instrument lights in the cockpit. I was an old hand at this, but it had been a while since my last night mission.

Finally, all the ground preparation was completed and we were on takeoff roll, single-ship. I was soon able to complete the join-up into close formation on Wendell's aircraft. He made the radio call to "Lion," our ground-based radar controller. "'Lion,' 'Lion,' 'Sherman' airborne Ubon, looking for the 'Cherry Anchor' tanker." "Lion" responded immediately with a vector requiring a small heading change as we continued our climb to the refueling altitude. Almost immediately my backseater acquired the tanker on our radar, and at about the same time the lead called, "Roger, 'Sherman' has radar contact." We were converging on the tanker from an exact reciprocal heading and with about a 20-degree offset with the KC-135 to our left. At precisely 26 nautical miles, "Sherman" directed the tanker to start his left turn to our heading. The timing was perfect and the tanker rolled out just in front of us and slightly above.

Wendell eased into the pre-contact position and I remained in formation with the tanker off its left wing while Wendell refueled. Then, with his refueling completed, he moved off the boom and slipped silently up onto the right wing of the tanker, leaving me space to slide down behind the KC-135 and plug into its flying boom. We too got our gas and departed the refueling track. We then received the radio call from "Sherman" Lead instructing us to change to the radio frequency for "Alley Cat" or "Moonbeam," the ABCCC EC-130E that kept track of us while we were in the combat area. They also had any mission change information for us. In this case it was a routine instruction to proceed to a Delta Point and contact a FAC on a coded radio frequency.

My memory of the night and the official report diverge at this point. The latter states that we rendezvoused with a C-130 or C-123 "Blind Bat" flare-ship to illuminate the target area. I recall that there was also a FAC involved. I don't remember any flares being used, nor do I remember seeing any ground fire. The official report stated that the flare-ship reported ground fire, and that "Sherman Lead" was shot down.

As I recall it, we entered the target area near Ban Topen and the FAC had dropped a log target identification tool, which was burning on the ground. It had created a point-of-light fire that the FAC used as a reference for directing the high-angle 30-degree dive delivery attacks favored by the fast-moving F-4s. We made 45-degree attacks in the daytime, weather permitting, but at night we used the shallower 30-degree dive-bombing profile.

The dialogue between the FAC and "Sherman Lead" went something like this. "'Sherman,' I have trucks for you. If you see my mark (log on the ground), aim 100 meters northeast of it. You are cleared hot under flight leader control with your hard ordnance." Wendell and I had set up in a right-hand wheel pattern, with each of us on the opposite side of our circle and with the target in the middle. The diameter of the wheel was determined to be the spacing needed for a 30-degree dive attack roll in. We expended our hard ordnance without incident or effect.

Next came the attack with the rockets. The wheel parameters were the same, and I delivered mine. The swoosh of the rockets and the instant change from total darkness to the blinding light from the projectiles' exhausts was very disorienting, especially when making a jinking 5g recovery back to level flight, followed by a climb up to wheel altitude. When expending rockets at night I always closed my eyes as I squeezed the pickle button that started the ripple sequence for the firing of the 19 rockets in each pod. I had a little timer in my head that told me when to start the dive recovery, along with a jink to change my flightpath out of the way of the expected AAA barrage.

The recovery was accomplished partially by looking outside and partially with reference to the aircraft's flight instruments to ensure I wasn't disoriented. I knew that if the guns were shooting they would be leading the point where the rockets had been observed firing and then perhaps placing a barrage on either side of our flightpath as indicated by the projectiles. The barrage would be an effort to hit us irrespective of which direction we turned. I continued my climb back into the right-hand wheel without incident, nor did I observe any ground fire. There were no new fires burning on the ground either. At this point I was approaching "San Diego" – the southwestern point in our wheel. Wendell called his position over "New York," with rockets for his last pass, which he said would be from "Miami" to "Seattle." As previously noted, we used the map of the United States, and its major city landmarks, to communicate to each other where our respective positions were.

Then time seemed to slow down in another example of temporal distortion. I knew where the target was supposed to be relative to the log on the ground, and that Wendell would be coming from the southeast. As a result of this information, I was looking at almost the exact point of his location when he fired the rockets. There was the blinding flash from the FFARs' exhausts and then the delay as the rockets streaked toward the target area. Then, the rockets impacted the target area and there was another blinding flash as their warheads exploded. Again, events continued in slow motion for what seemed like a long time, and then there was a tremendous explosion on the ground beyond the rocket impact point and in the same direction Wendell was supposed to be flying. My heart stopped.

Moments later I made a radio call, "'Sherman 1,' '2,'" but there was no response. Indeed, not a sound followed other than the breathing of my backseater and me into our individual oxygen mask microphones that were a part of our intercom system. My backseater that night was a WSO by the name of "Hoss" Cartwright. I called for "Sherman 1" again, and probably a couple more times. My hopeful wail was met with silence.

It was pitch black, and we saw no parachutes. If they had ejected we should have been hearing the screeching sound of the emergency radio beeper that was automatically activated upon leaving the jet. "'Hoss,'" I said to my backseater, "I think they went in." I have no recollection of the next few minutes. I am sure that we signaled the ABCCC "Alleycat" or "Moonbeam" and initiated a SAR mission, but I don't recall the details, nor do I remember the specifics of any conversation between "Hoss" and me. At some point we departed the area due to fuel and began the lonely ride home. Again, not a word was said.

We commanded a tremendous amount of attention during the debriefing back at Ubon. We went over the details once, twice, over and over and gradually the reality of the situation sunk in with our leadership and with us. Maj Keller was a highly experienced fighter pilot who had an ADC background, which included years of night operations in fighter aircraft. 1Lt Meroney was the son of Col Virgil "Mike" Meroney, a nine-victory P-47 Thunderbolt ace from World War II. Col Meroney had recently left Ubon, where he had served as the vice commander of the 8th TFW. "Little Mike" had been with Joel Rosensweig on our Silver Star mission just weeks earlier.

Eventually we were released, whereupon we went to the Officers' Club, where we got very drunk and I started smoking again. They were gone and would not be returned to us for decades. When they did return it was in a single casket.

9

Combat Skyspot and
Bad Weather Missions

In this chapter, I will explain in detail how we conducted warfare when the weather was really bad. That is a fair question, for during the annual monsoon season the weather in Southeast Asia was often very poor in either North Vietnam or in Laos, but usually not in both areas at the same time. There is a wealth of information about the *Combat Skyspot* radar-guided bombing equipment that we relied on during poor weather missions on the Internet for the reader who wants to "descend into the weeds" on this subject. My brief look at these sources indicated that the B-52s were a major user. Having read that, I have decided to relate what I remember being told about *Combat Skyspot* when at Ubon, and what I can recall about flying these missions in the F-4D.

We were informed that SAC graded its crews on bombing accuracy when training using a system referred to as Radar Bomb Scoring (RBS). A ground radar station would track the bombers on their mid- to high-altitude attack runs, and when the bomb(s) were simulated-released, the aircraft emitted a tone that was used by the RBS site to mark the exact release point on the radar track of the bomber. The RBS site then calculated the impact point on the ground, and thus was able to score the accuracy of the bomb run. In Southeast Asia, this system was turned around to a certain degree in that the ground radar site tracked and guided the F-4 and other bomber aircraft to a point in space that coincided with a release point for attacking a specific target on the ground. I don't remember exactly how the command to release a bomb load from an F-4 worked, but a couple of the "GIBs" in the squadron tell me that it was done on a verbal voice command from the *Combat Skyspot* controller.

We had less than affectionate nicknames for these missions. Two that come to mind were "Sky Dump" and "Sky Puke" missions. We didn't like flying in close formation in the weather or above a solid undercast, and, in our view, mindlessly dumping a bomb load on an unknown and unseen target. Nevertheless, sometimes we were fragged for *Combat Skyspot* and sometimes we were diverted from a fragged attack mission to perform an alternate *Combat Skyspot* mission.

The way I remember these missions unfolding is vague and subject to error, probably because we detested them so much. Upon the direction of the ABCCC, the flight leader of a formation of from two to four F-4s, all carrying a full load of bombs, would command the formation to switch over to the *Combat Skyspot* radio frequency. Radio contact was then made with the ground radar controller, while the flight lead navigated to an approximate point in space using Delta Points, the F-4's INS and on board AN/APN-154 radar beacons. Identification, Friend or Foe (IFF) systems were switched off in accordance with the ground radar controller's instructions, leaving only the flight leader's IFF on to reduce the possibility of multiple IFF responses from other members of the formation, which in turn caused ambiguity when locking onto the correct attack track.

Altimeter settings were passed from the ground radar controller, along with a firm altitude and calibrated airspeed for the level attack. As we proceeded inbound to the target, the radar controller provided heading changes to the flight leader in an effort to steer the formation to the exact pre-calculated bomb release point. This was similar to flying a high-speed GCA when in a landing recovery pattern.

The commands to select bombs ripple, ripple interval and the appropriate nose and/or tail fuse settings were passed to the aircraft in the formation. The Master Arm switch was selected in each aircraft when the flight lead directed. Sometimes, this was done one command at a time, while on other occasions it was a simple "Green them up" or "Fence check inbound" command, depending on the flight briefing prior to takeoff. At the appropriate time, the command "Pickle. Ready. Now" was given and the flight lead dropped his bombs, with all the wingmen in the formation following suit when they saw the ordnance drop off the lead aircraft.

The bombs were all carried on either MERs or TERs. The former could be fitted either on the F-4's centerline or outboard pylons and, theoretically, loaded with six Mk 82 500lb bombs. Practically, we carried only four bombs on a MER. TERs were attached to the inboard pylons, and they could be loaded with three Mk 82s. Sometimes, the three bombs on a TER and in the forward position on a MER had a 30in. extender tube screwed into the forward fuse well of the bomb. When in this configuration, we called the bombs "daisy cutters" because they would explode 30 inches or so above the target, laying out a shrapnel pattern that mowed down trees, bushes and any soft targets on the ground within the lethal range of the blast.

I don't recall ever receiving any post-strike BDA information following a *Combat Skyspot* mission. This lack of feedback on effectiveness added to our cynical attitude about these missions. I don't ever remember seeing any AAA during these missions either.

Following the bomb drop, each aircraft was checked for hung ordnance prior to the trek back to either the tanker or directly to Ubon for our recovery and landing. Ho hum – another "notch" for a *Combat Skyspot* mission.

"GHOST"

1Lt Mike "Ghost" Davison did an amazing job as a navigator from my back seat one day when the weather was bad, saving a mission in the process.

After I finished night flying I became fodder for the day schedule in the 433rd TFS. On one such mission I was scheduled to fly as No. 3 in a four-ship formation in support of the 25th TFS. A pilot from this unit was the scheduled leader for the mission, with three jets and crews from the 433rd on his wing. We were to drop anti-tamper weapons amongst the *Igloo White* sensors already on the ground. As previously explained, *Igloo White* was one of former Secretary of Defense Robert S. McNamara's schemes (allegedly) to detect North Vietnamese truck traffic traveling through the jungles of Laos. The sensors were capable of sending a response to a central authority that could then dispatch aircraft to attack the location. One of the problems encountered was that the bad guys would gather up the sensors and destroy them. So, the solution, as explained to the fighter pilots, was to seed the area surrounding the sensors with anti-tamper explosives designed to discourage the enemy from removing them.

The lead aircrew on this mission were trained to use the LORAN D equipment installed in the F-4Ds assigned to the 25th TFS, these systems allowing them to precisely locate the area where the sensors had been delivered. The three standard Phantom IIs from the 433rd were carrying canisters containing anti-tamper anti-personnel mines*.

The poor weather that can blanket Southeast Asia is known as either a southwest (June to September) or northeast (October to December) monsoon. This simple nomenclature describes the direction of the prevailing weather pattern. Because of the ocean areas to the east of Vietnam and to the south of Thailand, and the mountains in between, the end result of these geographical features was either good weather in Thailand and bad weather in eastern Laos and Vietnam, or vice versa.

On the day of this particular mission, the monsoon had clobbered eastern Laos with bad weather. We conducted our pre-strike air refueling without incident and headed east into what appeared to be solid cloud. As we entered the weather, our four-ship formation had to close up to barely wingtip spacing in order to maintain visual contact with the aircraft we were following. The No. 2 jet was on the right wing of the leader, while as No. 3, I was the alternate flight leader and on the leader's left wing, with No. 4 hanging on for dear life in the turbulence on my left wing.

Using the magic of their LORAN D, the lead crew made almost continuous corrections in their heading. Every little change rippled to those of us on their wing, and we bobbled around to hold our position and maintain visual contact with the jet in front of us. No. 4 could only sometimes see the

*Editor's Note: possibly BLU-42A/B 1.3lb wide-area anti-personnel weapons in SUU-34 or -38 dispensers.

leader through the murk, and hence was flying formation on me as No. 3. The turbulence was moderate, and at times the density of the cloud darkened the sky around us to near night-time conditions. I knew that our munitions had to be dropped from very low altitude, and it was a mystery to me why we were plowing around in the weather at probably at least 20,000ft AGL. But I was just No. 3, and my job was to be on the wing with my mouth shut. So it was.

Meanwhile, my good friend and navigator Mike Davison was busy in the back seat keeping track of both where we were and where we wanted to be. That was a huge task given the turbulence and the overall situation. Suddenly, we flew into a large cylinder of clear air embedded in the dense cloud. At the speeds we were flying at, the flight time from one side of the cylinder to the other was about 20 seconds. I know I breathed a sigh of relief at the respite from the intense concentration required when flying formation in the turbulent, heavy cloud. I expect the other pilots did also. Then, over the radio, the leader suddenly said "3, you have the lead," and he rolled inverted and pulled down in a vertical spiral into the cylinder of clear air.

I thought, "Holy shit, what's going on?" as I signaled Nos. 2 and 4 to close up the formation on me before we flew into the wall of cloud on the other side of the clear air bubble. The guys did a great job of getting into a tight formation on my wing and staying there.

I asked Mike, "You know where we are?" I welcomed his crisp reply of "Yep." Then I asked, "Can you get us back into that bubble of clear air?" and again he replied, "Yep." For the next minute or two I followed "Ghost's" commands as he skillfully steered me in a 90-degree turn in one direction followed by a 270-degree turn in the opposite direction.

In a perfect world this would put us on a reciprocal heading back toward the bubble of clear air, but it wasn't a perfect world, and thankfully "Ghost" was also monitoring our INS to determine our drift over the ground due to the wind. He gave me a couple of little heading changes to zero out the drift. "Ghost" then asked, "Boss which side of the bubble do you want or do you want the middle?" I replied, "Put us on the right side of the bubble," and "Ghost" gave me a minor heading change. We were still in a very tight three-ship V formation, with a 433rd jet on either side of us.

As if by magic we emerged into the clear bubble on the right side. I transmitted, "Hang on gang. We are going to make a left-hand spiral down into this hole." The boys hung on like they were glued to me. "Ghost" asked, "Boss, can you see the ground?" I said, "Yes." He replied, "Plan the spiral to emerge below the cloud from the middle of the cylinder of clear air on a heading of 135 degrees." And, as if in an afterthought, he said, "Tell 'em to arm up the weapons." Luck was with me, and I was able to comply with his instructions. As we leveled out under the weather "Ghost" asked if I had a mountain ridge at "12 o'clock" with a saddle slightly to the left. Amazed, I replied "Affirmative." "Good," "Ghost" said. "Put the wingmen in spread, hit the saddle and pickle the ordnance as you pass the crest." My reply to him was made over the radio to the wingmen, "Spread the formation, pickle on my ordnance and watch out for the mountains on either side."

By now we had accelerated to about 500 knots, zinging along about 500ft above the jungle. I could tell we would cross the saddleback in the mountain ahead at about 50–100ft AGL. It looked good. As we flew over the saddleback I pickled off my ordnance just as the ford in the river beyond the mountain appeared. "Ghost" yelled, "Shack!" as our weapons found their mark – not exactly as planned, but on target nonetheless. The wingmen collapsed back into close formation just as we re-entered the weather. The ride home was uneventful.

We never saw the flight leader again until we were on the ground being debriefed by our intelligence folks. He didn't have much to say for himself then, or in the years that have followed.

God, I was proud of "Ghost" and the stunning airmanship of my fellow 433rd pilots.

BURNING THE FIELDS

The monsoon sometimes caused us other problems as well. At the end of the crop-growing season and following the harvest, the farmers in Laos burned the residual debris from their fields. During those weeks, as a result, there was a thick smoke-induced haze that severely restricted visibility.

We had been fragged to attack an area in the vicinity of Tchepone, a town in central Laos. In these kinds of attacks, the target was usually described as a "suspected truck park."

The Ho Chi Minh Trail was the nickname for the North Vietnamese logistics pipeline into South Vietnam. The Trail exited southern North Vietnam through mountain passes on the border with eastern Laos. Two of these passes were particularly notable – Mu Gia and Ban Karai. Of the two, Mu Gia Pass was a favored northern exit from North Vietnam, while Ban Karai was situated further south. The mountains along the border were impressively rugged, and the trails through both of the passes were difficult to spot from the air due to multiple layers of jungle canopy. Ban Karai exited North Vietnam to the west and then "exploded" into a spider's web of trails that extended westward into Laos, before turning south and eventually back east into South Vietnam, flanking the DMZ that separated North and South Vietnam. Mu Gia Pass followed a deep canyon that first exited North Vietnam north of Ban Karai Pass in a westward direction and then turned south, with the trails joining the others that were an essential component of the supply route used and protected by the NVA.

Parts of this labyrinth extended into central Laos and the feared town of Tchepone, which seemed to be a major junction of these trails and had a serious reputation for the seemingly limitless numbers of AAA batteries that defended the area. As previously noted, our mission was to destroy a suspected truck park in the town. We joked about these often vague missions, calling them "monkey busters" and other less flattering names. Nevertheless, we took the enemy's defenses very seriously. We joked about the fact that we seldom caused much apparent damage, and even when we managed to get fires started on the ground, the results didn't seem to amount to much – especially given the risk involved in making the attacks.

Over the years that the war dragged on these kinds of targets along the Trail were repeatedly attacked, and the end result over time was the destruction of the jungle protection along large sections of the Trail. This left wide areas of red dirt pockmarked with bomb craters, with perhaps the faint trace of a vehicle trail winding through the area. Adjacent to these bombed-out areas was the seemingly eternal blanket of triple canopy jungle, which only disappeared when the next bomb craters came into view.

Often, bombed-out areas coincided where streams and small rivers had been bridged with primitive wooden structures or were shallow enough for vehicles to ford. In other cases, there were supposedly ferry boats used to move the vehicles across the river. I never saw a ferry boat myself, but we were reliably informed that they did indeed exist, and were almost exclusively used at night and then hidden away during the day. We were told that the ferry boats were often "sunk" during daylight hours to make them both invisible and virtually invulnerable and then refloated at night, permitting the never-ending movement of people and equipment south.

It is almost impossible to visualize the sheer number of these trails, and their attendant "crunch points," that existed as a part of the Ho Chi Minh Trail network.

Secretary of Defense Robert S. McNamara had attempted to interdict the Trail with a system of airdropped sensors (as part of *Igloo White*) that were designed to detect vehicle movement at various locations and then relay it in real time to an orbiting EC-121R of the 553rd Reconnaissance Wing, flying from Korat RTAFB. The information was then sent by radio link to the TFA communications center at NKP, whose technicians would analyze the data and then, theoretically, divert jets that were already over Laos on fragged mission to attack the trucks. Knowledge of such vehicular movements theoretically, at least, could allow our forces to make timely attacks. An entire organization was set up at NKP to oversee the running of *Igloo White*.

Regardless of the sensors, and the anti-tamper munitions sewn to protect them in a classical countermove, counter to the countermove campaign, the logistics continued to move either at night or under the cover of the jungle canopy during daylight along the Trail. And it went on, and on and on, and we went, as directed, and transformed jungle into splinters with our bombing attacks. When the farmers burned the fields, the reduced visibility made our job of turning jungle into rubble a lot tougher, and with that came the risk.

On the Tchepone mission I was the wingman, and the flight lead was one of our field grade officers – a West Pointer whom nobody ever much wanted to fly with. That day I guess it was just "my turn." We launched and got our typically excellent vector to the "Cherry Anchor" KC-135 tanker from Ubon's "Lion" GCI site. After getting our gas, the flight lead switched our radio frequency over to the ABCCC and checked in. We were cleared, as fragged, to the truck park target area near Tchepone, where we were to contact a FAC probably flying an O-2. It wasn't going to be fun for any of us.

From our transit altitude of about 12,000ft the ground was almost invisible due to the haze from the burning fields. At that altitude we could see each other okay, even from a mile or so apart in our combat spread formation. The ground, however, looked as though it was covered with a gray-green blanket. Every now and then the gunners on the ground would open up, basically shooting at noise I think. Even though the flak was not accurate, it was troubling to suddenly see a seven-round burst of 37mm AAA explode a mile or two in front of us, or between our aircraft and the flight lead.

We pressed on to the designated Delta Point and made contact with our FAC – I don't recall the details of the briefing the latter gave us about the target area. It was just the continuation of another mind-numbing mission attacking an unseen target that would be defended with a lot of aggressive AAA. We descended down to an altitude of about 7,000ft AGL that matched the preferred roll-in altitude for a 45-degree dive-bombing pass and set up a wheel pattern overhead the target area. With some difficulty, we spotted the

O-2, and the FAC radioed us that he was rolling in to mark the target with a 2.75in. white phosphorous-tipped rocket.

Moments later we observed a white puff as the rocket exploded in the top of the jungle canopy. As the FAC pulled out of his dive I saw a stream of tracers come up at him, and I made a mental note that the gun was probably a low-caliber AAA piece. Intelligence personnel called these guns ZSUs or ZPUs as I recall, and I seem to remember they fired 23mm and 14.5mm rounds, respectively, from a clip. There were far more shells in these clips than there were in seven-round clips for the larger-caliber 37mm AAA, and the inclusion of tracer rounds made the stream of bullets look like a red fire hose at night. Tracer was a lot harder to see in daytime, but if you were looking in the right location at the right time, they were clearly visible.

Either lead or my backseater transmitted on the radio that "They're shooting!" Following a brief period of silence, the FAC radioed asking if we could see the mark from the rocket he had just fired. Lead called "Tally Ho," as did I as No. 2. The FAC instructed us to aim about 100 meters north of his mark, clearing us to attack under flight leader control. Lead then called on the radio, "Let's go bombs single" with our 500lb Mk 82 ordnance. This meant four passes each as we were carrying four Mk 82s on our centerline MER. We were also armed with a single 19-shot pod of 2.75in. high-explosive rockets on one inner wing pylon and three CBU-24s on the other.

In the cockpit, we had five push buttons to select the different ordnance-carrying stations – centerline, left or right inboard stations and left and right outboard station. When pushed, the button illuminated with a yellow light. Additionally, there was a rotary switch that selected single, triple or ripple in respect to ordnance delivery. Bombs single obviously dropped one bomb off the pushbutton-selected station, triple dropped three bombs off the selected station at an interval determined by yet another switch and, finally, ripple saw all the weapons expended off the selected station. Another switch selected the fuse – nose, tail or both. The general-purpose bombs had a fuse in the nose for an instantaneous detonation and one in the tail that delayed it. With targets under a triple canopy of jungle, we usually didn't want the bombs to explode upon impacting the top layer of foliage because of the filtering effect of the lower layers and the potential for the target to therefore survive the attack. So, generally, either tail for the delay or both were selected.

The final switch was the master arm, which, when selected, energized the bombing circuits. Pressing the red button on top of the control stick released the selected ordnance. It was called the pickle button, and dropping ordnance was referred to as pickling.

Aiming involved an entirely different sequence of decisions that led to setting the depression angle on the gunsight and determining a release altitude above the target. The steeper the dive angle for that attack the more accurate the bomb delivery. Low-angle attacks were particularly difficult to perform accurately, and they also left the jet more vulnerable to AAA. Release air speed was usually 450 knots of calibrated airspeed. That day we started with 45-degree dive-bombing attacks and then reverted to 30-degree passes due to the poor visibility.

As expected, the bad guys were shooting everything they had at us, indicating that we might have found a target of some value. In our wheel orbit above the target area they were firing 37mm shells, and then during our pull off from dive-bombing the streams of 23mm and/or 14.5mm rounds came up at us every single time. In the Air Force, enlisted personnel just starting their career in the military perform at a basic skill level known as a 3-level. As the person gets more experienced they become qualified at 5-level and then 7-level and, finally, top out at 9-level. We graded the enemy gunners on the same scale.

The defenders on this mission appeared to be 3- to 5-level, and our jinking maneuvers kept us out of the stream of AAA they threw up in our direction. I didn't see any flak in the windshield of the aircraft during the diving attacks, but I did see the streams of tracers during the pull-out from the dive. I would pull right or left in a 60-degree bank, jinking with 4–5g for a second or two and then unload the jet to 0g, before either rolling or resetting the g in an attempt to be unpredictable, and thus spoil the lead the AAA gunner was using. I would look back behind us from the cockpit during the jinking turn to check the impact of the weapon just dropped, and that was when I saw the AAA. It was almost always coming up from behind the wing of the jet and then arcing off and over the wingtip or drifting in an arc behind us, never quite reaching our altitude. It is an impressive thing to see people shooting at you, I might add.

Our attack continued and we were about to wind things up with a last pass. I was already "Winchester," meaning I had no more ordnance. The leader rolled in and called "Last pass!" I could not pick him up visually in the haze as I studied the target area for evidence of fires burning on the ground or other signs of BDA for use in our debriefing with the intelligence folks back at Ubon. My search was disrupted with the reception of an eerie radio call, "Lead is off, HIT."

I responded, "No Tally, what's your position?" Silence followed. I failed to visually acquire the lead jet, and I couldn't ask the FAC for assistance as he had already departed the target area after we had told him that we would make our the final passes under flight lead control. "Lead, how do you hear?" Silence. I searched for a fireball on the ground but didn't see anything, nor was there a scream from the emergency beacon signaling an ejection. I didn't know what had happened or what was going on, and I felt compelled to take a closer look at the target area with the hope of somehow making contact with my flight leader.

I pulled the power back and descended down into the hazy murk, flying a zigzag pattern in case the bad guys started shooting again. They did. I selected afterburner to expedite my climb back up to a safer altitude, consuming what was now becoming precious fuel. More radio calls followed in an attempt to contact lead. Nothing! Several minutes went by. My fuel level mandated I depart the area and make my way back to the post-strike tanker. We were distraught and totally confused over the sequence of events. Then, like a bolt out of the blue, came a radio call from lead. "We made it to the Mekong River. I think we can make it to Udorn."

My reaction was, "You son-of-a-bitch. You could have gotten us killed trying to find you. Your sorry ass somehow got clanked up and you went mind-numb. I'll never fly with you again!" Unfortunately, I did have to fly with him again because it was my job to do what I was told to do. However, I had little trust in him, and I took no chances when faced with similar such antics on later missions.

10

Offset Bombing, Dive Toss
and "Wild Rides"

When I joined the 433rd TFS at Ubon most, if not all, of our backseaters were pilots. As the year passed we soon witnessed the arrival of both newly trained and older, seasoned navigators. Their assignment to the unit marked the true beginning of the WSO era in the F-4. The pilots were just as good at running the systems in the rear cockpit, but they were itching to move to the front seat of the Phantom II. The navigators had no such calling, being content to ride in the back seat and operate most of the aircraft's systems. Many later completed pilot training and became frontseaters, however.

All USAF Phantom IIs had radar except for the F-4Es flown by the Thunderbirds. The first model to see operational service with the Air Force was the F-4C, which aside from its Westinghouse AN/APQ-100 radar also had a fixed gunsight that could be depressed from roughly straight ahead of the jet to an angle that provided dive-bombing solutions for attacks made at 45 degrees or more. The number of mils of depression needed for a given set of attack parameters was contained in tables for bombing, rocketry and strafing in a document called the 1F-4-34 – christened the "Dash 34" by pilots and WSOs. The "Dash 34" listed a variety of combinations of mil settings for various ordnance and release parameters.

As time passed the young navigators learned numerous tricks of the trade from their older brethren, who were largely former ADC F-101 radar operators. The young ones had some great ideas of their own too.

Operating an airborne radar well is not an easily learned skill. Some people believe that radar "sees" everything in front of it, but that is simply not true. The system installed in the F-4 was a pulse radar that used a mechanically scanned antenna array. "Pulse" meant that the radar transmitted a burst of energy at the speed of light and then listened for a return or echo. "Mechanically scanned" meant that the radar antenna sweeps from side to side. Specifically, the F-4's antenna scanned 60 degrees either side of the nose of the jet for a total of 120 degrees in azimuth or direction. The antenna could also be set to look low, medium and high, or anywhere in between. This feature was called tilt.

The size of the antenna determines the size of the radar beam that is transmitted as it sweeps from side to side. A generally accepted rule of thumb for the beam width on a round or non-tapered antenna is 90 divided by the antenna diameter in inches. Using this approximation, the beam width for the F-4D's AN/APQ-109A radar in degrees was 90/36 = 2.5 degrees.[*] Another math tool used when calculating radar range is based on the fact that one degree at 60 nautical miles creates an arc of about one mile or 6,000ft long. So, a radar

[*]George W. Stimson III, *Introduction to Airborne Radar*, 2nd edition (SciTech Publishing: Raleigh, NC, 1998), page 97.

with a round antenna and transmitting a one-degree beam width pulse can see a target at 60 nautical miles as long as the target is within that 6,000ft diameter cone. The F-4D's beam width of just over two degrees widened this detection window to about 12,000ft. This is all approximate. Those with serious questions about these rules of thumb should consult George Stimson's book, *Introduction to Airborne Radar* (SciTech Publishing: Raleigh, NC, 1998).

To deal with the radar's range limitations, the tilt or angle above or below straight ahead with a mechanically scanning antenna could be adjusted by the radar operator. In practice, this meant in the air-to-air combat arena flight leads would typically search level, while their wingmen scanned either a little higher or lower.

The AN/APQ-109A also has application in the air-to-ground role, with both a radar-ranged mapping mode called MAP PPI and the dive toss computer-aided delivery. To understand the former, one more term needs to be introduced – gain. Gain, as explained in Chapter 1, can be loosely compared with intensity. The higher the gain the more the radar can see. But much of what it sees is clutter from returns of the radar signal bouncing back from the earth. Reduce the gain and reduce the clutter, thus improving radar detection of potential targets.

The backseaters, aided by the ASQ-91 weapons release computer in the F-4D, were able to use the radar to crisply define the tops of mountains, the elevations of which were known. They did this by searching for the mountain by lowering the antenna tilt and increasing the gain until clutter appeared at the approximate location of the mountain top. The jet's ASN-63 INS could provide a pointer to that general location. Once the mountain was broken out as a blob of clutter, the gain could be reduced and the tilt of the antenna raised until the summit was a precise dot. It took an enormous amount of preflight planning and topographic map study to create the expected radar picture. The process involved initially finding the mountain and then defining its top.

Armed with this information, and good preflight planning, the backseater could quickly insert the distance north or south and east or west between the mountain top and the target. These distances were then inserted into the N/S and E/W windows of the ASQ-91, along with the bomb range for a level delivery from a pre-planned altitude above the ground. This was called offset bombing. All of this was happening as the F-4 was flying toward the target at several hundred miles per hour, so time was precious.

When the location of the mountain top had been defined, the backseater scrolled out two connected cursors, one horizontal and one vertical. They were carefully placed on the exact dot of the radar return to signify the mountain top. The backseater then pressed a freeze button and the cursors began to track the mountain top. During this tracking, the placement of the cursors could be adjusted or refined to compensate for any initial placement errors. When the placement was satisfactory, the "GIB" pressed the insert button. With this action, the pilot in the front seat received precise steering information to the designated bomb release point based on the north/south and east/west preplanned distances.

The pilot's task was to "thread the needle" of the steering information while flying at the exact altitude and airspeed for the parameters put into the ASQ-91. Simultaneously, the pilot in the front set up the switches for the release of the bombs or other ordnance and turned on the master arm switch. As the bomb release point was approached, the backseater usually called "Cleared to pickle" over the intercom. The pilot then pressed and held down the bomb release button on the control stick until the ASQ-91 signaled that the release parameters had been met and the ordnance was automatically released from the aircraft. We considered an attack using the ASQ-91 computer in MAP PPI mode to be one of last resort due to the weather conditions. It could only be accomplished after a great deal of target planning, along with radar mapping plots. The navigator backseaters liked doing it, however.

The other mode using the radar for bombing was dive toss. There were a series of built-in-tests (BITs) that the backseater had to run through prior to takeoff to determine the "health" of the radar. The first four BITs verified various aspects of the radar's capability. BIT 5 was the test to check on the dive toss mode, and it was a critical BIT if that system was to be used for weapons delivery. When the pilot selected dive toss as his preferred method of delivery, the radar antenna went to the straight ahead boresight position. In the test, a target in the strobe of the radar display appeared, and it could be adjusted in intensity with the radar gain switch. If the BIT check was done properly, it provided an expectation as to how accurate the dive toss delivery would be when used to drop ordnance.

In practice, the pilot selected dive toss with switchology and rolled into a dive-bombing delivery, usually with a dive angle of between 30 and 45 degrees. When the antenna was working correctly, the backseater would see a ground return in the radar strobe. The ground return was refined to a dot by adjusting the radar gain, with the AN/APQ-109A being locked on to the return, providing radar range to the ground. When the backseater called "locked," the pilot adjusted the sight to the target and pressed the pickle button on the control stick. When the ASQ-91 calculated that the bombing solution had been reached, the weapon was automatically released from the aircraft.

Nobody except WSOs, and my great friend and Air Force Academy classmate Bob "Bevo" Baxter, enjoyed using the system. In an attempt to address the pilots' concerns about it, he wrote a published article he called, "Let's Get Serious About Dive Toss." "Bevo" is a Rhodes Scholar, and he was one of my instructors when I attended FWS a couple of years after returning from my combat tour. The problem with dive toss was one of training and experience, along with the fact that it was one of the first computerized dive-bombing systems to be seen in a combat aircraft. Next generation avionics installed in the F-15, F-16 and other frontline types have a variety of systems for the computer-delivery of weapons, one of which is called continuously computed impact point. With the proper switchology, the pilots of these next-generation aircraft can roll into a dive delivery, put the pipper on the target and push the pickle button, immediately after which they commence dive recovery. The jet decides when to release the bomb. These systems are very accurate. This was rarely the case with dive toss.

I used dive toss a few times in combat but I did not have the training or experience to employ it effectively. I generally relied on manual dive-bombing deliveries.

HUGH GOFORTH AND THE TURBO PORTER

A CIA pilot took me for a wild joy ride into a remote *Steel Tiger* airstrip in Laos. I didn't need to do that twice – actually ever! In reality, this didn't happen, but I have reconstructed such a trip in my mind so many times based on Hugh Goforth's stories that it is as if I had been there with him. Hugh Goforth flew PC-6 Turbo Porter utility aircraft on logistics missions for Air America, the air force of the CIA in Southeast Asia. We met at the bar one evening at the Officers' Club at Ubon and struck up a warm friendship. I learned that he had an American family in Bangkok and that his schedule permitted him to visit them often. He took me out to the flightline and gave me a tour of his aircraft. It was a turbine-powered single-engine tail dragger with a huge cargo compartment behind the pilot. We talked and joked about me going along with him in the co-pilot seat sometime when I could get a day off. It never happened.

One night he told me his wife was critically ill and that he needed to be with her and his children, but that Air America wouldn't give him leave or a pass to go to Bangkok. I asked, "What are you going to do?" He replied, "I quit and I'm leaving for Bangkok on the C-130 later tonight." I told him, "Holy shit, I'll really miss seeing you but that's great that you are willing to sacrifice your job and all." That was the end of the conversation and he departed soon after that. I never expected to see him again. A few weeks later Hugh was back at the bar. Dumbfounded, I asked about his wife and he said she had turned the corner and would be okay. Grateful for that news, I asked about his job and why he was back at Ubon. He casually replied, "Oh, they rehired me."

Years later I read that Hugh Goforth had been killed in an accident while flying a US Navy F8F Bearcat piston-engined fighter during an airshow off the coast of New Jersey.

Rest in Peace Brother Warrior.

11

"PDJ" and *Barrel Roll*

In the area north of eastern Thailand in the Kingdom of Laos, as we knew it then, and now known as the Lao People's Democratic Republic, lies the vast Plaine des Jarres. Christened the "PDJ" by fighter pilots at Ubon, its elevation is quite high and the population that is spread over this vast area (part of the Xieng Khouang Plateau) reside mostly in small villages. Our initial impression of the "PDJ" was that it was CIA territory and an area of operations that would not involve us as fast movers. Instead, we believed that the CIA was engaged in logistic support for the local Laotian resistance to the intrusion into their country by the NVA. This may or may not have been true, but it was our impression. Combat missions against the NVA and the communist Pathet Lao in the "PDJ" were flown as part of the highly secret Operation *Barrel Roll*, and when the 8th TFW was involved in them we usually worked with FACs that used the call-sign "Raven."

I learned later that my second cousin, Margaret Ann, was married to a CIA logistician named Tommy who specialized in aerial deliveries in support of friendly people. They lived in the capital of Laos, Vientiane, at approximately the same time that we were flying combat missions out of Thailand. Furthermore, some of my friends and at least one classmate, Capt Samuel James "Jim" Baker, flew T-28s with the 606th Air Commando (later Special Operations) Squadron over Laos long before I had my opportunity to participate in the war. Others flew World War II-era B-26s. Jim Baker was killed while test flying T-28D 49-1582 from NKP on October 23, 1966 (co-pilot Lt Col William J. Newton also perished).

Toward the end of my year in Thailand, and after I had finished flying nights, I undertook many missions into the *Barrel Roll* airspace and over the "PDJ." On one occasion I was directed to work with a "Raven" FAC that had a target he wanted struck. The details of how we got together with the FAC and the identity of the other F-4 participants in the mission have long been lost from my memory. However, the mental picture of the target remains vivid. As I overflew at medium altitude I spotted a single-story building – my target – that looked like a typical West Texas ranch house. It was a large and sprawling building, with the front door facing to the southeast. From the front door there was what appeared to be a wide sidewalk that from the air looked like a pointer to the front door. Vegetation was sparse in the immediate proximity, and what there was consisted of widely dispersed small trees and scrubby bushes.

The "PDJ" is at a pretty high elevation. In fact, the rolling hills were high enough that a fully fueled and bombed-up F-4 was unable to obtain a dive-bombing roll-in altitude that would permit a 45-degree dive-bombing angle while ensuring a 4,500ft AGL minimum altitude. In order to avoid the gunners on the ground, we typically planned 30-degree dive deliveries that did not require a roll-in altitude as high as that required for a 45-degree dive angle. And, while the level of AAA opposition in the "PDJ" was often hard to predict, the *Barrel Roll* RoE typically mandated that we adhere to the 4,500ft AGL minimum. That day was different, however.

The "Raven" FAC briefed me that defenses were low to non-existent, and to make one pass using a low-altitude and low-angle approach. By this point in the mission my only ordnance left was a pod of 19 2.75in. FFARs with high-explosive warheads. It seemed like an ideal scenario, and my fangs were out. I set up my switches to fire the entire pod of rockets in one burst and turned the master arm switch to arm. I was all set. The attack was to be almost like a traffic pattern, with a descending turn to a "downwind" position adjacent to the target pointing 180 degrees from the planned run in direction. After calling my position on the "downwind," the FAC cleared me hot and the next step was to continue the descending turn through another 180 degrees so as to be pointing at the sidewalk leading up to the front door of the building. I thought to myself, "This is going to be really cool."

Streaking toward the target with the gunsight set up with about 45 mils of depression for the low-angle rocket pass, I was only barely conscious of the importance of having g on the aircraft at the moment of launch. As the sight moved up toward the target I pressed the pickle button, firing all 19 rockets as the gunsight pipper crossed the front door. I thought how this was going to be a "ring of the doorbell" that the occupants would not soon forget if they lived to tell about it.

The rockets swooshed out of the LAU-3 launcher and I pulled hard on the control stick to recover from the dive, hesitated, unloaded the g and then rolled the aircraft to permit me to see the destruction. Frustratingly, every rocket hit the ground halfway down the sidewalk, leaving nothing but dust on the front door and the rest of the house. I think the FAC said something sarcastic over the radio like "Impressive." It was a long flight home that day. Nevertheless, it probably took a while for the people inside the building to compose themselves.

NAM OU RIVER

Although the Nam Ou River is north of the "PDJ," it was still in the area of operations covered by *Barrel Roll*. When looking east while overflying the Nam Ou target area, one could see over the ridge separating Laos from North Vietnam and view the general location of Dien Bien Phu. The fort at this infamous spot had been stoutly defended by French forces for 55 days until overwhelmed by besieging Viet Minh troops on May 7, 1954. Its capture effectively signaled the end of the First Indochina War and resulted in the withdrawal of French forces from the region.

We typically carried a mixed load of ordnance on missions to the Nam Ou River. The prime weapon was a 500lb Mk 82 high-drag bomb fitted with a fuse set to detect the magnetic field of a metal river boat. We were told that the NVA was shipping supplies down the Nam Ou at night, and that our mission was to interdict these supplies. Since it was somewhere between hard and impossible to catch these vessels in the act, the mining of the river with 500lb bombs appeared to be the only choice open to us.

As a wingman, I flew several missions to the Nam Ou. On every occasion I was left underwhelmed by the lack of tactical finesse displayed by the flight leads in charge of our missions. The river ran generally north to south and had mountain ridges on either side. Once the enemy worked out we were targeting shipping transiting the river, they quickly positioned AAA batteries on the ridges surrounding it and awaited our arrival. Although the ground fire opposing these missions steadily increased in intensity as a result, our major and lieutenant colonel flight leads insisted on "playing the same game" day after day. They were not, in the main, fighter pilots, having come to the unit after completing tours flying bombers with SAC. They continued to plan and lead as trained. It was as though they were on an undefended range somewhere in the US outside Nellis, or attacking targets on the Avon Park bombing range in central Florida. They didn't get any of us shot down, but on every mission we were fighting for our lives against AAA due to the predictable nature of our tactics.

I don't remember exactly how I got selected to lead one of these missions but it happened, and I was determined to change the way we were doing business. Instead of a square pattern, with all of the jets running in for their bomb drops on the same heading, I briefed a split up, wherein we all attacked sequentially, but from the four points of the compass, instead of all coming in from the same direction. It seemed to work because no one reported seeing any AAA fire. The gunners were confused, not knowing which way to look for us. I thought then, and continue to think now, that this is an example of the importance of varying tactics, especially when people are trying to kill you.

As the summer of 1969 progressed, Neil Armstrong and Buzz Aldrin went to the moon and I got checked out in the delivery of LGBs, specifically GBU-10s. This weapon was actually a 2,000lb Mk 84 general-purpose bomb that had a laser-guidance kit strapped to it. This early version of the LGB used a "bam-bam" type of guidance system. This meant that the guidance fins on the nose of the bomb unit moved to full deflection either up or down to vary the flightpath of the bomb as its traveled to the target. Viewed from the side, the trajectory of the bomb resembled a sine curve of tightly spaced ups and downs. The delivery was from high angle, either 30 or 45 degrees of dive angle, depending on the elevation of the target. Two GBU-10s were carried by the bomber, one each on the inboard pylons, with 370-gallon drop tanks on the outboard pylons.

Instead of attempting a precise dive angle with exact airspeed and release altitude, along with the correct mil setting in the gunsight, as required in a dumb bomb delivery, the LGB was dropped less exactly into what we called a basket. The basket resembled a cone, with its point being the target. As long as the bomb was dropped into the basket, it had enough energy to home in on the target with the "bam-bam" guidance that was built-in.

Guiding the bomb was another issue. The first guidance system was the AVQ-9 Pave Light, which was nicknamed the "Zot box" – this nickname was derived from the anteater character in Johnny Hart's famous "B.C." comic strip, the animal, called "Zot," deftly eating ants with his long tongue. Delivering LGBs required a second aircraft to illuminate the target with a laser. The rear cockpit of the F-4D was modified through the fitting of a box-like device mounted on the left canopy rail. The "Zot box" included a laser, a sighting eyepiece with crosshairs and a system of wires and pulleys that permitted the backseater to look through the eyepiece, acquire the target and then use a joy stick to point the laser at the target by superimposing the crosshairs over it. The laser was pointed 90 degrees to the flightpath of the aircraft in a line from the rear cockpit, over the left wing and to the distant target on the ground.

To make all of this work the pilot in the front seat of the F-4 was required to fly a circle around the target at an altitude of about 10,000ft above the ground. The laser-pointing device had forward-and-aft and up-and-down gimbal limits. Therefore, before takeoff, the pilot and backseater were required to calibrate the four gimbal limits to allow the crew to achieve the levels of coordination necessary for the backseater to acquire and then track the target while the pilot flew a steady level turn with about 30 degrees of bank angle. The calibration was accomplished in the arming area for the aircraft prior to takeoff, the latter typically being near the end of the departure runway. This was the location where the armorers pulled the safety pins and otherwise armed the ordnance prior to takeoff.

A second component of the pre-departure checklist was a comprehensive look over the aircraft for leaks or any other evidence that would indicate the F-4 was unworthy of flight.

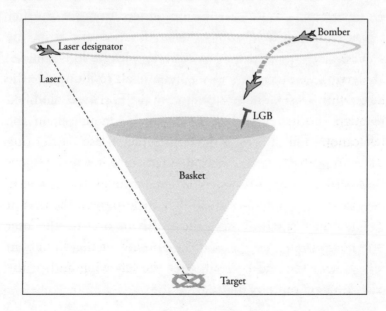

The calibration of the laser-pointing system was the final step in the preflight ritual, the backseater peering through the eyepiece moving the joy stick fully forward. He would then describe a distant building, tree or other notable feature visible through the eyepiece that represented the forward limit of the laser travel. The pilot in the front seat used a grease pencil to scribe a vertical line on the inside of his canopy to match this. This was repeated for the aft, upper and lower limits. When complete, the aircraft commander had a grease pencil-scribed rectangle on the inside of his canopy.

The pilot subsequently approached the target offset to the right and 10,000ft above the terrain. When line abreast of the target, the pilot entered a 30-degree banking turn toward it and kept the target as close to the center of the grease pencil calibration rectangle scribed on the canopy as possible while maintaining his turn. The backseater acquired the target through the eyepiece once the jet was established in the turn, duly using the joy stick to move the crosshairs so as to superimpose them over the aim point. A trigger was then squeezed by the WSO to fire the laser.

Various tactics were used by crews employing the "Zot box" designator, with the one generally preferred being for jets to enter the target area in close or route formation, with the bomber on the left wing of the designated F-4. Approaching an invisible line abreast of the target, the bomber would drop away from the "Zot box"-equipped aircraft in an initial dive-and-turn maneuver. When approximately over the target, the bomber would pull up and climb, crossing above and slightly behind the "Zot box" designator. The bomber would then roll in on the target, passing over the top of the "Zot box" designator. This was crunch time for the backseater. Final tweaking of the crosshairs over the target followed, along with a simultaneous trigger squeeze to fire the laser and a call over the radio that the bomber was cleared to drop.

The F-4 then released the 2,000lb GBU-10 into the basket and the bomb guided itself to the laser spot illuminating the target. The bomber recovered as if a normal dive-bombing pass had been made, with the pilot jinking to avoid ground fire. As soon as the bomb detonated, the "Zot box" also left the target area. The two F-4s then rejoined for either a second delivery of bombs and other ordnance or the return flight home.

So, with that as background, let's move onto a later mission to the Nam Ou River. On the day in question I was part of a four-ship being led by a major. As we were transiting at medium altitude over a village on the "PDJ," we came under intense fire from 37mm AAA. We were ready to attack in a protective reaction strike, but the flight leader would have none of it and we continued on to perform an uneventful bombing mission on the Nam Ou. Without exception, we were really angry with the major who refused to allow us to attack, and we let him know it. In the debrief, he indicated he had access to information that was above the security clearance level that all of the rest of us had, and that one of the notable buildings in the village from where the AAA had emanated was a Chinese "Cultural Center," thus making it strictly off limits. So, we dropped the issue.

The next day I was fragged as the bomber on a GBU-10 LGB mission and quickly realized that the target was the notable Chinese "Cultural Center" building from the previous day. The village it was located in was pretty small overall, although the notable feature was a fairly large building (at least compared to the other structures) with an orange-tiled roof. The structure looked like a pagoda, with a peaked roof and with the tips tilted up at each of its four corners.

The mission was on, and we headed for the "PDJ" after refueling with a "Cherry Anchor" KC-135. The subsequent attack all went exactly as briefed by the highly experienced "Zot box" designator flight lead. We entered the airspace overhead the village and split up as briefed, and I acquired the target while keeping track of the "Zot box" designator. The flight lead commenced his circular laser-designating orbit and I set up my switches for "bombs single," with nose and tail fusing adding redundancy to the weapon. Master arm switch was moved to arm and the mil setting was entered for the center of the basket, after which I gave the radio call, "Two is in hot." "Cleared hot Two," was the response I received from the flight lead.

I started my roll-in from a spot just aft and above the "Zot box" aircraft, its pilot having established his circular laser-designating orbit. My nose came down into the planned 30-degree dive angle, and as my speed increased I slowly retarded the throttles to idle, planning to hit the release altitude at 450 knots of calibrated airspeed with the pipper positioned below the center of the building's orange roof. The pipper inched up, the backseater was calling off altitudes and the seat of my pants knew we were in good delivery parameters. The "GIB" called, "Ready, pickle!" At that instant the pipper was on target and I pressed the button. The aircraft jerked from the effect of instantly becoming 2,000lb lighter as I pushed the throttles up to full 100 percent military power, made a hard turn and hauled back on the control stick to initiate the 5g recovery. Then, stick forward, unloading and rolling in the opposite direction, before resetting the g.

The roll allowed me to visually reacquire the target, which was then still in one piece. As I continued my gaze, along with the jinking dive, "time" seemed to shorten and then stand still. At first I saw a faint orange hue around the building. Then, as if in slow motion, the orange hue brightened and intensified. In the center of the building a fireball appeared and grew outward until the structure was totally consumed within what was now a huge smoke cloud that then lost the hue and billowed up vertically. I remember being mesmerized by this scene. I realized then that in spite of all the ordnance I had delivered in the previous months I had never actually witnessed a target suffering total destruction. The fireball and smoke cloud was symmetrically highlighted by expanding white spherical vapor circles that surrounded the scene. It was like a video run in reverse of onion rings magically being peeled back. Once the smoke cleared, there was nothing left of the building. I will never forget this visual experience.

We went home beating our chests over the mission. In the debriefing we learned that the target was not a Chinese "Cultural Center" at all, but rather a North Vietnamese communications center – hence the nearby AAA battery. We also learned that we had been denied our request to attack the building the previous day because an Operation *Hardnose* roadwatch team (probably CIA-generated) was on the ground conducting surveillance on the target in particular and the village in general.

This mission was one of only a handful I flew during my year at Ubon that left me feeling I had made a telling contribution to the war effort. Perhaps this was because I felt I had made amends for the "ranch house" caper that went wrong. It was also rewarding to target the bad guys that had shot at us the day before from the compound surrounding the "cultural center."

As far as I was concerned, none of my LGBs ever missed their target. Direct hits – all. When intel debriefers pushed back on my direct hit claims, suggesting a five- or ten-foot miss, I asked them if they knew the diameter of the fireball from a 2,000lb bomb. They didn't. End of discussion.

Later, during the *Linebacker* campaign against North Vietnam in 1972, great success was had with the AN/AVQ-10 Pave Knife experimental laser designator. This only confirmed my conviction that smart bombs were the way to go, and later while on duty in the Pentagon I had the opportunity to both brief Gen Alexander Haig, who was Supreme Allied Commander Europe at the time, on smart bombs, and then to champion the follow-on laser designator (which replaced the "Zot box" system). It was called AN/ASQ-153 Pave Spike and consisted of a pod that was housed within one of the F-4's AIM-7 missile bays. Pave Spike had a fully gimbaled turret-like device (similar to the experimental Pave Knife system) that permitted the aircraft to which it was fitted to deliver its own weapons. As a result, Pave Spike was also deemed suitable for use in heavily defended high-risk target areas, unlike AVQ-9 Pave Light.

A FIELD TRIP WITH T. R. GRAY

One evening shortly after my LGB experiences over "PDJ," I was socializing with T. R. and Estelle Gray when the former asked if I would be interested in a tour into the Thai countryside with him. I readily agreed, while at the same time asking whether it could take place when I next had no flying or squadron duties. T. R. indicated flexibility on the schedule, and so it was set.

I always enjoyed the personal one-on-one time with T. R., as he was a father figure to all of us at the 433rd, being a very positive and encouraging individual. After time with T. R. I always felt better about everything. Our field trip was no exception. I wore a flightsuit and met T. R. at his house downtown at the appointed time, after which the two of us headed out in his Land Rover-like vehicle. As we journeyed he explained the role of the United States and his employer, AID, in support of Thailand. We drove by rice paddies and occasionally stopped and got out of the vehicle to inspect irrigation ditches, dykes and dams. The details he imparted were fascinating to me, and a wonderful distraction from months of combat operations.

At one point we visited a Buddha in one of the villages we drove through and chatted with the locals. I spoke no Thai other than to say hello and goodbye. T. R., on the other hand, was able to converse with them in their language, and he graciously kept me informed about the content of their conversations.

When the tour was over and we had returned to Ubon for cocktails and dinner at home with Estelle, I felt an immense relief. The day with T. R. had been a much-needed catharsis – one that I had no understanding of how much I had needed it at the time.

12

"Jeb" Stewart is Down

It really hurts when you lose anyone, but the pain is especially severe when you lose a squadronmate that you trained with, flew with, partied with, knew his wife and felt as close to as a brother.

"'Jeb' Stewart is down!" The mission planning room in the TOC at 8th TFW HQ at Ubon froze with the unexpected announcement. Someone asked, "Where?" The intelligence officer answered, "Mu Gia Pass." "Chute and beeper?" "Yep, they are talking to him. He is hurt pretty bad* but was able to hole himself up in a cave on the side of a wall of karst. It's too late for a SAR mission tonight. He will hunker down and we'll try to snatch him out in the morning."

The following day (May 18, 1969), after long and fierce resistance from enemy forces in the area that included a nearby AAA battery, a USAF pararescueman (PJ) from the 40th Aerospace Rescue and Recovery finally got to him. According to one report, 1Lt "Jeb" Stewart was already dead, his body wedged in a crevice. His status became killed in action, body

---

*Editor's Note: he reported that he had a broken arm and leg.

not recovered – the lone PJ was unable to recover the body due to NVA troops closing on his position. As far as I am aware, that status still hasn't changed.

We had to know what had happened during the armed reconnaissance mission over the Mu Gia Pass on May 17, and the story soon unfolded. "Jeb" was flying with Maj Paul Albritton when they took a hit from ground fire that either ejected "Jeb" or led to his decision to eject, thinking that was the only option he had available to save his life. We will never know. The aircraft commander, Albritton, was able to maintain control of the F-4 and return safely to Thailand, but without "Jeb." End of story.

Judy Stewart had just had a baby, their first child, a little girl named Kimberly who would never know her dad other than by reputation and family memory.

The entry for "Jeb" Stewart on the *Find a Grave* website reads as follows:

Virgil Grant "Jeb" Stewart*
Birth: October 9, 1942
Death: May 17, 1969 (Laos)

STEWART, VIRGIL GRANT
CAPTAIN, AIR FORCE
BATON ROUGE, LOUISIANA
BODY HAS NOT BEEN RECOVERED

1Lt Virgil Grant "Jeb" Stewart was married to Judy Keturah Bond and had a daughter Kimberly who was born in 1969. "Jeb" was a pilot assigned to the 433rd TFS "Satan's Angels" of the 8th TFW, flying F-4D fighters.

---

*Text taken from https://www.findagrave.com/cgi-bin/fg.cgi?page=gr&GRid=42003494. Reproduced by kind permission of Mike Davison and Find A Grave.com.

On May 17, 1969, 1Lt Stewart was the WSO of an F-4D in the area of the Mu Gia Pass, Khammouane Province, Laos, when his aircraft sustained battle damage. He ejected from his aircraft and reported to rescuers that he was on the ground with a broken arm and leg. Rescue forces had a visual sighting of him. A hostile gun position was located south of his position and it was attacked by SAR forces. A pararescue specialist later landed in the area and found him dead. Hostile ground fire prevented recovery of his body. He was declared killed in action, body not recovered. He was posthumously promoted to captain.

From Mike ["Ghost"] Davison at The Vietnam Veterans Memorial:

"Jeb" was my best friend at Ubon RTAFB in 1969. We built the 433rd's party hooch together, had a friendly rivalry at radar bombing (which I should have been better at, being a navigator) and we killed way too many brain cells together in the Officers' Club after missions. "Jeb" had a handmade knife that his father had crafted for him that he always carried when he flew. I hope that whoever has it today appreciates it. We hung a memorial brass bell in the party hooch with a quote from Confederate Gen J. E. B. Stuart that read, "I'd rather die than be whipped." I think that "Jeb" would have liked it, but I would have liked it better if we wouldn't have had to do it. Rest in peace, old friend.

Vietnam Memorial Wall Panel 24W – Line 34.

Mike Davison continued in an e-mail to me and others from the squadron:

I've always thought it strange that I knew so little about "Jeb's" last mission, considering that he was my best friend at the time. Here's what I do remember. The aircraft landed at NKP after the ejection, that being the closest emergency runway. I don't think that anyone really knows why "Jeb" ejected that day. To my knowledge, there was no damage to the aircraft [actually, according to Paul Albritton, an engine was shot out]. "Jeb" was a pretty cool-headed guy, and I cannot imagine him making a panicky decision. Still a mystery as far as I know.

I heard about the incident just as I was briefing for an LGB mission, and I fully expected that by the time I returned "Jeb" would be back as well. After dropping some "smart" iron on some insignificant piece of dirt in Laos, I went straight to the TOC and asked Maj Rooney, who was on duty that day, if they had rescued "Jeb" yet, and he just shook his head and said "KIA." Nothing else. I turned back into the hallway, sank down against the wall and cried. After a few minutes I got up and started to walk toward the door when the other "GIB" on the flight, Steve Hubert, said that we had to debrief the mission. I said, "I don't think so" and left. I had fully intended on NOT going to the bar that night and lasted until about nine or ten o'clock before breaking down, walking over and getting very drunk.

At the back of the "C" Flight hooch area there was a large patio that was pretty much unused. I don't know whose idea it was to turn it into a party hooch, but I do know that at least initially, "Jeb" and I did the lion's share of the work, building the walls with stones and cement, putting up the walls behind the bar, mounting the "Satan's Angel's" sign above the bar, sweating gallons and replacing it with equal quantities of Singha beer. Obviously, there were many others involved, but in my memory it was "Jeb's" and my project.

A day or two after the incident, the houseboy for the "C" Flight living area, a young Thai man named Prasit, asked me when 1Lt Stewart would be coming back. When I told him what had happened, and that 1Lt Stewart would not be coming home, he kicked the dirt with his bare feet and said,

"Ho Chi Minh No. 10." Yes, I assured him, Ho Chi Minh was indeed No. 10.

When he flew, "Jeb" always carried a handcrafted knife that his father had made for him. It had an aluminum handle and a serrated blade that was razor sharp. He was very, very proud of it. You can see it on his hip in the photo from the newspaper article announcing his death.

Finally, there is a Dick Jonas song called "The Ballad of Jeb" that tells the story of "Jeb" Stewart's death, although since Jonas wasn't at Ubon at the time, there must have been a lot of dramatic license taken.

That's all I've got. Guys, go ahead and change any incorrect statements if your collective memories serves you differently.

Over and out,
"Ghost"*

The following is a newspaper report that featured in the November 1, 2012 edition of *The Picayune Item* after a robbery at a house owned by the brother of "Jeb" Stewart. The names of the suspects, and the Stewart family members, have been removed from the articles:

Stolen guns had sentimental value
By Jeremy Pittari, Staff Writer, *The Picayune Item*

Two stolen guns from a Henleyfield home held more than monetary value, they are reminders of a brother lost during the Vietnam War. Pearl River County deputies were called to a home on September 26 in response to a break-in where two guns, handmade in Thailand, were taken, said Chief Deputy Shane Tucker. Also taken in the burglary

---

*From an e-mail sent by Mike Davison to Gail Peck, approximate date February 2013. Reproduced by kind permission of Mike Davison.

was an oxygen cutting rig, copper tubing and a window air conditioning unit. The suspects entered the home by breaking out a window pane on the rear door before taking two black powder, 0.38cal rifles and the air conditioning unit. The oxygen cutting rig and copper tubing were taken from an outside storage unit, Tucker said.

Detective Marc Ogden was assigned the case but did not have a lot of evidence to go on. Fortunately, a community tip led him to the suspects. The investigation showed the suspects were responsible for breaking into the home and stealing the items. The investigation showed one suspect sold the guns to an individual in another state, but they have since been recovered. The investigation also recovered the oxygen cutting rig and copper tubing in the woods behind one suspect's home, but the air conditioning unit is still missing, Tucker said. Two suspects were charged with residential burglary and the third has been charged with burglary accessory after the fact, Tucker said.

The story behind the guns was a driving force for Ogden to continue to investigate a case that started with little evidence, Tucker said. The guns belong to a man who lost his brother in the Vietnam War. Virgil Grant Stewart was an F-4 Phantom II jet pilot during the Vietnam War. During Grant Stewart's time overseas, he came across a gunsmith in Thailand who was known for crafting guns by hand for people in the area who used them to hunt game for food. The guns were unique items. Not only are they entirely handmade, but they include rosewood and materials from water buffalo, according to the brother.

During his tour in Vietnam, Grant Stewart sent the guns home, one for himself and another as a gift to his brother. "But he never made it home," the brother said. During his 266th mission, weeks away from finishing his tour and heading home to meet his newborn daughter, Grant Stewart's plane was hit while flying over enemy territory near the North Vietnamese border in May of 1969, his brother said. Grant Stewart ejected from the jet fighter and suffered injuries that would lead to his death about four hours later. He was 26 years old. The brother said the military knew Grant Stewart was initially still alive due to continued emergency radio contact with him.

The guns are considered to be showpieces, and he is grateful to Ogden for putting in the extra work to locate the guns and catch the individuals responsible. "These guys did a lot of investigative work to track these (guns) down," Grant Stewart's brother said. "He made my day when he called me on that."*

The following text is from a posting on June 26, 2011 in the Gainesville, Florida, *News Column* attributed to Brig Gen (Ret.) Paul Albritton, "Jeb's" aircraft commander that fateful day:

During that year, he had "two bad incidents, the worst of which was on May 17, 1969," he said. "We were hit by ground fire, and my backseater ejected and died on the ground about five hours later." He remembered the harrowing details. His comrade fell into a "most-heavily defended target in Laos – Mu Gia Pass." Though the rescue team made contact via radio and sent helicopters in, their efforts were to no avail. "They went in about the seventh hour and determined he was already dead, so his body's still there," he said. The attack cost Albritton an engine, too, but he was able to guide the plane back safely.†

---

*Text from http://picayuneitem.com/local/x699481539/Stolen-guns-had-sentimental-value. Reproduced by kind permission of *The Picayune Item*.
†Text from http://www.gainesvilletoday.com/2011-july/2011/06/26/into-the-wild-blueyonder/.

13

More R&R and a Staff Posting

My second spell of R&R while at Ubon was spent in Hawaii, where I met up with my wife. Prior to meeting her, however, I had to get an F-4 back to Ubon from Clark AB. I took off and headed west, only to have one of the aircraft's generators fail. So, even though the bus-tie breaker closed as it was supposed to, permitting the remaining generator to power the aircraft's entire electrical system, I nevertheless returned to Clark to have it fixed. The next time I took off the same thing happened, and again using good judgment, I returned to Clark and another confrontation with the aircraft maintenance team there that was responsible for fixing broken transient jets. Again, it took several days before maintenance declared the jet airworthy. The time for my flight to Honolulu was drawing close, and I was increasingly impatient and anxious to get back to Ubon and then on my way for the R&R.

The third time the generator failed partway across the Gulf of Tonkin, so I said to myself, "To hell with it!" and continued on to Ubon. We arrived just fine with no other issues, and soon thereafter I was on my way for the long-awaited rest and relaxation leave in Honolulu and a reunion with the mother of my children. However, things just didn't seem quite right during our reunion. Nothing specific. There were loving moments, but things were just not quite right. I could not put my finger on it. The week quickly passed and soon I was on my way back to Ubon for my final three months in combat.

8TH TFW STAFFER

I had become a pretty close friend with Maj Remo Nicoli while in Thailand. Remo was assigned to our squadron and regularly flew with us, although his primary job was on the wing staff. Remo started making suggestions that I would fit well into a vacancy that had opened up on the wing staff and I was intrigued by the idea. Although my colleagues in the squadron were very much against me going, I listened to Remo's pitch about how important the job was and how it could be helpful to my career in the future. I thought long and hard about it and when the time came for a decision I decided to become a "Wing Weenie." Our Operations Officer, Lt Col Bill Strand, a lifelong friend, never completely forgave me for leaving the 433rd. Nevertheless, I found my new job rewarding, and am not sorry I went that way.

One of my major duties at wing HQ was to support and, to some degree, supervise the barrier crew. At Ubon we had seven jet barriers that stretched across the full 125ft width of the 8,000ft-long runway. There were MA-1A barrier nets that could be raised across either end of the runway that we dubbed "rabbit catchers." When in the raised position, the barrier would trap a jet that was overshooting the runway and plowing into the overrun. Each end of the barrier was connected to a large chain that was laid out in the same direction as the overrun. Thus, when a jet engaged the barrier it tugged on increasing links of chain, slowing the aircraft until it finally stopped.

There were also three Barrier Arresting Kit (BAK) 12s, with one several hundred feet from either end of the runway and the third in the middle. These barriers took the form of cables stretched across the runway and held several inches above its surface by heavy rubber disks. The disks had a slit to a central hole, which meant that they could be easily twisted until the cable slipped into said hole, thus ensuring a snug fit over the steel barrier cable. The disks were positioned every few feet, and they allowed the cable to be raised high enough for the aircraft's tail hook to be snared as the jet rolled over it, much like on an aircraft carrier.

The ends of the BAK-12 cable extended beyond the runway edges in a trench until they reached the barrier "shack," which housed a huge spool with more cable on it. Running along a path at the edge of the runway was a system of rollers that allowed the snared cable to follow the rapidly decelerating jet down the tarmac while more cable spun off the spool in the barrier shack along a line perpendicular to the runway. Within the shack, in addition to the large spool with more cable wrapped around it, was a brake system from an F-104 fighter that acted like a clutch on the spool. As more and more cable was pulled off by the engaged but decelerating aircraft, the clutch brake engaged increasing pressure on the spool from a much larger brake assembly from a B-52.

There were two other barriers that were also routinely used to recover our aircraft, as the BAK-12s and MA-1As were primarily kept for emergencies only. We needed the remaining two barriers because of the nature of the runway at Ubon and the monsoon weather that routinely hit the airfield. The 8,000ft runway was grooved like many Interstate freeways. It was also highly crowned to help the water run off quicker during the monsoon rains that were prevalent for much of the year. If it was raining heavily it was very difficult to keep an F-4 on the highly crowned runway.

Running off the tarmac in a big jet fighter and plunging into a muddy mire on either side of the runway was clearly not a preferred option. Add a crosswind to the already slick runway, and directional control became almost impossible because the drag 'chute tended to cause the aircraft to weathervane into the wind and onto a runway departure trajectory. Snagging the barrier cable prevented this from happening, so we trapped the jets like on an aircraft carrier when the weather was really nasty.

The remaining two barriers at Ubon were the M-2 Mobile Arresting Gear (MOREST), used by the US Marine Corps, and the BAK-13. Both were capable of being quickly recycled, allowing the trapping of a stream of fighters making approaches with just a few miles of spacing between them. However, neither of these barriers was as rugged as the BAK-12, so use of the drag 'chute was essential to slow the F-4 down to a speed that the MOREST and BAK-13 were capable of handling. For example, as I recall, the maximum engagement speed for the MOREST was 139 knots. The F-4 flew its final approach at 19.2 units angle-of-attack or about 150 knots, plus a few extra knots depending on fuel and overall gross weight. The best technique was to hold the 19.2 units angle-of-attack until the aircraft touched down. The drag 'chute was then immediately deployed. The impact of the aircraft touching down on the runway and the initial deceleration due to the drag 'chute was enough to slow the jet to less than 139 knots, unless the pilot was "hot" in airspeed or landed long.

The MOREST was positioned about 800ft down the runway. An aircraft making a proper engagement with the MOREST slowed to taxi speed very quickly, and after raising the tail hook the pilot could taxi clear of the runway during the time it took a well-drilled crew to recycle the barrier and be ready for the next jet in the stream. If a pilot missed the MOREST or broke it, the BAK-13 was a bit further down the runway, allowing the aircraft recovery stream to continue barrier engagements. The BAK-13 was more robust than the MOREST but it did not recycle as quickly.

So, catching the jets when they came home with battle damage or in bad weather was a never-ending challenge, and along with the task of making the jet recoveries happen, there was the companion logistics challenge of maintaining the barriers. Like seemingly everything else, spare parts were always in short supply and that was especially true with the barrier parts. Soon after I took the job at the wing and became the officer-in-charge of the barrier operation, our MOREST was damaged badly and became inoperable. We depended on the Marine Corps for spare parts, but had no easy or clear logistics channel for getting them.

The senior NCOs on the barrier team identified the parts we needed and sent messages and made phone calls in an to attempt to source them. Usually, our source was the Marine air base at Chu Lai in South Vietnam, with Da Nang AB, also in South Vietnam, occasionally being tapped for parts. Eventually, the NCOs found what we needed at the latter site, and it became my job to get them to Ubon. We had two C-47s under the control of the 8th TFW for this very reason, and I was able to schedule one of the twin-engined prop-driven transports for a quick trip east across the combat zones of Laos and South Vietnam.

A couple NCOs and I embarked on our journey to Da Nang, not realizing it was the eve of Tet 1969. Tet 1968, on January 30, had been a major event in the war, and one would have thought that we might have been warned or otherwise cued to be prepared for trouble by the wing's intelligence folks. We weren't. After arriving at Da Nang, the NCOs went about the business of hooking up with the Marines, and I was to meet them on the Marine Corps side of the airfield (which was principally a USAF base) later that evening. As agreed, just before dusk, I made my way toward the Marine side of the air base and was walking up a hill to the meeting point when I heard the unmistakable sound of a developing rocket attack. I was in a flightsuit and wearing a baseball cap, unarmed and totally without situational awareness. Fortunately, two young Marines, both heavily armed, took it upon themselves to protect me at all cost. They directed me into a shallow trench and took up defensive positions at either end. Meanwhile, the rockets were whistling overhead as the bad guys attempted to blow up the bomb dump at Da Nang as a part of their new Tet offensive.

We had no idea whether or not the enemy was coming over the wire into the area where we were hunkered down, and my Marine protectors spared no caution, so we sat it out in the trench that entire evening. We all survived, as did our spare parts, and the next day my NCOs and I made our way back to Ubon via our trusty C-47 with yet another war story to tell.

Having really bonded with the barrier crew, I was often out by the runway when they were trapping jets in the pouring rain. When those braking contraptions were in steady use, the spools areas engaged by the B-52 brake (in the case of the BAK-12) glowed red hot. It was hard and dangerous work, and I would have had no idea about the barrier crew element of our combat team if I hadn't taken the job at the wing.

I still had my combat moustache when I became a staffer. At that point I was in the process of applying to fly with the Thunderbirds, and as part of the application process you had to submit a professional portrait photograph. I shaved off the moustache for the photo, prompting one of the barrier crew to write the following short poem:

> From Fighter Jockey
> to "Barrier Crew."
> They took his PRIDE.
> His moustache too.
> He is the one who saves the crew.
> The same they used to laugh with too.
> Little is known of his quiet nature,
> but he's "Number One" this is true.

TACTICS CONFERENCE

One of the perks of my assignment to the 8th TFW staff was that I attended the Red River Valley Fighter Pilots' Association (also known as the "River Rats") tactics symposium at Udorn on behalf of the wing in the early summer of 1969. This event culminated with a party in Bangkok. The delegates from the 8th TFW loaded up one of our C-47s and headed for Udorn for the formal component of the symposium.

The "River Rats" had been established by senior commanders in Thailand (Howard "Scrappy" Johnson and Robin Olds, among others) as a tool for hammering out troubling details of Thirteenth Air Force's day-to-day combat operations that were conducted from different bases in Thailand. We had a confusing chain of command in-theater because we belonged to Thirteenth Air Force but were fragged on a daily basis for combat operations by Seventh Air Force, with its HQ in Saigon.

Each of Thirteenth Air Force's bases in Thailand had either different aircraft and missions or variations of the same mission. For example, the F-105 bases at Korat and Takhli flew both strike bombing missions and *Wild Weasel* SAM suppression and destruction missions. The Phantom IIs based in Thailand included recce RF-4s flying alongside strike and fighter F-4s at Udorn, while the 8th TFW had night attack jets, LORAN D-equipped F-4Ds, fighters and LGB bombers operating from Ubon. The 8th TFW's *Igloo White* Phantom IIs of the 25th TFS had a particularly confusing tasking structure. TFA at Nakhom Phanom monitored the sensors the 25th implanted on the Ho Chi Minh Trail and passed that information directly to the planners in Saigon. It was all very hush-hush, and officers with my security clearance level were not in the know in respect to details.

Our SAR forces in Thailand, flying A-1s and helicopters while coordinating defense suppression with fast-moving strike aircraft, often had to work with unfamiliar units based in South Vietnam while attempting to rescue downed aircrew in Laos. The "River Rats" conference gave personnel from this community the opportunity to meet senior officers from the units assigned to Seventh Air Force, and they could then discuss how best to work together in a predictable fashion during critically important SAR extractions.

Finally, KC-135 tanker units were also represented at Udorn, as both pre-strike and post-strike aerial refueling were major components of our daily operations. For example, the last thing we needed when we were coming out of North Vietnam short of fuel and possibly with battle damage was to find our tanker at the far end of a 100-mile-long tanker orbit, instead of circling as close to the combat zone as possible.

With the almost continuous turnover of personnel in-theater, these meetings were vital, and thus were held every six months or so. Typically, topics discussed at the conference included a lot of information on "old business" and the lessons from the many years of combat that the new guys needed to know, along with new thoughts, challenges and issues that had more recently surfaced. I have long since forgotten the exact agenda for the symposium, but it probably flowed pretty quickly so that the delegates could get on with the "two-part" party.

Part one consisted of a major parade at Udorn. The SAR helicopter guys all dressed in their green party suits and looked like the Jolly Green Giant of canned vegetable fame – they had costumed-up complete with green face makeup. Their HH-3 helicopters were also called Jolly Greens Giants, mainly due to their shape and jungle camouflage paint scheme. There were young Thai women, largely from the Udorn Officers' Club staff, that were scantily dressed, with messages scrawled across the butt of their panties warning off predators. There were elephants and floats. The parade was hilarious and a true hoot! A lot of alcohol went into the pre-parade preparations, which added to the festive mood of the event.

The next day we all assembled on the flightline at Udorn for a C-130 flight to Bangkok for the real "practice party" – it was called this because the "River Rats" intended to have a proper party in the US when the PoWs were liberated and able to attend alongside their more fortunate colleagues. The real party subsequently happened in Las Vegas in 1973 after the guys came home.

There were ice chests full of beer and Bloody Mary cocktails were in abundance as we sat and sweated beneath the wings of the C-130 while awaiting the signal to board. Eventually we were ushered into the aircraft.

I sat on a troop seat near the forward cockpit ladder and left exterior door of the Hercules. Next to me was a major who introduced himself as "Moody." Maj Richard M. "Moody" Suter was the 366th TFW's weapons officer at Da Nang. The F-4 wing there was somehow tasked with supporting elements of operations in both Laos and North Vietnam. I never did fully understand the Seventh/Thirteenth Air Force arrangement. That experience, meeting and listening to "Moody" Suter, set the stage for much of my thinking and future career. He had recently graduated from the FWS after an earlier tour flying F-101s, followed by a spell in ATC as an instructor. I quickly realized that "Moody" was the "real deal," and I listened closely to what he had to tell me. He started by saying something like, "We have to get a handle on training. It is idiotic that we are sending 'Blue 4' out to serve as cannon fodder, half-assed trained and with marginal leadership. We must fix this." That was the theme of his message, and it came at me like a lecture over and over, with slight variations.

At the same time drunk fighter pilots had started to play Tarzan in the cargo compartment of the C-130, swinging above us and jumping around like crazy people. "Moody" was undaunted, totally ignoring the chaos around us as he explained things to me. At one point a full colonel came out of the flightdeck door and attempted to restore order and quieten things down. He was met with jeers and a barrage of ice cubes to the extent that he finally gave up and went back to the cockpit. Nobody was mad, not even the colonel. It was one of the craziest hours of my life; all the while I was trying to absorb this apparently important lesson from the Da Nang wing weapons officer.

"Moody" and I went on to become great friends. He was my mentor in many ways in that he ran the air-to-air flight at the FWS when I attended as a student, and was still the air-to-air flight commander when I returned to work for him as an instructor. We talked about training and training programs, and every possible angle and component of what we needed to do to mature the USAF in this important area. "Moody" subsequently successfully advocated the Aggressor program, and after leaving Nellis for an assignment at the Pentagon, invented *Red Flag*, one of the greatest air combat training programs ever devised. I was fortunate enough to replace him as the air-to-air flight commander at the FWS.

During his next assignment at the Pentagon, "Moody" was secretly managing Air Force training with real Soviet MiG jet fighters. I had flown the MiG-17 when I was stationed at Nellis working for him. I was next assigned to the same office in the Pentagon. "Moody" was rewarded for inventing *Red Flag* with a new assignment as the commander of the 555th Fighter Training Squadron (FTS) at Luke AFB, Arizona – the 555th's mission was to train new pilots to fly the F-15 Eagle. I again inherited "Moody's" job, this time with the MiGs. This opportunity led to my advocacy of a program we named *Constant Peg*. "Constant" was the call-sign of Maj Gen Sandy Vandenberg, my boss at the Pentagon, and "Peg" was the name of my second wife, Peggy.

Constant Peg established a secret airfield at the Tonopah Test Range (TTR) in the R-4809 restricted area of the Nellis ranges. The airfield was equipped with a fleet of restored MiG fighters, and the American pilots flying these Soviet jets were tasked with training American aircrews on how to dogfight and win against these aircraft. I landed the first of these Soviet aircraft (a MiG-21) at the TTR in July 1979. *Constant Peg* lasted almost ten years, generated more than 15,000 MiG sorties and trained almost 6,000 USAF, US Navy and US Marine Corps aircrew in how to fight the MiG-17, MiG-21 and MiG-23 and win.

So, meeting "Moody" Suter on the C-130 in Thailand was a major event in my life.

DOWNTOWN WITH THE CHILDREN

Contrary to what I have written in this book, I didn't spend my entire time while in-theater during my year of combat either flying strike missions or attending booze-fueled parties. I am not sure how it came to pass, but my initial roommate at Ubon, Nelson E. "Ed" Cobleigh from Chattanooga, Tennessee, and the officer with whom I flew my first combat mission, somehow hooked up with a Thai organization that I seem to recall was an orphanage.

One of "Ed's" favorite getaway past times was to go to downtown Ubon and play with the children at the orphanage. I went with him on more than one occasion, and we always found the visits to be uplifting, especially given our routine daily tasks of planning for, conducting or debriefing war.

14

Home Stretch

As the end of my combat tour approached, my focus began to change in anticipation of the next chapter in my life. The most important of these concerns was renewing my connection with my family and planning for our next assignment. I dreaded the idea of returning to ATC as an instructor and feared the possibility I could be sent to SAC to fly bombers. I desperately wanted to continue to fly fighters, any fighters, any place in the world. The assignment finally came through and I was thrilled to learn I was being sent to the 81st TFW at RAF Bentwaters near Ipswich, in Suffolk, England. And, better still, I was to continue flying the Phantom II. Great news, and with that objective met, I relaxed a bit and began to enjoy my final missions, and the social contact with our US Army colleagues that were stationed with their families in the town of Ubon.

Our squadron established a warm relationship with the Army crowd. Our prime social event was volleyball, and we competed with a vengeance. As these contacts developed, light chit chat expanded into deep conversations about career objectives and, to some degree, disappointments. At one point

I confessed my dismay at not being able to attend parachute training as a cadet at the Air Force Academy and earn my Jump Wings. The Army guys immediately informed me that they could make that happen. Thus, I entered into training in my off duty time, with the goal of five quick parachute jumps leading to the award of the coveted Jump Wings. All proceeded smoothly as I increased my physical conditioning by running daily and engaging in strenuous calisthenics. Meanwhile, I continued to fly those missions that were leading up to my final combat flight.

My squadronmates made fun of my obsession with Jump Wings and few, if any, of them took it seriously. But as the time approached a few made plans of their own to disrupt and prevent my folly. The day finally came, and Steve Mosier and I were scheduled together for our last combat mission. It was totally unremarkable and I have no memory of the details – that is, until we returned to Ubon. According to Steve we took a very long and uneventful trip to *Barrel Roll* that was highlighted by hung ordnance due to the wingman's switchology. The wingman happened to be our night partner Norm Fogg, who got to brief the wing about his error. He concluded with a smart remark that got him in the "dog house" again. But we all survived, and the colonel that put Norm in the penalty box disappeared very soon thereafter. No one was sorry to see him go.

After landing and parking our Phantom II, we were met with the traditional "fini-flight" cast of squadron members and other friends for the champagne toast and the "parade" back to the squadron area. As we dismounted our jet we were liberally sprayed by a fire hose, totally soaking us and all of our equipment. Then, someone charged up while we were wiping the water out of our eyes and jerked the two little tabs on our emergency life preservers, inflating the orange bladders that were now were protruding forward and aft from under our arms. Finally, at plane side, came the champagne, some of which we drank, some of which was poured on our heads and some of which we squirted at the crowd after vigorously shaking the bottle.

Then we mounted the 433rd's samlor, which was adorned in squadron colors and equipped with large flags that signaled our successful combat accomplishment, and the parade was on. Our squadron commander, Lt Col Jack Bennett, drove the samlor, and we made our way to the squadron building through a gauntlet of well-wishers. It was a thrilling moment. That night we had a going away party and memories of that event are a total fog. I do know that the plan my squadronmates had hatched was to prevent me from pursuing my Jump Wings because early the next morning, when I was scheduled to join our Army friends for my big event, I found the door to my room nailed shut. This had obviously been accomplished by drunks, and it took little or no effort to force the door open and get on my way.

The plan was to grab our jump gear and board one of the base C-47 aircraft and make five quick jumps in one day, do the award of the Jump Wings paperwork and be done with it. The overall mission was an integrated jump, with the parachutists under the command of local Thai Army personnel, with the US personnel serving as advisors.

Since we were doing a static line jump from a C-47, we needed a static line extender to ensure that as jumpers we would be able to fall clear of the aircraft's tail and tailwheel before the static line hooked to the plane automatically pulled our parachute rip cord. This is a typical combat-type jump. The aircraft had a steel cable that ran down the length of the cabin at about eye height when seated. Each jumper could then be seated on either side of the cabin, with their backs to the windows, and reach out and hook up their static line to the steel cable. When the time to jump approached all jumpers stood up and faced aft. The jump master stood at the aft edge of the aircraft door, and upon reaching the drop zone signaled the first jumper to go. Then, each jumper followed the one in front in quick succession. When all the jumpers were out, the jump master pulled all of the static lines back into the aircraft. The jump master was a Thai NCO on this mission, while the jumpers were a combination of Thai and US Army personnel, plus me. I was seated at the far aft end of the cabin in the No. 1 jumper position, with my US Army instructor sitting next to me.

All went according to plan right up until time for takeoff, when the C-47 pilot announced a problem with the aircraft that required a ground abort. That was the bad news. The good news was that we had a spare C-47 that day, and the mission would continue after a change of equipment. The other bad news was that the spare C-47 was a VIP aircraft that had airline seats instead of troop seats and was not equipped with the steel cable down the cabin for static line attachment. Instead, a heavy nylon loop was tied to a cargo tie down connector on the floor of the aircraft under the left heel of the Thai jump master. We loaded up, and each jumper carefully compressed the spring latch opening the end of the static line hook and connected it to the loop on the floor. I don't remember the details of the hook-up, but it worked and we were all set to go again. The big difference was that the static line was now about four or five feet longer since it was attached to the floor instead of the steel cable at eye height in the cabin. This detail was about to become very important to the rest of my life.

We took off and climbed to jump altitude as the pilot aligned the aircraft for the approach to the jump zone. Upon receiving the signal from the jump master, as the No. 1 jumper I moved to the open door of the aircraft, with my instructor right behind me, and the Thai jump master on my left. I don't really know why what occurred next happened, but the story I was told later is that the Thai NCO confused me and my instructor, assumed I was fully qualified and allowed me to go out the door unsupervised. This was important because the static line extender was attached with a heavy metal clamp. The static line, with its extra length, went out in front of me, formed a loop and I fell head first into it. As the loop tightened it began to peel the flesh from my chest. When it was done I was raw meat from the nipples on my chest to the tip of my chin and my jaw was broken in three places. I was lucky it hadn't ripped my head off.

There was no pain, nor did it knock me out. I had the sensation that my face was somehow distorted, which it was. Nevertheless, I steered my 'chute down to the large white X that had been laid out on the ground. I actually won a case of beer, which I never drank, for landing the closest to the X of all the jumpers.

The team on the ground quickly realized I had been injured, loaded me into a jeep and rushed me to Ubon AB. I eventually ended up in the dental clinic. Squadronmates were all around as the dentist cut my flightsuit off, exposing the raw meat otherwise known as my chest. Next, he administered iodine or some other antibiotic and that was the first time I felt pain. Excruciating pain, and my squadronmates held me back into the dental chair to prevent me from bolting. Thankfully, the burning pain subsided and a fast-paced series of events followed.

Firstly, the US Army awarded me the Jump Wings, but I never wore them. Secondly, I was loaded onto the same C-47 I had jumped out of and flown to the hospital at Korat AB, where I underwent surgery to reduce the mandibular fracture. The surgeons installed arch bars on my upper and lower teeth and then wired them together, using my upper teeth as a splint for the broken lower jaw. Several teeth had been broken off in the accident, including one of my front teeth – probably by the metal buckle from the static line extender. I recovered pretty quickly, and learned that my Air Force Academy classmate and fellow swim team member Rip Blaisdell was also in the Korat hospital. Rip had broken his wrist while playing football during his second or third combat tour, this time flying the F-105.

After a few days I was airlifted to Clark AB on a medical evacuation and then eventually sent on to the hospital at Travis AFB, near San Francisco. All my possessions had been left behind at Ubon. Some eventually found their way to me, but others never did – amongst the things I lost were my 433rd TFS baseball cap, my flying helmet and my "Howdie Hat." Some of my clothing, including my party suit and a 433rd white party shirt, did eventually show up, however.

I was home at last, and instead of my new destination being RAF Bentwaters, I learned that my assignment to England had been cancelled and I was being sent permanently to the Wilford Hall Air Force Hospital in San Antonio, Texas. I was anxious to get home to my family, but had no clue how that would unfold given my hospital pipeline status to San Antonio. I tried to call home but got no answer. By this time I was completely ambulatory and able to negotiate a pass out of the Travis hospital. I called my brother Jim, who was training to become a navigator at Mather AFB near

Sacramento, California, and since it was a weekend and I had a pass, he retrieved me. Our plan was to go to Reno for a couple of days.

Jim duly picked me up and we headed for Reno. We hadn't seen each other in over a year, and a lot had happened to both of us during that time. Jim had finished college at the University of Texas, graduating with an aerospace engineering degree, and was accepted into the Air Force Officer Candidate School (OCS). Upon completion of OCS, he had obtained an assignment to Mather AFB to train as a navigator. He filled me in on all the details and, as brothers do, we swapped "war stories" with great enthusiasm. Jim later completed pilot training and flew both the F-4 and the F-15. As we were approaching Donner Pass on the interstate highway to Reno, he suddenly paused, reached into his pocket and handed me a letter. He said that my wife Jeannie had sent it to him to pass on to me because she knew he would see me soon after my planned arrival in California. The broken jaw had delayed that event by a few weeks. I opened the letter, and within the first paragraph I understood why there had been no answer to the telephone at home. "Dear Gail, I cannot believe you do not already know this but I want a divorce."

We went to Reno, gambled a little, drank too much and returned to the Bay area. Soon, Jim was back at Mather finishing his training and I was back at Travis awaiting my fate. The medical people confirmed that my assignment to RAF Bentwaters had been cancelled and that I would be transported to the hospital in San Antonio on another air evacuation aircraft. After arriving at Wilford Hall I learned that I faced another operation to properly set my jaw. That went without incident and pretty soon I was up and around, anxious to get to Las Vegas and finalize the divorce.

One day I challenged the doctors, who were making their rounds, by asking for a convalescent leave from the hospital. They informed me that I could not survive with my mouth wired shut unless I had hospital care. I asked for a day pass and arranged for a friend in San Antonio to pick me up and take me to the Base Exchange at nearby Lackland AFB. There, I purchased a blender, and on the way back to the hospital, I bought a complete Mexican dinner to go. The next day, when the doctors came around, I told them I could survive outside the hospital and was prepared to demonstrate how. Somewhat amused, they played along and pretty soon I was dumping Mexican food into the blender and adding just enough water to make the concoction a liquid.

My injury included that broken front tooth, which allowed me to insert a straw into my mouth. I had liquid Mexican food for lunch and the doctors said, "Okay, you can have a month's leave. Here are some surgical scissors that you can use to cut the wires on your teeth that are holding your lower jaw to the upper, just in case you start to choke." I was free for a month to go and do exactly what I wanted to. First stop was Las Vegas, and divorce. I was not happy about this, and the process was not a pleasant experience.

The next step was to try to figure out the rest of my life. I traveled to Tucson, Arizona, and visited Davis-Monthan AFB, where I met up with former Lt Col and now full Col "Hoot" Gibson, who had been my first squadron commander at Ubon. Col "Hoot," whose new job was Deputy Commander for Operations of the F-4-equipped 4453rd Combat Crew Training Wing, treated me like a long-lost brother, understood my plight and offered me a job as a Phantom II instructor supporting the Replacement Training Unit (RTU) pipeline for aircrew destined to see combat in

Southeast Asia. Aside from F-4 training that was taking place at Davis-Monthan, there were other Phantom II RTUs at George AFB, near Victorville, California, and at MacDill, where I had been trained. Knowing I had a job flying fighters waiting for me in Tucson, I decided to finish my hospital leave by going to Tampa for a "hospitality check" with Tom Saylor, my original F-4 instructor.

Tom and I had a great time telling war stories and just hanging out. One day, we were going into the Officers' Club at MacDill for lunch when an officer in a red Firebird convertible made a high-speed entry into the club parking lot. Tom said, "Oh, that's 'Firecan.' I want you to meet him!" After those initial greeting formalities were over, "Firecan" looked at me and said, "What's wrong with your mouth?" I was still wired up with the braces. I told him the short version of the story and he said, "No shit?" and I responded in an identical fashion. With that and a few other war stories, "Firecan" and I bonded, but at that point I didn't know it. "Firecan," also known as the "Firelad" and Daniel O'Brien Walsh, became my mentor.

When I got back to Wilford Hall for my final evaluation and to get my braces off, I called the Personnel Center at Randolph to inquire about my future assignment fate. I was told they had been looking all over the Air Force for me to let me know they had received a by-name assignment for me to go to MacDill as an F-4 instructor. Hooray! As it turned out, jumping out of that "Gooney Bird" in Thailand and breaking my jaw was the best thing that ever happened to me in that it set the stage for the rest of my professional life.

The divorce had left me without resources: no car, no house and my meager savings having been cashed in to make the down payment on a property that I no longer owned. But

I did have a job and a steady pay check. So, I went to see my Uncle James who was the President of the Mercantile Bank in San Antonio. He arranged for the financing I required to allow me to purchase a burnt orange-colored Plymouth Barracuda. I have no idea why I selected an orange car with black and white hound's tooth bucket seats, but I did, and I drove that car until I made major and could afford a 1974 Corvette, which I still own to this day.

I showed up at MacDill, was assigned to "Firecan's" squadron and got recurrent in the F-4. When I arrived in Florida I didn't have enough Phantom II flying time to be an instructor according to the TAC rules, so "Firecan" sent me on non-stop TDYs ferrying new aircraft to Europe and moving our F-4s around the US for various improvement modifications, thus building my flight time accordingly.

For the first year or so I lived in the bachelor officers' quarters at MacDill – I had a two-room suite with a kitchenette. My "bachelor pad" became a popular party hang-out for a lot of my friends, along with the girls we met at the Officers' Club on Friday nights. Life was getting really good.

One day we received word that the squadron and the wing at MacDill were being converted into an operational unit and the RTU was being shut down. "Firecan" assigned me the extra duty of mobility officer. It was my job to ensure the squadron was ready to deploy on a moment's notice. I had two young officers, Mike Evans and John Gonda (both navigators and Air Force Academy classmates), along with several very efficient NCOs, on my mobility team. About three months later we absolutely aced a major inspection.

Meanwhile, I was winning a lot of quarters on the gunnery range with the F-4, and I started to lobby for one of those cherished slots attending the FWS at Nellis. "Firecan" had graduated from the F-100 FWS some years earlier, and he proudly wore his "patch" on the left shoulder of his flightsuit. Graduates returned to their fighter squadrons and became the chief instructor responsible for preparing their unit for war. The more time passed the more I wanted an FWS "patch" too. "Firecan" eventually made that happen when he selected me ahead of several other very deserving pilots to go to Nellis for the FWS class that ran from September to December 1970. After FWS, I returned to MacDill and the 46th TFS, which shortly thereafter was re-designated as the 27th TFS. In the late spring of 1972, I received orders to return to Nellis as an air-to-air instructor with the school.

This book has been almost exclusively about combat, so the rest of my career in the Air Force is not a part of that story. Suffice it to say that I enjoyed a 26-year career in the USAF. I instructed at the FWS in the F-4E, was present when the first Air Force aggressor squadron was created and became a full "card-carrying aggressor pilot" flying F-5Es. I then flew as an adversary in a lot of *Red Flag* combat training exercises and had the opportunity to command a USAF squadron of aggressors where we operated real Russian MiG-17s and MiG-21s (I flew both). Check out my book *America's Secret MiG Squadron*, also published by Osprey, for further details. "Firecan" and other senior officers continued to steer my career after that, and I was fortunate to be in charge of operations for the 18th TFW at Kadena AB, Okinawa, where I flew both the F-15C and the RF-4C. Finally, it was a true privilege to command an RF-4 wing in Europe during the height of the Cold War.

Along the way a wonderful woman named Peggy came into my life. She had lost her husband in combat while he was flying out of Cam Ranh Bay in South Vietnam. We seemed to fit perfectly, and after a multi-year courtship she agreed to marriage and blessed me with wonderful support and 27 years of true happiness, along with two absolutely beautiful and loving daughters, Jennifer and Elizabeth. Our family truly came together with my previous family when Peggy agreed to our taking custody of Jack and Kayte, my two older children from my marriage to Jeannie. It was golden. When Peggy and I married we had our wedding reception in Las Vegas at the home of Peggy's close friend Carol. After Peggy's death in 2002, Carol entered my life again and in 2004 we married and are currently living out the dream.

I did have a career of ups and downs, filled with thrills and disappointments, but I routinely landed on my feet and I would eagerly live the entire sequence again given a return to my youth.

> When once you have tasted flight, you will forever walk the earth with your eyes turned skyward, for there you have been, and there you will always long to be.*

Read the final chapter. It is the rest of the story.

*Leonardo da Vinci

15

Final Chapter

Fast forward to the 21st century. I am a retired Air Force civilian instructor assigned contract duties with the 433rd Weapons Squadron (WPS) at the USAF Weapons School at Nellis. It is a position I have held since May 1998. My duties include some teaching and the periodic revision of all F-15C and F-22A academics, syllabi and phase manuals.

I was sitting at my desk when my phone rang. On the other end was the 433rd WPS commander, Lt Col John "Krusty" Kent. He asked me, "Have you ever heard of 433rd guys from the Vietnam timeframe named Wendell Keller and Mike Meroney?" My reply was, "Absolutely. They were squadronmates of mine at Ubon in 1968–69. In fact, I was their wingman the night they were lost."

"Krusty" then told me that their remains had been recovered from a crash site in Laos but were not separable. As a result, they were shipped back to the US in a single casket under an American flag. He went on to elaborate that he had subsequently received a phone call from a colonel at Dover AFB, Delaware, who told him that DNA had been used to separate the remains. Each set, again under new American flags, had now been prepared for shipping to their respective families for a final interment. The colonel had also told "Krusty" that his team had researched the 433rd TFS, found it to be an active squadron at Nellis AFB, and, as a result, he wondered if the unit would be interested in receiving the original flag that repatriated the combined returns.

I went into some detail from my memory about these two officers and their fateful final mission. As the chat was nearing completion, we decided that it would of course be appropriate for the 433rd to accept the flag on behalf of all aircrew lost by the squadron in the Vietnam War. At the time, we envisioned some sort of memorial display being created in the squadron building, with the flag as a center point. The identification team at Dover duly sent an incredibly sharp officer to Nellis to present the flag to the squadron. We had a brief ceremony attended by current 433rd WPS pilots, and I spoke about the circumstances of the loss and then turned the program over to the officer from Dover, who presented the flag to Lt Col Kent.

The next step was to design a fitting memorial display and organize a dedication ceremony. Our graphic artist on the academic support contract team, Christine Biederer, led the way and came up with a design and pencil sketches in the likeness of the two fallen officers. In addition to the flag, it was decided to include other artifacts from the crash site. Time passed and artwork was completed, along with the construction of an appropriate display case.

Families of the two lost officers, as well as squadronmates that lived in the general western United States area, were contacted and a date for the ceremony was set as May 23, 2013. On that date families, former squadronmates from Ubon and current members of the 433rd WPS gathered in the squadron building for the dedication ceremony. I again had a speaking role, my task being to set the stage with a summary of the events we had lived through in Thailand during our time in the Vietnam War. I proceeded as follows:

Gen Strand, Fellow "Satan's Angels" and Friends,
I'm going to lead a little trip down memory lane for those of you that experienced Ubon, Thailand, and the Vietnam War. I will try to paint a picture in your minds for the rest of you here today about the way it was.

During my year there I flew with many great warriors who became lifelong friends. We fought as our Nation directed and we experienced life with a gusto that I have not since known. The 433rd had come to Ubon many years before I was honored to become a member of the squadron. The "Satan's Angels" arrived at Ubon after being constituted at George AFB, California, and then deployed to the war as a unit. I believe J. B. Spencer, who is with us today, was either with that group or followed soon thereafter. Dick Jonas was with us also. It is great to have you both here today.

I arrived at Ubon on a hot and humid day in August 1968 and was met by "D. J." Alberts as I stepped off the C-130 from Bangkok. We went by the 433rd TFS and then to the hooch area. I knew I was going to the 8th TFW at Ubon, but had no previous clue as to squadron assignment. Several of us who got off the C-130 that day were assigned to the 433rd. Others went to the remaining fighter squadrons on base. There were four fighter squadrons at Ubon at that time, the 433rd TFS, 435th TFS, 25th TFS and 497th TFS, the latter being a squadron dedicated to night operations. Additionally, there were O-2 FACs with the call-sign "Nail," and during our time the AC-130 Spectre gunships also arrived.

With our F-4Ds, we fought the enemy in North Vietnam and then in Laos under the control of the FACs, and we also escorted the AC-130 gunships, protecting them from the AAA during their night missions. The Thais operated T-28s from Ubon too. So, it was a busy place for a single 8,000ft-long crowned and grooved runway that was only about 125ft wide. It was grooved to expedite the rain runoff during the monsoon season. The runway had five barriers, plus the "rabbit catcher" barriers at either end. We used them a lot when it was wet.

I flew 20 or so missions into North Vietnam in the weeks that followed my arrival.

One day, my flight commander, Maj Roger Johnson, called a "C" Flight meeting in the hooch day room. Maj Johnson announced to all of us that the 8th TFW's combat tasking for night operations had been increased and would exceed the capacity of the 497th TFS "Night Owls" to fill the schedule. Therefore, a small group of the 433rd aircrews would pick up an expanded and dedicated night mission. The "C" Flight share was one crew, and Maj Johnson asked for a captain aircraft commander to volunteer for this duty. I looked around and realized I was the only captain aircraft commander in the flight. That's how my assigned back seat pilot, Steve Mosier, and I got into the night-flying business.

Night flying had its challenges because it was dark! No one had ever even heard of night vision goggles like you guys have today. The way we checked out was an experienced night crew, in my case consisting of Brian McMahon and Dickie Dull, swapped out with Steve Mosier and me. Dickie got in my back seat and Steve got in Brian's, and I flew on Brian's wing until he felt Steve and I were ready to fly together. Then, Brian started checking Steve and me out as flight leaders. When that was done, Brian and Dickie went back to day flying and Steve and I started the same routine to check out Norm Fogg and Roger Govett at night. Once Norm and Roger were up to speed and checked out, we flew together just about every night, taking turns as leaders.

There were a lot of mostly illegal, but memorable, events on those night sorties, like post-strike basic fighter maneuver training over Ubon using minimum afterburner so we could keep track of each other.

One night mission in particular stands out in my memory. I think Norm was leading and we were fragged into North Vietnam to conduct armed recce along the coastal highway. We were cleared to attack any targets we came across. The weather was pretty rotten that night, so we went out over the Gulf of Tonkin and let down through the clouds in close formation over the water, using our radar altimeters to gauge our height above the sea. We broke out under about a 500ft ceiling, and the backseaters used the map mode of our radar to find the point on the coast for the start of our recce. Once that was sorted out Norm directed me to drop back a couple miles in trail behind him. He was carrying flares and I had CBU-2s, which dispensed bomblets like dropping little hand grenades. Norm's job was to find any movers along the highway and drop a flare so I could see the target. Then I was to lay down a carpet of death on the movers as I flew over them, all of this happening under the 500 to 1,000ft ceiling in pitch black, other than the light from the expected flare.

The backseaters were truly busy, with the lead navigating and Steve using our air-to-air radar to keep track of Norm. It was one helluva plan. We took some AAA, especially Steve and me back in trail. Norm woke them up so they could shoot at the wingman, but it was all pretty much barrage fire versus aimed fire, and therefore low threat. We didn't see "Jack" and ended up jettisoning our ordnance because you couldn't bring CBU-2s home. It was judged to be too dangerous because of the nature of the munitions and the dispenser. The bomblets had a propensity to hang up in the exit chute of the dispenser. The last thing we needed was a bomblet falling to the ground upon landing and blowing up under the jet during the landing roll. No BDA that night, but it was a memorable experience nevertheless, and we swore we would NEVER do it again.

The dusk and dawn patrols were a different story. We were high enough that it was daylight where we were and bad guys could see us. It was pitch black on the ground, however, and all we could see were AAA muzzle flashes and any fires that we got going off with the explosion of our ordnance.

We usually landed late at night, debriefed intel and headed for the Officers' Club at Ubon for dinner and refreshments. There wasn't much else to do. The club was open 24 hours a day, seven days a week. The bar was large and usually well attended. Most nights, there were four, five, or six craps dice games going on in the back room bar, while the dining room offered a complete menu. Our least favorite waitress was a young Thai girl we came to call "Two Step." She would go to great extremes to take our orders for dinner, turn around toward the kitchen, take two steps, forget the entire order and bring everyone a chili-cheese omelet.

Lt Col (later Gen) Bill "Padre" Strand was our Operations Officer in the 433rd at Ubon, and as we flew more and more at night we got better and better at beating up the bad guys. This made the squadron look good and made Bill Strand happy. We had come to call ourselves sewer rats because we did our job in the dark like rodents in the bowels of an underground sewer. One day, the "Padre" was bragging about our night efforts, and he referred to us as his "Sewer Doers." So, J. J. Winters, one of our young back seat pilots, designed an appropriate emblem and we had patches made up for our flightsuits and plaques for us to subsequently hang on the walls of our "I love me" dens at home. We felt good about the job we were doing. When I talked to Dickie Dull the day before this dedication, he reminded me that out by the original "Inferno" squadron bar in the hooch area at Ubon was a stolen manhole cover placed in a conspicuous place to recognize the "Sewer Doers."

In addition to Wendell Keller and Mike Meroney, who are specifically remembered today with this dedication ceremony, Dickie Dull also reflected on "Jeb Sewart," Paul Bannon and Peter Pike – three other "Satan's Angels" we lost during the 1968–69 period that I was at Ubon. Dickie went on to say, "I do know that those of us who cannot be there in person will all be there strong in thought, heart and prayer – prayers of thankfulness that these two warriors can be honored today."

Returning to the tales about Ubon, the O-2 FACs stationed there were often the same guys we were working with in Laos, and as evenings progressed so did the rivalries. We had a favorite bar game that some called "sockey" and others call "hocker." It was sort of a combination of soccer and hockey. Instead of a ball or a puck, we used a crushed beer can, and the tool to move the beer can was the combat boot. Two bar stools at each end of the barroom were the goals. Fighter pilots versus FACs was the name of the game. Just to make it more interesting a couple of pitchers of beer were usually splashed on the barroom floor to get it nice and slippery. And then the tournament began. Sometimes, as the cock crowed and sun crept over the eastern horizon at dawn, a colonel or two would wander through the bar, shake their heads at the carnage before them and continue on their way to breakfast.

So, thus it was. A year of intense combat, some terrifying and some routine. We interrupted the sequence of great adventures with a lot of rowdy behavior, moustaches that far exceeded regulations, letters received and letters written home. We loved Jefferson Airplane and songs like "Downtown" and "We Gotta Get Out of this Place." They were the days of our youth. I finished my night detail and started flying days, mostly dropping laser-guided 2,000lb bombs that were guided by our laser designator crews, one of whom was Col Earl Haney, who is here with us today.

"Mr Earl" and I always synced well together in the air, seldom having to sort out on the radio what to do next. We grooved and I enjoyed flying with him, as well as the change of pace from night flying.

But, they were not all good days. My lifelong friend "J. D." Allen was the normal night partner for the night crew of Wendell Keller and Mike Meroney. "J. D." went to Bangkok for a few days of much needed R&R, and I was scheduled to fly Keller and Meroney's wing on that night sortie on March 1, 1969.

At this point I turned the microphone over to Lt Col Kent for appropriate words and the formal unveiling and dedication of the memorabilia and the US Flag that covered the single casket on the homeward trip of Wendell Keller and Mike Meroney. Christine Biederer made the memorial display happen. She did a magnificent job in the design and supervision of the memorial, and all who were present were amazed at the product.

Family members expressed their gratitude with heart-rending comments, we drank a toast to those no longer with us, and when we were done with formalities, our fighter pilot colleague and professional music writer and musician Dick Jonas led a traditional 433rd "song fest" with all of his bawdy creations from the past and present. The very capable young airmen from the Nellis *Bullseye* newspaper recorded the event in the following article:

433rd WPS welcomes home, honors fallen wingmen

Posted 6/4/2013 Updated 6/4/2013
by Staff Sgt. Michael Charles
99th Air Base Wing Public Affairs

6/4/2013 – **NELLIS AIR FORCE BASE, Nev.** Airmen from the 433rd Weapons Squadron held a heritage hallway dedication May 23 at the US Air Force Weapons School for two recently repatriated Airmen who were missing in action following their service in the Vietnam War.

Citing the need to honor their fallen comrades, the 433rd WPS invited past wingmen and family members of Col Wendell R. Keller and Capt Virgil K. Meroney to the dedication. "It is important to take time to reflect and honor our fallen comrades that have made the ultimate sacrifice in service to their country," said Lt Col John Kent, 433rd WPS commander.

The F-4D Phantom II pilot Maj Wendell R. Keller and WSO 1Lt Virgil K. Meroney, assigned to 433rd Tactical Fighter Squadron at Ubon Royal Thai Air Force Base, Thailand, were tasked with a night interdiction mission against a heavily defended supply route and storage area complex near the Ban Karai Pass, on the border between Laos and Vietnam, on March 1, 1969. During this mission Keller, Meroney and their wingman from the 433rd TFS came under fire. Keller and Meroney attacked and destroyed the threatening enemy gun positions. Their aircraft was hit by hostile fire and crashed during the attack. There were no parachutes seen or emergency beacons sent. Keller and Meroney were declared Missing In Action.

"It [March 1, 1969] was not a good day," said retired Air Force Col Gail Peck, former Tonopah commander and 433rd TFS member. "These weren't just my wingmen, they were my brothers."

The Department of Defense announced that it had found the remains of Keller and Meroney and would be returning them home in October 2012. However, due to the time and the effects of the elements, their remains had fused to each other, requiring them to be transferred to Dover Air Force Base, Delaware, in one coffin and covered by a single

American flag. Once the remains were separated, a flag was presented to each family to honor their loss. The single flag that covered the coffin of Keller and Meroney during transfer was donated to the 433rd WPS for its newly dedicated heritage hall and a shadow box was constructed by the 99th Force Support Squadron Arts and Craft Center filled with pictures and personal items from the men.

"When asked by Dover Mortuary Affairs if our squadron would like to display the flag that covered our two comrades on their trip home, I responded with four words, 'We would be honored,'" Kent said. "With their help, and that of the arts and craft center, we were able to create a memorial which depicts the importance of honoring those who have lost their lives in the line of duty."

The families also took an opportunity to meet squadron members and share a few words. "For years I wished my father would come home; now he has," said Michael Keller, son of Col Keller. "Now he will never be forgotten."

"My brother was proud to serve in the military," said Doug Meroney, who was noticeably fighting back tears. "A veteran is somebody who writes a check to the nation for the amount of up to that individual's life. Both Col Keller and my brother are heroes, and I couldn't be more proud of both of them."

The two were interned into Arlington National Cemetery in Washington, D.C., in October 2012 in a group burial. According to Doug Meroney, the families came to the conclusion that it was only fitting that the two enter Arlington the same way they have spent the last 40+ years – together.

As of May 29, 2013, following the repatriation of Keller and Meroney, there are still five 433rd TFS personnel listed under the Department of Defense classification of Missing In Action from the Vietnam War.

The old 433rd guys who were able to make the event sat around after the formal ceremony, drank a few cocktails with the much younger F-15C and F-22 instructor pilots from the 433rd WPS, and relived moments from their past.

The words of Ford Smartt remind us of our profession and of the deeds of our past: "A fighter jock is quite a phenomenon."*

We thought those days would never end.

But, they did.

---

*The rest of Mr. Smartt's observations, in the essay entitled "What Is A Fighter Pilot," can be viewed on the website https://fightersweep.com.

Appendices

APPENDIX 1

The 433rd Weapons Squadron
Satan's Angels

Vietnam Memorial Dedication

In Honor of

Col Wendell R. Keller,
Capt Virgil K. Meroney III,
and all of the fallen members of the 433 TFS

23 May 2013

<u>Attending Family</u>

Mike Keller
Son of Wendell Keller

Kelly Meroney
Son of "Mike" Meroney

Doug Meroney
Brother of "Mike" Meroney

Program

Welcome
Col (Ret) Gail "Evil" Peck

Opening Comments
Lt Col John "Krusty" Kent
Commander, 433rd WS

Family Comments
Doug Meroney
Brother of 'Mike' Meroney

Mike Keller
Son of Wendell Keller

Revealing of the Memorial

Reception

The 433 TFS in Vietnam

The 433 Tactical Fighter Squadron, was deployed to Ubon Royal Thai Air Force Base in December 1965, becoming part of Pacific Air Forces Thirteenth Air Force. The 433rd was assigned to the 8th Tactical Fighter Wing and engaged in combat operations over Southeast Asia. The squadron's mission included bombardment, ground support, air defense, interdiction, and armed reconnaissance.

Beginning in May 1967, the 433rd was reequipped with new F-4D aircraft. This gave the unit the distinction of being the first in Southeast Asia to be operationally equipped with the improved Phantom II. In May 1968, the squadron employed laser-guided bombs (LGBs) in combat for the first time. During its final years of combat, the unit used F-4Ds for fast-forward air control, interdiction, escort, armed reconnaissance, and other special missions. The squadron continued combat in Vietnam until mid-January 1973, in Laos until 22 February 1973, and in Cambodia until 15 August 1973. Satan's Angels remained in Thailand until July 1974 when the squadron was inactivated.

01 MARCH 1969

On March 1, 1969, the 433rd Tactical Fighter Squadron was tasked with a night combat mission over Laos. The 433rd F4D Phantom departed from Ubon RTAFB, Thailand and was piloted by Maj Wendell R. Keller and weapons systems officer (WSO) 1Lt Virgil K. Meroney.

Keller and Meroney were tasked with a night interdiction mission against a heavily defended supply route and storage area complex near the Ban Karai Pass. During this mission Keller and Meroney and their wingman came under fire. Keller and Meroney attacked and destroyed the threatening enemy gun positions. During the attack Keller and Meroney's aircraft was hit by hostile fire and crashed. No parachutes were seen and no emergency beacons were heard. Keller and Meroney were declared missing in action.

On 15 October, 2012, the Department of Defense announced that their remains had been recovered and identified. Repatriation of Col Wendell Keller and Capt Virgil K. Meroney III's remains was completed on 19 October 2012.

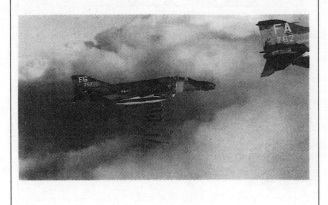

Col Wendell R. Keller

Wendell Keller was born on 19 May 1934 in Fargo, North Dakota. An avid model airplane builder as a youth, Wendell pursued a lifelong interest in aviation and electronics. He majored in Electrical Engineering at NDSU and graduated with an AF ROTC commission in 1956. Following pilot training in Texas and Oklahoma, Keller flew F-86's at Sioux City, Iowa; C-21's at McClellan AFB, Ca; and F-101's in Grand Forks, ND. As American involvement in Vietnam escalated, Wendell volunteered to fly F-4's in support of the war effort and was assigned 433rd Tactical Fighter Squadron in September 1968. Keller is remembered by those who knew him as a man of few words who was always gentle and caring towards his family. Wendell is survived by his wife Jacqueline, and his two sons, Greg & Mike. Wendell Keller was posthumously promoted to the rank of Colonel.

Capt Virgil K. Meroney III

Virgil "Mike" Meroney was born on 22 May 1943 in Pine Bluff, Arkansas. He was commissioned a 2d Lt through the Air Force ROTC Program on 21 March 1967, and was awarded his pilot wings at Webb AFB, Texas, in March 1968. After completing F-4 Phantom II Combat Crew Training and F-4 Pilot Systems Operator training, Lt Meroney was assigned to the 433rd Tactical Fighter Squadron of the 8th Tactical Fighter Wing at Ubon Royal Thai AFB, Thailand. Meroney's father, Col Virgil K. Meroney (1921-1980), was a World War II fighter ace and flew two combat missions with his son in Southeast Asia before Mike was killed in action. Mike is survived by his wife Connie (1944-2008), son Kelly, and daughter Kim. Mike Meroney was posthumously promoted to the rank of Captain.

433 TFS POW/MIA/KIA

1965
Capt Robert D Jeffrey---POW-R
1Lt George I. Mims Jr.---KIA-BNR

1966
Major Samuel R. Johnson---POW-R
Capt Larry J. Chesley---POW-R
Capt Donald L. King---MIA
1Lt Frank Ralston III---MIA
Capt Armand V. Meyers---POW-R
1Lt J.L. Borling---POW-R
Capt Douglas B. Peterson---POW-R
1Lt Pernard L. Talley---POW-R
Capt. William R. Andrew---KIA-RR 1990

1967
Lt Col Frederick A. Crow---POW-R
1Lt Henry Fowler---POW-R
1Lt Charles D. Austin---MIA
Maj Herman L. Knapp---MIA
Maj Jack VanLoan---POW-R
1Lt Joseph Milligan---POW-R
1Lt Richard Brazik---KIA-BNR
Capt Richard Claflin---KIA-BNR

1968
1Lt John H. Crews---MIA
Capt Dean P. St Pierre---MIA
Col C. Crumpler---POW-R
Capt Mike T. Burns---POW-R

1969
Maj Wendell R. Keller---KIA-RR
1Lt Virgil K. Meroney III---KIA-RR
1Lt Peter X. Pike---KIA-BNR
Maj Paul Bannon---KIA-BNR
1Lt Grant Stewart---KIA

<u>433 TFS POW/MIA/KIA</u>

<u>1970</u>
Capt Albin E. Lucki—MIA
1Lt Robert A. Gomez—MIA

<u>1971</u>
Maj Lawrence G. Stolz—KIA-BR
1LT Dale F. Koons—KIA-BR

<u>1972</u>
1Lt James McCarthy—KIA-RR
Capt Charles Jackson—POW-R

<u>Abbreviations</u>
BNR—Body Not Recovered
BR-Body Recovered
RR—Remains Repatriated
R—Repatriated

<u>High Flight</u>

Oh! I have slipped the surly bonds of Earth
And danced the skies on laughter-silvered wings;
Sunward I've climbed, and joined the tumbling mirth
Of sun-split clouds, — and done a hundred things
You have not dreamed of — wheeled and soared and swung
High in the sunlit silence. Hov'ring there,
I've chased the shouting wind along, and flung
My eager craft through footless halls of air. . . .

Up, up the long, delirious burning blue
I've topped the wind-swept heights with easy grace
Where never lark, or ever eagle flew —
And, while with silent, lifting mind I've trod
The high untrespassed sanctity of space,
Put out my hand, and touched the face of God.

— John Gillespie Magee, Jr

APPENDIX 2

The following note was sent to me from the squadron after my broken jaw event.

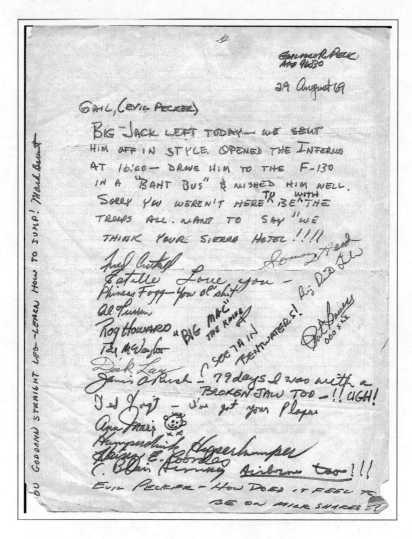

APPENDIX 3

Typical Flying Schedule

This was sent to me, with the note in Appendix 2 on the reverse side. The handwritten note from "Mr. Earl" is from squadronmate Earl Haney, who was teasing me by suggesting that I would need a Standardization Check Ride (for poor judgment?) in the *Barrel Roll* area of Laos following my post-combat tour broken jaw "caper" while parachuting with the US Army in an attempt to get my Jump Wings.

C. O. TRAYLOR	8TFW DAILY SCHEDULE 433rd FPS		DATE: 30 AUG 67		
			WG AIRCREW MEETING 1200 & 1600		
MOBILE	0900-1200	ROSE	25th SQDN BRF ROOM.		
TOWER	1200-1500	FISHER			
	1500-1800	WILLIAMS	DRIVER's REFRESHER BRIEFING		
DUTY	0700-1230	SORENBERGER	THEATRE 1500		
	1230-1800	WOODELL			
	1800-END	BENDLIN	JUSMAG VOLLEYBALL 1530		
			TRUCK DEPARTS HOOTCH 1515		
	AC	PILOT		AC	PILOT
0630/0700 BENNETT	ARNBERGER VOIGT *	JOHNSON WESTON	1530/1600 COACH	FOGG ALLEN PRICE	MCCLEAD KANASTER LARSON
BR Cov			*ESC*		
0730/0800 COBALT	COL DRIVEN L/C MCCLURE	WARNER HUBERT	1600 T/O SATAN	VAYDA	MEYER
BR Cov					
0930/1000 BANYAN	HANEY MCINERNEY HOWARD	LAW PILL CLASON			
0930/1000 HORNET	TURRIN DINGMAN L/C ALBRITTON	DAVISON HENNEMAN JACKSON			
			Mr Earl		
	APPROVED BY:				
	James P. Albritton				
	JAMES P. ALBRITTON, Lt Col, USAF Operations Officer			1st day	
	* THEATRE INDOCTRINATION CHECK				

8TFW (SCOTT) Form 0-73, 12 Jul 58

APPENDIX 4

Citation to Accompany the Award of the Silver Star to Gaillard R. Peck, Jr

Capt Gaillard R. Peck, Jr distinguished himself by gallantry in connection with military operations against an opposing armed force in Southeast Asia on January 25, 1969. On that date, Capt Peck, an aircraft commander of an F-4D Phantom II, conducted a most determined and heroic series of attacks against a lethal concentration of anti-aircraft defenses. These defenses had been established as a deadly trap and had succeeded in destroying several aircraft just prior to this mission. Disregarding all considerations of his own personal safety, Capt Peck made repeated devastating attacks against the gun positions until the threat was eliminated. In doing so he was subjected to some of the most intense and accurate anti-aircraft artillery fire ever experienced by aircrews in Southeast Asia. These actions enabled subsequent missions of great importance to the United States Air Force to be successfully conducted. By his gallantry and devotion to duty, Capt Peck has reflected great credit upon himself and the United States Air Force.

APPENDIX 5

F-4 Tailcodes, Ubon RTAFB, circa 1967–72[*]

The following two-digit letters were painted on the vertical stabilizer of aircraft assigned to the respective fighter squadrons within the 8th TFW:

FA – 25th TFS

FG – 433rd TFS

FO – 435th TFS

FP – 497th TFS

[*]nam.wz.cz/letadla/tailcodes_usaf.html

Glossary

ACRONYMS

AAA	Anti-Aircraft Artillery
ABCCC	Airborne Battlefield Command & Control Center
ACM	Air Combat Maneuvering
ADC	Air Defense Command
ADI	Attitude Directional Indicator
AFB	Air Force Base
AGL	Above Ground Level
AGM	Air-to-Ground Missile
AID	Agency for International Development
ATO	Air Tasking Order
BDA	Bomb Damage Assessment
BFM	Basic Fighter Maneuvers
CBU	Cluster Bomb Unit
CIA	Central Intelligence Agency
DFC	Distinguished Flying Cross
DMZ	Demilitarized Zone
EGT	Exhaust Gas Temperature

FAC	Forward Air Controller
GBU	Guided Bomb Unit
GCA	Ground-Controlled Approach
GCI	Ground-Controlled Intercept
"GIBs"	Guys in Back
GPS	Global Positioning System
ID	Identification
INS	Inertial Navigation System
IP	Instructor Pilot
IR	Infrared
KIA	Killed in Action
LADD	Low-Angle Drogue Delivery (nuclear weapon)
LGB	Laser-Guided Bomb
LORAN	Long Range Navigation
MAP PPI	F-4 radar mode for mapping
MARS	Military Affiliated Radio System
MER	Multiple Ejector Rack (up to six bombs)
MIA	Missing in Action
MSL	Mean Seal Level
NCO	Non-Commissioned Officer (enlisted)
NKP	Nakhon Phanom RTAFB
NVA	North Vietnamese Army
OCS	Officer Candidate School
"PDJ"	Plaine des Jarres
PIT	Pilot Instructor Training
POL	Petroleum, Oil, Lubricants

PoW	Prisoner of War
RoE	Rules of Engagement
RPM	revolutions per minute (calibrated in percent in US jets)
RSU	Runway Supervisory Unit
RTAFB	Royal Thai Air Force Base
RTU	Replacement Training Unit
SAC	Strategic Air Command
SAM	Surface-to-Air Missile
SAR	Search and Rescue
SOS	Squadron Officer's School
TAC	Tactical Air Command
TDY	Temporary Duty
TER	Triple Ejector Rack (three bombs)
TFA	Task Force Alpha
TFW	Tactical Fighter Wing
TOC	Tactical Operations Center
UHF	Ultra-High Frequency
UPT	Undergraduate Pilot Training
USAF	United States Air Force
WSO	Weapon Systems Operator

TERMS

1st, 2nd, 3rd, 4th Class – Classes of cadets (1st Class – Seniors) at the Air Force Academy

"Alleycat" – Night call-sign for (northern orbit) C-130 ABCCC

Arc Light – SAC B-52 bombing raids

Arm – Master switch setting (on), enabling delivery of ordnance

"Bam-bam" – GBU guidance system (controls only go to full deflection)

Barrel Roll – Combat theater in northern Laos

Bingo – Fuel state mandating either return to base or aerial refueling

"Blind Bat" – Call-sign for the EC-130E flare aircraft

"Blue Chip" – Call-sign for Seventh Air Force command post in Saigon that issued the ATO or daily frag order

Bolo – Mission devised and led (on January 2, 1967) by Col Robin Olds, CO of the 8th TFW, that inflicted heavy losses on North Vietnamese MiGs

Button – Term used inflight by flight lead pilots for commanding the other fighters to change to preset UHF radio frequencies (as in "Pintail, go Button 3" or "Button 13," etc.)

"Cherry Anchor" – Aerial refueling orbit northeast of Ubon along the Mekong River

Constant Peg – USAF training program in Nevada using actual MiG fighters as adversaries

"Cricket" – Day call-sign for (northern orbit) C-130 ABCCC

Delta Point – Commonly used classified geographic locations on the ground in the combat area of responsibility. It was used for rendezvousing with FACs and other targeting

Downwind – Position in either the gunnery or landing traffic pattern that is 180 degrees opposite the landing or ordnance delivery direction

"Feet Wet" – Flight position over water

Gain – Radar rheostat switch used for refining a radar return

Guard – Emergency radio frequency of 121.5 VHF and 243.0 UHF

"Hillsboro" – Day call-sign for (southern orbit) C-130 ABCCC

Hooch – Our nickname for our billets at Ubon

"Hot" – Word used to indicate that an impending delivery pass would expend ordnance. Can also mean excessively fast, as in a join-up into formation or in an aerial attack, either visually or using radar

Igloo White – Codename for Secretary of Defense McNamara's plan to seed the Ho Chi Minh Trail in Laos with sensors to detect truck traffic

Jink – Aggressive maneuvering by a fighter designed to spoil a gun attack from either another aircraft or AAA on the ground

"Judy" – Radio call made by a fighter to ground radar indicating the fighter has radar contact with the target, is taking over the intercept and is expecting no further assistance from the GCI controller

Koch – Fasteners used to connect seat belts and aircrew harnesses to the ejection seat and parachute

Linebacker – Bombing campaign against North Vietnam that started on May 9, 1972

"Lion" – Call-sign for the GCI radar at Ubon RTAFB

"Mayday" – Radio call indicating a dire emergency in flight

"Misty" – Call-sign of F-100F FACs

"Moonbeam" – Night call-sign for (southern orbit) C-130 ABCCC

"Nail" – Call-sign of the O-2 FACs stationed at Ubon RTAFB

"Pappa Wolf" – Nickname for the leader of the "Wolf" FACs at Ubon RTAFB

Pave Knife – An experimental laser designator carried into combat in Route Package VI that enabled aircraft to both designate a target and drop an LGB on it

Pave Spike – A follow-on operational laser designator that enabled the carrying aircraft to both designate a target and drop an LGB on it

Paveway – Original LGB program using the "Zot box" laser designator and employed by the 433rd TFS as early as 1968

"Pickle" – Directive for the pilot to push the button on the control stick that releases weapons

"Pintail" – One of the flight call-signs assigned to the 433rd TFS for combat operations

"Raven" – Call-sign used by CIA FACs in *Barrel Roll*

Red Flag – Combat training exercise at Nellis AFB invented by then Lt Col "Moody" Suter

Rolling Thunder – Bombing campaign against North Vietnam that ended on November 1, 1968

Route Package – North Vietnam was divided into geographic sectors called Route Packages. Route Package I was closest to the DMZ. Route Package VI had two parts, VIA Hanoi (USAF target area) and VIB Haiphong (US Navy target area)

"Sherman" – One of the call-signs assigned to the 433rd TFS for combat operations

Skip – Low-altitude delivery typically used with non-finned napalm

Spectre – Call-sign assigned to the AC-130 for combat operations

Steel Tiger – Combat theater in southern Laos

Strafe – Gun attack against a target on the ground

Switchology – The "art" of having the correct switch settings for the intended delivery of ordnance

Sync – Synchronize (function of aligning the INS)

"Tally Ho" – The area of Route Package I that was just north of the DMZ

"Winchester" – Radio call indicating that an aircraft was out of ammunition or ordnance

"Wolf" – Flight call-sign, plus a number, assigned to the 8th TFW "Wolf" FACs for combat operations

"Zot box" – Laser designator used with the Paveway LGB system

List of Illustrations

6   While an instructor pilot in the T-38 at Randolph I was the squadron information officer, and in that capacity I had the privilege of flying author Herbert Molloy Mason, Jr in the back seat of the T-38 on several missions. I subsequently made the cover of his book. (*Gail Peck collection*)

7   1Lts Grant "Jeb" Stewart, Bill Schnittger and Steve Mosier were three of the back-seat F-4 pilots in my RTU at MacDill AFB, Florida. They were photographed with their faces suitably camouflaged during our survival school course at Fairchild AFB, Washington. "Jeb" Stewart was later killed in action on May 17, 1969. (*Steve Mosier collection*)

8   My jungle survival school class (both officers and NCOs) pose for a group photograph with one of our Negrito instructors near Mount Pinatubo, on the Philippine island of Luzon. Steve Mosier is standing fourth from the right in the back row, and I am on Steve's left. (*Gail Peck collection*)

9   Legendary World War II ace Col Robin Olds is carried on the shoulders of his men to the Officers' Club at Ubon after completing his final combat mission as CO of the 8th TFW on September 23, 1967. At the party that was held to celebrate his "100th," Olds gave his crews a detailed summary of his time at Ubon, listing the many achievements but also naming all 72 men who had been shot down during that period, and warning his audience to stay alert and avoid complacency. The influence he had on the "Wolf Pack" was still very much in evidence when I joined the wing almost exactly a year later to the day. (*Gail Peck collection*)

10 An aerial view of the 8th TFW's flightline revetments at Ubon AB. These were hastily built at Thai air bases to protect the aircraft from sabotage following a series of devastating attacks by the Viet Cong on airfields in South Vietnam. The risk of such attacks in South Vietnam became so great that "wonder arch" steel and concrete shelters were eventually erected to deter sapper and rocket attacks – these were never seen in Thailand. Post-war, some of the disused steel-walled revetment components at South Vietnamese bases were shipped to North Vietnam for MiG airfields. (*Gail Peck collection*)

twin pusher/puller engines gave it an 80mph speed advantage over the single-engined O-1 Bird Dog. The O-2A could also carry more weapons, but it was less maneuverable. Ubon not only hosted O-2As from the 23rd Tactical Air Support Squadron (the aircraft seen here, flying over Laos, was from this unit), but also a detachment of B-models from the 9th Air Commando Squadron. The aircraft of the latter unit were modified for psychological warfare, dropping leaflets and broadcasting propaganda messages as a "voice in the sky." (*Gail Peck collection*)

18 Mk 82 500lb GP bombs with conical fins are seen pre-loaded on a TER. The nearest F-4D is armed with Mk 82 bombs with 36in. "daisy cutter" fuse extenders. Note also the AN/ALQ-87 ECM pod on an adapter carried in the jet's forward Sparrow missile well. Col Olds noted that the advent of ECM pod-equipped F-4Ds from May 8, 1967 improved the 8th TFW's combat situation, as it became possible to escort F-105 Thunderchiefs to high-risk targets in the Hanoi SAM belt in bomb-armed Phantom IIs. (*Peter E. Davies collection*)

19 A pair of bombed-up 433rd TFS F-4Ds take their turn on a KC-135's air refueling boom. The aircraft on the left appears to have completed refueling, as excess JP 4 is venting from its starboard wing "overflow" pipe. Night-time refueling was one of the biggest challenges for an F-4 crew, helped by a pattern of color-coded lights beneath the tanker to assist in positioning the fighter. The "boomer" was also in radio contact with the F-4, and color-coded markings on the boom assisted positioning in daylight. (*Peter E. Davies collection*)

20 A mountain pass on the border with Laos looking into North Vietnam. The steep karst protrusions that dominate this panoramic view were an extreme hazard to flying at night or in poor visibility, and to any aircrew who landed on their sharp surfaces after bailing out of a stricken aircraft. F-105D pilot and MiG killer 1Lt Karl Richter was among several pilots who died from injuries sustained after hitting a karst following a parachute descent. (*Gordy Jenkins*)

21 Some said the North Vietnamese called us "Yankee Air Pirates," so we had patches that proudly proclaimed this manufactured locally for our flight suits. (*Gail Peck collection*)

an airman, prepares to hose down a fellow "Satan's Angel" who has just returned from his final combat mission. (*Mike Davison collection*)

30   Dickie Dull skillfully hurdles a beer can pyramid that has been carefully assembled on one of the sidewalks in the party hooch area during a squadron pig roast. The pyramid became a challenge to the former track athletes among us, with many vaulting it between beers and while waiting for the pig to cook. (*Gail Peck collection*)

31   Wendell Keller (bottom right) and Grant "Jeb" Stewart (standing in the center of the photograph holding a newspaper) at one of the squadron pig roasts. Sadly, both pilots were killed in action in 1969. (*Gail Peck collection*)

32   8th TFW staff officers, and friends, prepare to board the base C-47 prior to heading to the Red River Valley Fighter Pilots' Association tactics conference at Udorn AB, followed by a party in Bangkok, in the early summer of 1969. (*Gail Peck collection*)

33   For $5.00, "Sideburns" – a bartender at the Officers' Club at Ubon – created pencil portraits from our "I love me, the war hero" photographs. (*Gail Peck collection*)

34   A "Satan's Angels'" F-4D loaded with Mk 82 bombs on the inboard pylons, each with "daisy cutter" fuse extenders, and standard Mk 82s on the centerline station. (*Peter E. Davies collection*)

35   Jeannie, Jack and Kayte bidding me farewell from Las Vegas after Christmas leave in January 1969, midway through my tour of duty at Ubon. (*Gail Peck collection*)

36   Maj Wendell Keller, left, with the "Howdy Hat," and his backseat pilot 1Lt "Little Mike" Meroney, the crew of "Sherman Lead" that fateful night of March 1, 1969. (*Meroney family collection*)

37   F-4D 66-7750, which was my assigned jet, provides an impressive backdrop for my squadron photograph at Ubon. The aircraft was a MiG killer for the 433rd TFS's Maj William L. Kirk and 1Lt Theodore R. Bongartz as "Buick 01" on October 24, 1967. They brought down the 921st Fighter Regiment MiG-21 flown by Dong Van Song (who ejected

safely) using their external SUU-23/A gun pod – the two AIM-7s that Kirk had fired moments earlier both missed the target. The Phantom II was later transferred to the Republic of Korea Air Force following post-Vietnam War service with USAFE and the USAF Reserve's 507th Tactical Fighter Group. (*Gail Peck collection*)

38   These Mk 82 low-drag general purpose bombs have been fitted with "daisy cutter" fuse extenders to make them explode above ground for maximum blast effect, rather than burying themselves in soft terrain and then detonating. Originally conceived as a field modification using lengths of water pipe, the extensions (in 18, 24 or more usually 36in. versions) used an M904 fuse and wiring on a variety of bomb types. On "Wolf Pack" F-4Ds, they were usually carried on the inboard TERs, combined with Mk 82s with standard M904 nose fuses on the centerline MER. (*Peter E. Davies collection*)

39   The "Disappearing River" – a target on the North Vietnamese/Laotian border. What looks like the mouth of a cave in the jungle-covered hillock in the center of the photograph appears to have been bombed in the recent past. (*Gail Peck collection*)

40   1Lt "Little Mike" Meroney poses with a T-38 from the 3560th FTW at Webb AFB, Texas, during his pilot training in 1967–68. (*Meroney family collection*)

41   P-47 ace Col Virgil K. "Mike" Meroney, 8th TFW vice commander, and his son 1Lt "Little Mike" Meroney flew a mission together from Ubon on January 14, 1969. This event was recorded by a USAF photographer. (*Meroney family collection*)

42   The small cadre of 8th TFW "Wolf" FACs in 1968–69. "Pappa Wolf" CO Maj Ray Battle is standing in the back row, far right, with Maj Paul Bannon to his right and 1Lt Steve Mosier at far right in the front row. (*Steve Mosier collection*)

43   The "Satan's Angels'" bar in the squadron hooch area at Ubon, built almost exclusively by the backseaters (specifically 1Lts Mike "Ghost" Davison and "Jeb" Stewart). The bar sign has been "zapped" in the bottom left corner by visiting pilots from Sabre-equipped No. 79 Sqn, Royal Australian

Air Force. This unit flew from Ubon in the airfield defense role between May 1962 and August 1968. (*Mike Davison collection*)

44 "Pappa Wolf" Maj Ray Battle nurses F-4D 66-0249 back to Ubon after its nose was shot off by AAA near Tchepone, Laos, on November 18, 1968. His backseater, 1Lt Kenny Boone, ejected from the aircraft while Ray struggled to regain control. Kenny was rescued the next day after spending the night in the Laotian jungle. (*Bob Irvine collection*)

45 "Pappa Wolf" wisely chose to extend the F-4's tail hook in the hope he could engage the approach end barrier upon landing at Ubon. The main landing gear was disabled, probably as a result of the AAA hit, forcing Maj Battle to land the jet on its belly. The tail hook failed to engage the approach end barrier wire, and instead the jet careened down the runway on its belly. (*Bob Irvine collection*)

46 Maj Battle eventually departed Ubon's narrow runway in a huge cloud of dust and dirt, before finally coming to a stop not too far away from one of the 8th TFW's two C-47s. It took more than two-and-a-half years to return 66-0249 to airworthiness, the jet resuming service with the 8th TFW in June 1971. (*Bob Irvine collection*)

47 F-4D 66-8815 was one of eleven D-models fitted with the AVQ-9 Pave Light "Zot box" laser designator (seen here attached to the inside of the rear left canopy rail) to "lase" guided bombs while the aircraft maintained an orbit to the left and another F-4D dropped its LGB into the laser "basket" to home onto the laser mark on the target. (*Peter E. Davies collection*)

48 With its "Satan's Angels" squadron insignia proudly displayed on its left air intake, F-4D 66-7639 cuts through the clouds with a combat camera hung under its right inner pylon. Flying as a "Wolf" fast FAC on an April 23, 1970 *Steel Tiger* mission near the Ban Karai Pass, this aircraft – which had by then been transferred to the 497th TFS – was seen to crash after suffering AAA hits. Capt Albin Lucki (pilot) and 1Lt Robert Gomez (WSO) were presumed killed, as no ejections were observed. (*Peter E. Davies collection*)

among 72 Block 32-33 F-4Ds of the 8th TFW that were equipped with ITT ARN-92 LORAN from 1967 as part of the Pave Phantom project. Its "towel rail" antenna structure above the rear fuselage was linked to the aircraft's INS and its Lear Siegler ballistics computer that contained the flight characteristics of most US ordnance. LORAN compared fractional time differences between signals from three ground station transmitters to update the INS for accurate ordnance delivery. Although the aircraft has black "night owl" undersurfaces, its GBU-10 has probably been dropped using a "Zot box" laser marker in daylight conditions. (*Peter E. Davies collection*)

55 A GBU-10 LGB up close. The forward fins guided the bomb to the laser spot on the target. The guidance was "bam-bam," meaning the fins deflected fully one way or the other during guidance, causing the bomb to fly a path similar to a sine wave. The LGB's laser seeker head opened immediately after it was dropped, and it then sought the laser mark from a "Zot box" target marker F-4D. It had to be dropped within a 1,500ft x 500ft "box" on the ground in order to detect the laser "dot" on the target. The marker aircraft, equipped with a "Zot box" or later a Pave Knife pod, orbited at around 10,000ft AGL, marking targets for as long as its fuel allowed. The 8th TFW arrived at Ubon on December 8, 1965, and its first combat use of LGBs was in May 1968. (*Mike Davison collection*)

56 This bombed-out area of what had previously been Laotian jungle was called the "Dog's Head" because it faintly resembled the cartoon character Snoopy. A bend in the river southwest of the Mu Gia Pass, the "Dog's Head" was on the Laotian side of the country's border with North Vietnam. (*Mike Davison collection*)

57 Later model GBU-12 LGBs with different tail fins. The fins on this bomb were folded during carriage and then popped open after the weapon was released. The GBU-12 was based on a Mk 82 500lb GP bomb with an MX-602 fin kit that used short wings for attacks from medium altitude. Twelve 433rd TFS F-4Ds were wired for the "Zot box's"

successor, the Ford Aeroneutronic AN/AVQ-10A Pave Knife, a banana-shaped external laser designator hung beneath the left inner pylon. It gave the lasing F-4D more flexibility in maneuvering while marking its target than the "Zot box" had previously allowed. (*Peter E. Davies collection*)

58   Capt Steve Mosier and I shake hands after completing our final combat mission in August 1969. We had flown F-4D 66-7767 on that day, and the jet remained in USAF service for a further 20 years. (*Mike Davison collection*)

59   A hug and a kiss from Estelle Gray after flying the final mission. My life preserver's water wings had been inflated with a tug on the lanyard by a squadron mate – a longstanding tradition in the wake of a "fini flight." (*Steve Mosier collection*)

60   Squadron CO Lt Col Jack Bennett pedaled the squadron samlor around the ramp at Ubon after our final mission, giving us a parade-like ride back to the squadron HQ building while we drank champagne from the bottle. The ride eventually ended when we rolled through the gates that surrounded the 433rd TFS HQ building and were deposited outside. We then walked inside and began our final intelligence debriefing. (*Steve Mosier collection*)

61   Steve and I receive congratulations after completing the last mission. The lanyards around each of our necks were Thai leis, boasting wonderful smelling flowers, including jasmine. (*Steve Mosier collection*)

62   Estelle Gray with Capt Mike "Ghost" Davison following his last mission. Note the RTAF T-28 in the background. This photograph was taken shortly after I had returned home. (*Mike Davison collection*)

63   A somber procession carrying the casket of "Little Mike" Meroney to his final resting place after so many years. The funeral was held at Fairview Memorial Gardens in Fayetteville, Arkansas on June 9, 2012 following the recovery of "Sherman Lead's" remains. (*Meroney family collection*)

64   Final moments of the flag-folding ceremony for "Little Mike" Meroney. (*Meroney family collection*)

65   The bikers came to honor "Little Mike" and saluted the missing-man flyby, performed by four A-10 Thunderbolts of

the Arkansas Air National Guard's 188th FW. (*Meroney family collection*)

66   A display case honoring the Meroney family of warriors in Arkansas. (*Meroney family collection*)

67   A memorial to the fallen warriors of the 433rd TFS "Satan's Angels" was dedicated in the 433rd WPS area at Nellis AFB on May 23, 2013. I was honored to be asked to be one of the dedication speakers. Many family members of the deceased as well as squadron mates from Thailand and Nellis dignitaries attended, along with F-15C and F-22 pilots from the current 433rd WPS. Part of the dedication ceremony display featured a large framed print – seen here to my right – of the 433rd TFS at Ubon in the fall of 1968 when Lt Col Ralph "Hoot" Gibson was CO. (*Gail Peck collection*)

68   Mike Keller, son of "Sherman Lead" pilot Col Wendell Keller, views the memorial display during the dedication ceremony in the 433rd WPS area at Nellis AFB. It contains pencil likenesses of Col Keller and Capt Meroney created by graphic artist Christine Biederer, the single flag that covered the pilots' remains during their final journey home, and various labeled artifacts recovered from the crash site in Laos. (*Gail Peck collection*)

Acknowledgments

I owe so much to so many for their support and encouragement as I prepared this book. It actually goes back to the preparation for the combat tour. Our training was conducted at MacDill AFB in Tampa, Florida, and the units were the 45th and 46th Tactical Fighter Squadrons (TFSs). A tip of the hat to the leadership and the combat-hardened instructor pilots of these two squadrons. They equipped us by sharing every "arrow in their quivers of combat proven tools." I will always be especially grateful to Tom "Sinbad" Saylor, my instructor.

Then, on to the war. "D. J." Alberts met me at Ubon Royal Thai Air Force Base (RTAFB), in Thailand, and smoothed the trail for my integration into the 433rd TFS – the "Satan's Angels." Ed Cobleigh had the courage to take me on my first combat mission. We were roommates for a while, and later were instructors together at the Fighter Weapons School (FWS) at Nellis AFB, Nevada. Steve Mosier was my PSO (pilot systems operator) for our entire period of night flying after Brian McMahon and Dickie Dull got Steve and me checked out. We also flew together a lot on other sorties and, most meaningfully, on our last combat mission. Roger Govett was there in Norm "Phineas" Fogg's back seat for those night capers we shared over and over as "Sewer Doers," as Lt Col Bill "The Padre" Strand called us. I just wish "Phineas" and "The Padre" had lived to see this story published.

My hat is off to the "Guys in Back" ("GIBs") that rode in the back chair with me on so many adventures. I wish I could name them all, but in addition to Steve Mosier, Mike "Ghost" Davison, Dickie Dull, Doug Henneman, Jimmy Hoffman and "Hoss" Cartwright stand out in my memory. There were others, and I apologize that time has faded my recall of their names.

"J. D." Allen has been my friend and colleague from the early days of our combat tour and onward through the FWS as classmates and instructors until this day when, tonight, I hope to meet him for dinner at the Order Of Daedalians' meeting at the Nellis Club. Maj Gen Jeff Cliver, another FWS colleague, helped me with the manuscript for this book, as he did for my earlier book, *America's Secret MiG Squadron*, published by Osprey in 2012.

Steve Mosier went through the manuscript a couple of times and pointed out my errors, and advised me on ways to better explain a situation or event. Then he sent me priceless pictures. I owe you brother! Steve also proposed several short stories from his observations during our year of combat. I have placed them throughout the manuscript at what seemed to me to be appropriate places. Steve's stories strengthen the book, and I am grateful for his contributions.

Mike "Ghost" Davison came to my rescue with gems from his fantastic photographic collection. He could have been a professional photographer. I'm glad he didn't become one. A tip of the hat to you too mate. Over the years Gordy Jenkins has told me many stories about his personal experiences and the contribution of the F-105 to the war in Southeast Asia. I am grateful that he let me use the stunning picture of a mountain pass looking into North Vietnam (included in the plates section) from his F-105 briefing. My close friend Bob Irvine, also known as "Fleagle," provided the incredible pictures of Ray Battle nursing home a battle-damaged F-4. The pictures were given to Bob by the photographer Pat Clark, who is now deceased. By the way, "Fleagle" is what we started calling Bob when he made major. It was our way of calling our military senior a field-grade lackey! Without the photographs so generously loaned to me for publication by "Ghost," Steve, Gordy, "Fleagle," and British aviation historian and fellow Osprey author Peter E. Davies, and others, the stories I have written about in this book would have relied on memory and imagination when it came to their illustration. Photographs supplant imagination and bring stories to life. I am indebted to all of you.

Col Gaillard R. Peck, Jr (USAF) Ret.

September 2018

Index